WINTER

A Book
for the
Season

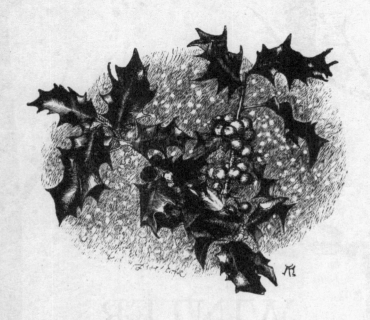

First published 2016

Amberley Publishing
The Hill, Stroud
Gloucestershire, GL5 4EP

www.amberley-books.com

Copyright © Felicity Trotman, 2016

The right of Felicity Trotman to be
identified as the Author of this work
has been asserted in accordance with the
Copyrights, Designs and Patents Act 1988.

ISBN 978 1 4456 6474 3 (hardback)
ISBN 978 1 4456 6475 0 (ebook)

British Library Cataloguing in Publication
Data.
A catalogue record for this book is
available from the British Library.

Typesetting and Origination by Amberley
Publishing.
Printed in the UK.

CONTENTS

THE OLD YEAR

CHRISTMAS, SACRED AND SECULAR

THE NEW YEAR

ABOUT THE EDITOR

Felicity Trotman was born in Belfast, moving to Wiltshire as a child. A history graduate, she was a fiction editor at Puffin and at Macmillan Children's Books. Eventually turning freelance, she added history and military history to her children's speciality. She is a churchwarden and school governor, and has spent many happy years as a member of the English Civil War Society.

THE OLD YEAR

THE ENGLISH WINTER

The English winter – ending in July,
To recommence in August

George Gordon, Lord Byron
Don Juan, XIII, xlii

George Gordon, Lord Byron (1788–1824) was a poet whose work included satire and romance. He gave his name to 'the Byronic hero' – dark, moody and passionate. Byron's first work was poorly received, but after the publication of the long poem 'Childe Harold's Pilgrimage' became very famous. A scandal caused him to leave Britain for Europe, where he spent the rest of his life. Having helped revolutionaries in Italy, he went to Greece to help their fight against the Turks, dying of fever at Missolonghi.

SONNET LXXXIII

That time of year thou mayst in me behold
When yellow leaves, or none, or few, do hang
Upon those boughs which shake against the cold,
Bare ruined choirs, where late the sweet birds sang.
In me thou see'st the twilight of such day
As after sunset fadeth in the west;
Which by and by black night doth take away,
Death's second self, that seals up all in rest.
In me thou see'st the glowing of such fire,
That on the ashes of his youth doth lie,
As the death-bed, whereon it must expire,
Consumed with that which it was nourish'd by.
 This thou perceiv'st, which makes thy love more strong,
To love that well, which thou must leave ere long.

William Shakespeare
Sonnets

William Shakespeare (1565–1616) is universally regarded as one of the world's greatest playwrights and poets. His sonnets divide into those clearly addressed to a man, and those addressed to a woman, the Dark Lady. In published form 'Mr W. H.' was named as 'the only begetter' – the mystery of who these people were has puzzled scholars ever since.

THE WINTER GARDEN

God Almighty first planted a garden. And indeed it is the purest of human pleasures. It is the greatest refreshment to the spirits of man; without which, buildings and palaces are but gross handiworks; and a man shall ever see, that when ages grow to civility and elegancy, men come to build stately sooner than to garden finely; as if gardening were the greater perfection. I do hold it, in the royal ordering of gardens, there ought to be gardens, for all the months in the year; in which severally things of beauty may be then in season. For December, and January, and the latter part of November, you must take such things as are green all winter: holly; ivy; bays; juniper; cypress-trees; yew; pine-apple-trees; fir-trees; rosemary; lavender; periwinkle, the white, the purple, and the blue; germander; flags; orangetrees; lemon-trees; and myrtles, if they be stoved; and sweet marjoram, warm set. There followeth, for the latter part of January and February, the mezereon-tree, which then blossoms; crocus vernus, both the yellow and the grey; primroses, anemones; the early tulippa; hyacinthus orientalis; chamairis; fritellaria.

Sir Francis Bacon
Of Gardens

Francis Bacon, Viscount St Albans (1561–1626) was a philosopher, scientist and statesman. He was an MP and held many important offices, including those of solicitor general, attorney general, and Lord Chancellor. Accused of taking bribes, he was fined, imprisoned and banished from parliament and court. He was soon released, and then pardoned, but never held public office again. As a scientist, he believed in careful observation, and has been called the father of empiricism. He argued that making a garden was a more ambitious and perfect activity than constructing a building – without a garden, 'Buildings and Pallaces are but Grosse Handyworks'. He died after catching cold conducting an experiment in which he stuffed a chicken carcase with snow to see if frozen meat would keep as well as salted meat.

LAMENT OF THE FLUTES
FOR TAMMUZ

At his vanishing away she lifts up a lament,
'Oh my child!' at his vanishing away she lifts up a lament;
'My Damu!' at his vanishing away she lifts up a lament.
'My enchanter and priest!' at his vanishing away she lifts up a
    lament,
At the shining cedar, rooted in a spacious place,
In Eanna, above and below, she lifts up a lament.
Like the lament that a house lifts up for its master, lifts she up
    a lament,
Like the lament that a city lifts up for its lord, lifts she up a
    lament.
Her lament is the lament for a herb that grows not in the bed,
Her lament is the lament for the corn that grows not in the ear.
Her chamber is a possession that brings not forth a possession,
A weary woman, a weary child, forspent.
Her lament is for a great river, where no willows grow,
Her lament is for a field, where corn and herbs grow not.
Her lament is for a pool, where fishes grow not.
Her lament is for a thicket of reeds, where no reeds grow.
Her lament is for woods, where tamarisks grow not.
Her lament is for a wilderness where no cypresses (?) grow.
Her lament is for the depth of a garden of trees, where honey
    and wine grow not.
Her lament is for meadows, where no plants grow.
Her lament is for a palace, where length of life grows not.

Sir James Frazer
The Golden Bough

This ancient Babylonian hymn honours Tammuz, the Sumerian god of corn
and vegetation. It was sung at the beginning of winter, when Tammuz was
thought to die, to be revived again in the spring. His story has similarities
with those of Adonis and Persephone.

WHY THE CHICKADEE GOES CRAZY ONCE A YEAR

A long time ago, when there was no winter in the north, the Chickadees lived merrily in the woods with their relatives, and cared for nothing but to get all the pleasure possible out of their daily life in the thickets. But at length Mother Carey sent them all a warning that they must move to the south, for hard frost and snow were coming on their domains, with starvation close behind. The Nuthatches and other cousins of the Chickadees took this warning seriously, and set about learning how and when to go; but Tomtit, who led his brothers, only laughed and turned a dozen wheels around a twig that served him for a trapeze.

"Go to the south?" said he. "Not I; I am too well contented here; and as for frost and snow, I never saw any and have no faith in them."

But the Nuthatches and Kinglets were in such a state of bustle that at length the Chickadees did catch a little of the excitement, and left off play for a while to question their friends; and they were not pleased with what they learned, for it seemed that all of them were to make a journey that would last many days, and the little Kinglets were actually going as far as the Gulf of Mexico. Besides, they were to fly by night in order to avoid their enemies the Hawks, and the weather at this season was sure to be stormy. So the Chickadees said it was all nonsense, and went off in a band, singing and chasing one another through the woods.

But their cousins were in earnest. They bustled about making their preparations, and learned beforehand what it was necessary for them to know about the way. The great wide river running southward, the moon at

height, and the trumpeting of the Geese were to be their guides, and they were to sing as they flew in the darkness, to keep from being scattered. The noisy, rollicking Chickadees were noisier than ever as the preparations went on, and made sport of their relatives, who were now gathered in great numbers, in the woods along the river; and at length, when the proper time of the moon came, the cousins arose in a body and flew away in the gloom. The Chickadees said that the cousins all were crazy, made some good jokes about the Gulf of Mexico, and then dashed away in a game of tag through the woods, which, by the by, seemed rather deserted now, while the weather, too, was certainly turning remarkably cool.

At length the frost and snow really did come, and the Chickadees were in a woeful case. Indeed, they were frightened out of their wits, and dashed hither and thither, seeking in vain for someone to set them aright on the way to the south. They flew wildly about the woods, till they were truly crazy. I suppose there was not a Squirrel-hole or a hollow log in the neighbourhood that some Chickadee did not enter to inquire if this was the Gulf of Mexico. But no one could tell anything about it, no one was going that way, and the great river was hidden under ice and snow.

About this time a messenger from Mother Carey was passing with a message to the Caribou in the far north; but all he could tell the Chickadees was that he could not be their guide, as he had no instructions, and, at any rate, he was going the other way. Besides, he told them they had had the same notice as their cousins whom they had called "crazy"; and from what he knew of Mother Carey, they would probably have to brave it out here all through the snow, not only now, but in all following winters; so they might as well make the best of it.

This was sad news for the Tomtits; but they were brave little fellows, and seeing they could not help themselves, they set about making the best of it. Before a week had gone by they were in their usual good spirits again, scrambling about the twigs or chasing one another as before. They had still the assurance that winter would end. So filled were they with this idea that even at its commencement, when a fresh blizzard came on, they would gleefully remark to one another that it was a "sign of spring," and one or another of the band would lift his voice in the sweet little chant that we all know so well:

Another would take it up and re-echo:

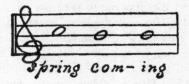

and they would answer and repeat the song until the dreary woods rang again with the good news, and people learned to love the brave little Bird that sets his face so cheerfully to meet so hard a case. But to this day, when the chill wind blows through the deserted woods, the Chickadees seem to lose their wits for a few days, and dart into all sorts of odd and dangerous places. They may then be found in great cities, or open prairies, cellars, chimneys, and hollow logs; and the next time you find one of the wanderers in any such place, be sure to remember that Tomtit goes crazy once a year, and probably went into his strange retreat in search of the Gulf of Mexico.

Ernest Thompson Seton
Lives of the Hunted

Ernest Thompson Seton (1860–1946) was born in Britain, but went to Canada at the age of six when his parents migrated. He loved nature and wildlife, and this is reflected in his many stories about animals and in his artwork. Seton was one of the pioneers of the Scouting movement in America. This story was published in *Our Animal Friends*, the organ of the American Society for the Prevention of Cruelty to Animals.

THE GREAT STORM

Before we come to examine the Damage suffer'd by this terrible Night, and give a particular Relation of its dismal Effects; 'tis necessary to give a summary Account of the thing it self, with all its affrightning Circumstances.

It had blown exceeding hard, as I have already observ'd, for about fourteen Days past; and that so hard, that we thought it terrible Weather: Several Stacks of Chimneys were blown down, and several Ships were lost, and the Tiles in many Places were blown off from the Houses; and the nearer it came to the fatal 26th of November, the Tempestuousness of the Weather encrease'd.

On the Wednesday Morning before, being the 24th of November, it was fair Weather, and blew hard; but not so as to give any Apprehensions, till about 4 a Clock in the Afternoon the Wind encreased, and with Squauls of Rain and terrible Gusts blew very furiously.

The Collector of these Sheets narrowly escap'd the Mischief of a Part of a House, which fell on the Evening of that Day by the Violence of the Wind; and abundance of Tiles were blown off the Houses that Night: the Wind continued with unusual Violence all the next Day and Night; and had not the Great Storm follow'd so soon, this had pass'd for a great Wind.

On Friday Morning it continued to blow exceeding hard, but not so as that it gave any Apprehensions of Danger within Doors; towards Night it encreased: and about 10 a Clock, our Barometers inform'd us that the Night would be very tempestuous; the Mercury sunk lower than ever I had observ'd it on any Occasion whatsoever, which made me suppose the Tube had been handled and disturb'd by the Children.

But as my Observations of this Nature are not regular enough to supply the Reader with a full Information, the Disorders of that dreadful Night having found me other Imployment, expecting every Moment when the House I was in would bury us all in its own Ruins; I have therefore subjoin'd a Letter from an Ingenious Gentleman on this very Head, directed to the Royal Society, and printed in the Philosophical Transactions, No. 289. P. 1530. as follows.

A Letter from the Reverend Mr. William Derham, F.R.S. Containing his Observations concerning the late Storm.

SIR,

According to my Promise at the general Meeting of the R.S. on St. Andrews Day, I here send you inclos'd the Account of my Ingenious and Inquisitive Friend Richard Townely, Esq; concerning the State of the Atmosphere in that Part of Lancashire where he liveth, in the late dismal Storm. And I hope it will not be unaccepable, to accompany his with my own Observations at Upminster; especially since I shall not weary you with a long History of the Devastations, &c. but rather some Particulars of a more Philosophical Consideration.

And first, I do not think it improper to look back to the preceding Seasons of the Year. I scarce believe I shall go out of the way, to reflect as far back as April, May, June and July; because all these were wet Months in our Southern Parts. In April there fell 12,49 l. of Rain through my Tunnel: And about 6, 7, 8, or 9, l. I esteem a moderate quantity for Upminster. In May there fell more than in any Month of any Year since the Year 1696, viz. 20,77 l. June likewise was a dripping Month, in which fell 14,55 l. And July, although it had considerable Intermissions, yet had 14,19 l. above 11 l. of which fell on July 28th and 29th in violent Showers. And I remember the News Papers gave Accounts of great Rains that Month from divers Places of Europe; but the North of England (which also escaped the Violence of the late Storm) was not so remarkably wet in any of those Months; at least not in that great proportion more than we, as usually they are; as I guess from the Tables of Rain, with which Mr. Towneley hath favoured me. Particularly July was a dry Month with them, there being no more than 3,65 l. of Rain fell through Mr. Towneley's Tunnel of the same Diameter with mine.

From these Months let us pass to September, and that we shall find to have been a wet Month, especially the latter part of it; there fell of Rain in that Month, 14,86 l.

October and November last, although not remarkably wet, yet have been open warm Months for the most part. My Thermometer (whose freezing Point is about 84) hath been very seldom below 100 all this Winter, and especially in November.

Thus I have laid before you as short Account as I could of the preceding Disposition of the Year, particularly as to wet and warmth, because I am of opinion that these had a great Influence in the late Storm; not only in causing a Repletion of Vapours in the Atmosphere, but also in raising such Nitro-sulphureous or other heterogeneous matter, which when mix'd together might make a sort of Explosion (like fired Gun-powder) in the Atmosphere. And from this Explosion I judge those Corruscations or Flashes in the Storm to have proceeded, which most People as well as my self observed, and which some took for Lightning. But these things I leave to better Judgments, such as that very ingenious Member of our Society, who hath undertaken the Province of the late Tempest; to whom, if you please, you may impart these Papers; Mr. Halley you know I mean.

From Preliminaries it is time to proceed nearer to the Tempest it self. And the foregoing Day, viz. Thursday, Nov. 25. I think deserveth regard. In the Morning of that day was a little Rain, the Winds high in the Afternoon: S.b.E. and S. In the Evening there was Lightning; and between 9 and 10 of the Clock at Night, a violent, but short Storm of Wind, and much Rain at Upminster; and of Hail in some other Places, which did some Damage: There fell in that Storm 1,65 l. of Rain. The next Morning, which was Friday, Novem. 26. the Wind was S.S.W. and high all Day, and so continued till I was in Bed and asleep. About 12 that Night, the Storm awaken'd me, which gradually encreas'd till near 3 that Morning; and from thence till near 7 it continued in the greatest excess: and then began slowly to abate, and the Mercury to rise swiftly. The Barometer I found at 12 h. ½ P.M. at 28,72, where it continued till about 6 the next Morning, or 6¼, and then hastily rose; so that it was gotten to 82 about 8 of the Clock, as in the Table.

How the Wind sat during the late Storm I cannot positively say, it being excessively dark all the while, and my Vane blown down also, when I could have seen: But by Information from Millers, and others that were forc'd to venture abroad; and by my own guess, I imagin it to have blown about S.W. by S. or nearer to the S. in the beginning, and to veer about towards the West towards the End of the Storm, as far as W.S.W.

The degrees of the Wind's Strength being not measurable (that I know of, though talk'd of) but by guess, I thus determine, with respect to other Storms. On Feb. 7. 1698/9. was a terrible Storm that did much damage. This I number 10 degrees; the Wind then W.N.W. vid. Ph. Tr. No. 262. Another remarkable Storm was Feb. 3. 1701/2. at which time was the greatest descent of the ☿ ever known: This I number 9 degrees. But this last of November, I number at least 15 degrees.

As to the Stations of the Barometer, you have Mr. Towneley's and mine in the following Table to be seen at one View.

A Table shewing the Height of the Mercury in the Barometer, at Townely and Upminster, before, in, and after the Storm.

Townely				Upminster			
Day	Hour	Height of ☿		Day	Hour	Height of ☿	
	7	28	98		8	29	50
Nov. 25	3		64	Nov. 25	12		39
	9½		61		9		14
	7		80		8		33
26	3		70	26	12		28
			9				10
	9⅛		47		12½	28	72
	7		50		7½		82
27	3		81	27	12	29	31
	9½		95		9		42

	7	29	34		8		65
28	3		62	28	12		83
	9		84		9	30	07
29	7		88	29	8		25

As to November 17th (whereon Mr. Towneley mentions a violent Storm in Oxfordshire) it was a Stormy Afternoon here at Upminster, accompanied with Rain, but not violent, nor ☿ very low. November 11th and 12th had both higher Winds and more Rain; and the ☿ was those Days lower than even in the last Storm of November 26th.

Thus, Sir, I have given you the truest Account I can, of what I thought most to deserve Observation, both before, and in the late Storm. I could have added some other particulars, but that I fear I have already made my Letter long, and am tedious. I shall therefore only add, that I have Accounts of the Violence of the Storm at Norwich, Beccles, Sudbury, Colchester, Rochford, and several other intermediate places; but I need not tell Particulars, because I question not but you have better Informations.

Thus far Mr. Derham's Letter.

It did not blow so hard till Twelve a Clock at Night, but that most Families went to Bed; though many of them not without some Concern at the terrible Wind, which then blew: But about One, or at least by Two a Clock, 'tis suppos'd, few People, that were capable of any Sense of Danger, were so hardy as to lie in Bed. And the Fury of the Tempest encreased to such a Degree, that as the Editor of this Account being in London, and conversing with the People the next Days, understood, most People expected the Fall of their Houses.

And yet in this general Apprehension, no body durst quit their tottering Habitations; for whatever the Danger was within doors, 'twas worse without; the Bricks, Tiles, and Stones, from the Tops of the Houses, flew with such force, and so thick in the Streets, that no one thought fit to venture out, tho' their Houses were near demolish'd within.

The Author of this Relation was in a well-built brick House in the skirts of the City; and a Stack of Chimneys falling in upon the next Houses, gave the House such a Shock, that they thought it was just coming down upon their Heads: but opening the Door to attempt an Escape into a Garden, the Danger was so apparent, that they all thought fit to surrender to the Disposal of Almighty Providence, and expect their Graves in the Ruins of the House, rather than to meet most certain Destruction in the open Garden: for unless they cou'd have gone above two hundred Yards from any Building, there had been no Security, for the Force of the Wind blew the Tiles point-blank, tho' their weight inclines them downward: and in several very broad Streets, we saw the Windows broken by the flying of Tile-sherds from the other side: and where there was room for them to fly, the Author of this has seen Tiles blown from a House above thirty or forty Yards, and stuck from five to eight Inches into the solid Earth. Pieces of Timber, Iron, and Sheets of Lead, have from higher Buildings been blown much farther; as in the Particulars hereafter will appear.

It is the receiv'd Opinion of abundance of People, that they felt, during the impetuous fury of the Wind, several Movements of the Earth; and we have several Letters which affirm it: But as an Earthquake must have been so general, that every body must have discern'd it; and as the People were in their Houses when they imagin'd they felt it, the Shaking and Terror of which might deceive their Imagination, and impose upon their Judgment; I shall not venture to affirm it was so: And being resolv'd to use so much Caution in this Relation as to transmit nothing to Posterity without authentick Vouchers, and such Testimony as no reasonable Man will dispute; so if any Relation come in our way, which may afford us a Probability, tho' it may be related for the sake of its Strangeness or Novelty, it shall nevertheless come in the Company of all its Uncertainties, and the Reader left to judge of its Truth: for this Account had not been undertaken, but with design to undeceive the World in false Relations, and to give an Account back'd with such Authorities, as that the Credit of it shou'd admit of no Disputes.

For this reason I cannot venture to affirm that there was any such thing as an Earthquake; but the Concern and Consternation of all People was so great, that I cannot wonder at their imagining several things which were not, any more than their enlarging on things that were, since nothing is more frequent, than for Fear to double every Object, and impose upon the Understanding, strong Apprehensions being apt very often to perswade us of the Reality of such things which we have no other reasons to shew for the probability of, than what are grounded in those Fears which prevail at that juncture.

Others thought they heard it thunder. 'Tis confess'd, the Wind by its unusual Violence made such a noise in the Air as had a resemblance to Thunder; and 'twas observ'd, the roaring had a Voice as much louder than usual, as the Fury of the Wind was greater than was ever known: the Noise had also something in it more formidable; it sounded aloft, and roar'd not very much unlike remote Thunder.

And yet tho' I cannot remember to have heard it thunder, or that I saw any Lightning, or heard of any that did in or near London; yet in the Counties the Air was seen full of Meteors and vaporous Fires: and in some places both Thundrings and unusual Flashes of Lightning, to the great terror of the Inhabitants.

And yet I cannot but observe here, how fearless such People as are addicted to Wickedness, are both of God's Judgments and uncommon Prodigies; which is visible in this Particular, That a Gang of hardned Rogues assaulted a Family at Poplar, in the very Height of the Storm, broke into the House, and robb'd them: it is observable, that the People cryed Thieves, and after that cryed Fire, in hopes to raise the Neighbourhood, and to get some Assistance; but such is the Power of Self-Preservation, and such was the Fear, the Minds of the People were possess'd with, that no Body would venture out to the Assistance of the distressed Family, who were rifled and plundered in the middle of all the Extremity of the Tempest.

It would admit of a large Comment here, and perhaps not very unprofitable, to examine from what sad Defect in Principle it must be that Men can be so destitute of all manner of Regard to invisible and superiour Power, to be acting one of the vilest Parts of a Villain, while infinite Power was threatning the whole World with Disolation, and Multitudes of People expected the Last Day was at Hand.

Several Women in the City of London who were in Travail, or who fell into Travail by the Fright of the Storm, were oblig'd to run the risque of being delivered with such Help as they had; and Midwives found their own Lives in such Danger, that few of them thought themselves oblig'd to shew any Concern for the Lives of others.

Fire was the only Mischief that did not happen to make the Night compleatly dreadful; and yet that was not so every where, for in Norfolk the Town of —— was almost ruin'd by a furious Fire, which burnt with such Vehemence, and was so fann'd by the Tempest, that the Inhabitants had no Power to concern themselves in the extinguishing it; the Wind blew the Flames, together with the Ruines, so about, that there was no standing near it; for if the People came to Windward they were in Danger to be blown into the Flames; and if to Leeward the Flames were so blown up in their Faces, they could not bear to come near it.

If this Disaster had happen'd in London, it must have been very fatal;

for as no regular Application could have been made for the extinguishing it, so the very People in Danger would have had no Opportunity to have sav'd their Goods, and hardly their Lives: for though a Man will run any Risque to avoid being burnt, yet it must have been next to a Miracle, if any Person so oblig'd to escape from the Flames had escap'd being knock'd on the Head in the Streets; for the Bricks and Tiles flew about like small Shot; and 'twas a miserable Sight, in the Morning after the Storm, to see the Streets covered with Tyle-sherds, and Heaps of Rubbish, from the Tops of the Houses, lying almost at every Door.

From Two of the Clock the Storm continued, and encreased till Five in the Morning; and from Five, to half an Hour after Six, it blew with the greatest Violence: the Fury of it was so exceeding great for that particular Hour and half, that if it had not abated as it did, nothing could have stood its Violence much longer.

In this last Part of the Time the greatest Part of the Damage was done: Several Ships that rode it out till now, gave up all; for no Anchor could hold. Even the Ships in the River of Thames were all blown away from their Moorings, and from Execution-Dock to Lime-House Hole there was but our Ships that rid it out, the rest were driven down into the Bite, as the Sailors call it, from Bell-Wharf to Lime-House; where they were huddeld together and drove on Shore, Heads and Sterns, one upon another, in such a manner, as any one would have thought it had been impossible: and the Damage done on that Account was incredible.

Together with the Violence of the Wind, the Darkness of the Night added to the Terror of it; and as it was just New Moon, the Spring Tides being then up at about Four a Clock, made the Vessels, which were a-float in the River, drive the farther up upon the Shore: of all which, in the Process of this Story, we shall find very strange Instances.

The Points from whence the Wind blew, are variously reported from various Hands: 'Tis certain, it blew all the Day before at S.W. and I thought it continued so till about Two a Clock; when, as near as I could judge by the Impressions it made on the House, for we durst not look out, it veer'd to the S.S.W. then to the W. and about Six a Clock to W. by N. and still the more Northward it shifted, the harder it blew, till it shifted again Southerly about Seven a Clock; and as it did so, it gradually abated.

About Eight a Clock in the Morning it ceased so much, that our Fears were also abated, and People began to peep out of Doors; but 'tis impossible to express the Concern that appear'd in every Place: the

Distraction and Fury of the Night was visible in the Faces of the People, and every Body's first Work was to visit and enquire after Friends and Relations. The next Day or Two was almost entirely spent in the Curiosity of the People, in viewing the Havock the Storm had made, which was so universal in London, and especially in the Out-Parts, that nothing can be said sufficient to describe it.

Another unhappy Circumstance with which this Disaster was join'd, was a prodigious Tide, which happen'd the next Day but one, and was occasion'd by the Fury of the Winds: which is also a Demonstration, that the Winds veer'd for Part of the Time to the Northward: and as it is observable, and known by all that understand our Sea Affairs, that a North West Wind makes the Highest Tide, so this blowing to the Northward, and that with such unusual Violence, brought up the Sea raging in such a manner, that in some Parts of England 'twas incredible, the Water rising Six or Eight Foot higher than it was ever known to do in the Memory of Man; by which Ships were fleeted up upon the firm Land several Rods off from the Banks, and an incredible Number of Cattle and People drown'd; as in the Pursuit of this Story will appear.

It was a special Providence that so directed the Waters, that in the River of Thames, the Tide, though it rise higher than usual, yet it did not so prodigiously exceed; but the Height of them as it was, prov'd very prejudicial to abundance of People whose Cellars and Ware-houses were near the River; and had the Water risen a Foot higher, all the Marshes and Levels on both sides the River had been over-flowed, and a great part of the Cattle drowned.

Though the Storm abated with the rising of the Sun, it still blew exceeding hard; so hard, that no Boats durst stir out on the River, but on extraordinary Occasions: and about Three a Clock in the Afternoon, the next Day being Saturday, it increas'd again, and we were in a fresh

Consternation, lest it should return with the same Violence. At Four it blew an extreme Storm, with Sudden Gusts as violent as any time of the Night; but as it came with a great black Cloud, and some Thunder, it brought a hasty Shower of Rain which allay'd the Storm: so that in

a quarter of an Hour it went off, and only continued blowing as before.

This sort of Weather held all Sabbath-Day and Monday, till on Tuesday Afternoon it encreased again; and all Tuesday Night it blew with such Fury, that many Families were afraid to go to Bed: And had not the former terrible Night harden'd the People to all things less than it self, this Night would have pass'd for a Storm fit to have been noted in our Almanacks. Several Stacks of Chimneys that stood out the great Storm, were blown down in this; several Ships which escap'd in the great Storm, perish'd this Night; and several People who had repair'd their Houses, had them untiled again. Not but that I may allow those Chimneys that fell now might have been disabled before.

At this Rate it held blowing till Wednesday about One a Clock in the Afternoon, which was that Day Seven-night on which it began; so that it might be called one continued Storm from Wednesday Noon to Wednesday Noon: in all which time, there was not one Interval of Time in which a Sailor would not have acknowledged it blew a Storm; and in that time two such terrible Nights as I have describ'd.

And this I particularly noted as to Time, Wednesday, Nov. the 24th was a calm fine Day as at that time of Year shall be seen; till above Four a Clock, when it began to be Cloudy, and the Wind rose of a sudden, and in half an Hours Time it blew a Storm. Wednesday, Dec. the 2d. it was very tempestuous all the Morning; at One a Clock the Wind abated, the Sky clear'd, and by Four a Clock there was not a Breath of Wind.

Thus ended the Greatest and the Longest Storm that ever the World saw.

Daniel Defoe
The Storm

The Great Storm of 1703 was one of the worst ever to hit Britain. It was an extratropical cyclone, which did a huge amount of damage in central and southern England. Some two thousand chimney stacks were blown down in London alone – Queen Anne had to take refuge in a cellar because of the danger when chimneys fell and part of the roof of St James's Palace collapsed. Lead was torn off the roof of Westminster Abbey, and many thousands of trees were blown down. HMS *Association* was blown from Harwich to Gothenburg in Sweden. Daniel Defoe (1660–1731) lived through the storm, and subsequently wrote a book about it. The calendar has changed since 1703: the storm was then dated 26–29 November. Today its dates are 7–10 December.

HARD FROSTS IN ENGLAND

In the year

220. Frost lasted 5 months.

250. The Thames frozen 9 weeks.

291. Most rivers frozen 6 weeks.

508. The rivers frozen 2 months.

695. The Thames frozen 6 weeks; booths built on it.

759. Frost from October the 1st, till February 26th, 760.

827. Frost for 9 weeks.

923. The Thames frozen 13 weeks.

987. Frost lasted 120 days.

998. The Thames frozen 5 weeks.

1035. Frost on Midsummer Day so vehement that the corn and fruits were destroyed.

1063. The Thames frozen for 14 weeks.

1076. Frost from November to April.

1114. Several wooden bridges carried away by the ice.

1407. Frost for 15 weeks.

1434. Thames frozen down to Gravesend; 12 weeks frost.

1683. Frost for 13 weeks.

1739. Frost for 9 weeks.

1788. Frost from November to January 1789, when the Thames was crossed opposite the Customhouse, the Tower, Execution Dock, Putney, Brentford, &c. It was general throughout Europe.

1796. Frost the most severe on Dec. 25th that had ever been felt in the memory of man.

1814. Severe frost, Thames frozen, and tremendous falls of snow.

P. T. W.
The Mirror of Literature, Amusement and Instruction, Vol. 13, No. 355,
Feb. 7, 1829

The Mirror of Literature, Amusement and Instruction was a periodical; published weekly from 1822 to 1847, it cost 2d. In 1847 its title was *The Mirror Monthly Magazine*, then from 1849–1850 it became *The London Review*.

JOLLY GOOD ALE AND OLD

I cannot eat but little meat,
My stomach is not good;
But sure I think that I can drink
With him that wears a hood.
Though I go bare, take ye no care,
I nothing am a-cold;
I stuff my skin so full within
Of jolly good ale and old.

Back and side go bare, go bare,
Both foot and hand go cold;
But, belly, God send thee good ale enough,
Whether it be new or old.

I love no roast but a nut-brown toast,
And a crab laid in the fire;
A little bread shall do me stead;
Much bread I not desire.
No frost nor snow, no wind, I trow,
Can hurt me if it would,
I am so wrapped and throughly lapped
Of jolly good ale and old.

Back and side go bare, go bare,
Both foot and hand go cold;
But, belly, God send thee good ale enough,
Whether it be new or old.

And Tib, my wife, that as her life
Loveth well good ale to seek,
Full oft drinks she till ye may see
The tears run down her cheek.
Then doth she troll to me the bowl,
Even as a maltworm should,
And saith, "Sweetheart, I took my part
Of this jolly good ale and old."

Back and side go bare, go bare,
Both foot and hand go cold;
But, belly, God send thee good ale enough,
Whether it be new or old.

Now let them drink till they nod and wink,
Even as good fellows should do;
They shall not miss to have the bliss
Good ale doth bring men to.
And all poor souls that have scoured bowls
Or have them lustily trolled --
God save the lives of them and their wives,
Whether they be young or old.

Back and side go bare, go bare,
Both foot and hand go cold;
But, belly, God send thee good ale enough,
Whether it be new or old.

William Stevenson
Gammer Gurton's Needle

William Stevenson (?1530 – 1575) was a Fellow of Christ's College.
Cambridge. There he put on plays, and he probably wrote *Gammer
Gurton's Needle*, the earliest surviving English comedy, from which this
drinking song comes.

FROST FAIR

On the 20th of December, 1688 [misprint for 1683], a very violent frost began, which lasted to the 6th of February, in so great extremity, that the pools were frozen 18 inches thick at least, and the Thames was so frozen that a great street from the Temple to Southwark was built with shops, and all manner of things sold. Hackney coaches plied there as in the streets. There were also bull-baiting, and a great many shows and tricks to be seen. This day the frost broke up. In the morning I saw a coach and six horses driven from Whitehall almost to the bridge [London Bridge] yet by three o'clock that day, February the 6th, next to Southwark the ice was gone, so as boats did row to and fro, and the next day all the frost was gone. On Candlemas Day I went to Croydon market, and led my horse over the ice to the Horseferry from Westminster to Lambeth; as I came back I led him from Lambeth upon the middle of the Thames to Whitefriars' stairs, and so led him up by them. And this day an ox was roasted whole, over against Whitehall. King Charles and the Queen ate part of it.

Eyewitness of the 1683/84 Frost Fair

From the seventeenth century to the early part of the nineteenth century, during a period known as the Little Ice Age, there were winters in Britain so severe that the Thames froze over. Traders set up stalls, and sports and shows took place, as many people came to see and enjoy the phenomenon.

In the pedestrian tunnel under the south bank of Southwark Bridge, there is an engraving by Southwark sculptor Richard Kindersley, made of five slabs of grey slate, depicting the frost fair.

The frieze contains an inscription that reads (two lines per slab):

> Behold the Liquid Thames frozen o're,
> That lately Ships of mighty Burthen bore
> The Watermen for want of Rowing Boats
> Make use of Booths to get their Pence & Groats
> Here you may see beef roasted on the spit
> And for your money you may taste a bit

There you may print your name, tho cannot write
Cause num'd with cold: tis done with great delight
And lay it by that ages yet to come
May see what things upon the ice were done

This text, taken from handbills printed on the Thames during frost fairs, has been engraved by the Southwark sculptor Richard Kindersley. It appears on plaques placed on the wall of the pedestrian tunnel under the south bank of Southwark Bridge.

LA BELLE DAME SANS MERCI

'O what can ail thee, knight-at-arms,
  Alone and palely loitering?
The sedge has wither'd from the lake,
  And no birds sing.

'O what can ail thee, knight-at-arms,
  So haggard and so woe-begone?
The squirrel's granary is full,
  And the harvest's done.

'I see a lily on thy brow,
  With anguish moist and fever-dew,
And on thy cheeks a fading rose
  Fast withereth too. '

'I met a lady in the meads,
  Full beautiful, a fairy's child;
Her hair was long, her foot was light,
  And her eyes were wild.

'I made a garland for her head,
  And bracelets too, and fragrant zone;
She looked at me as she did love,
  And made sweet moan

'I set her on my pacing steed,
  And nothing else saw all day long,
For sidelong would she bend, and sing
  A faery's song.

'She found me roots of relish sweet,
  And honey wild, and manna-dew,
And sure in language strange she said—
  "I love thee true!"

'She took me to her elfin grot,
  And there she wept and sighed full sore,
And there I shut her wild, wild eyes
  With kisses four.

'And there she lullèd me asleep,
  And there I dreamed—Ah! woe betide!—
  The latest dream I ever dreamt
On the cold hill's side.

'I saw pale kings and princes too,
  Pale warriors, death-pale were they all;
Who cried—"La Belle Dame sans Merci
  Hath thee in thrall!"

'I saw their starved lips in the gloam,
  With horrid warning gapèd wide,
And I awoke and found me here,
  On the cold hill's side.

'And this is why I sojourn here,
  Alone and palely loitering,
Though the sedge is wither'd from the lake,
  And no birds sing.'

John Keats

John Keats (1795–1821), poet and surgeon, only wrote fifty-four poems in his twenty-five years of life, but was one of the most influential of the Romantic poets. His ballad 'La Belle Dame Sans Merci' combines a simplicity of structure with a very enigmatic story, firing the imagination of the reader.

BATH BIRDS

When staying in Bath in the winter of 1898-9 I saw a good deal of bird life even in the heart of the town. At the back of the house I lodged in, in New King Street, within four minutes' walk of the Pump Room, there was a strip of ground called a garden, but with no plants except a few dead stalks and stumps and two small leafless trees. Clothes-lines were hung there, and the ground was littered with old bricks and rubbish, and at the far end of the strip there was a fowl-house with fowls in it, a small shed, and a wood-pile. Yet to this unpromising-looking spot came a considerable variety of birds. Starlings, sparrows, and chaffinches were the most numerous, while the blackbird, thrush, robin, hedge-sparrow and wren were each represented by a pair. The wrens lived in the wood-pile, and were the only members of the little feathered community that did not join the others at table when crumbs and scraps were thrown out.

It was surprising to find all or most of these birds evidently wintering on that small plot of ground in the middle of the town, solely for the sake of the warmth and shelter it afforded them, and the chance crumbs that came in their way. It is true that I fed them regularly, but they were all there before I came. Yet it was not an absolutely safe place for them, being much infested by cats, especially by a big black one who was always on the prowl, and who had a peculiarly murderous gleam in his luminous yellow orbs when he crouched down to watch or attempted to stalk them. One could not but imagine that the very sight of such eyes in that black, devilish face would have been enough to freeze their blood with sudden terror, and make them powerless to fly from him. But it was not so: he could neither fascinate nor take them by surprise. No sooner would he begin to practise his wiles than all the population would be up in arms—the loud, sharp summons of the blackbird sounding first; then the starlings would chatter angrily, the thrush scream, the chaffinches begin to pink-pink with all their might, and the others would join in, even the small hideling wrens coming out of their fortress of faggots to take part in the demonstration. Then puss would give it up and go away, or coil himself up and go to sleep on the sloping roof of the tiny shed or in some other sheltered spot; peace and quiet would once more settle on the little republic, and the birds would be content to dwell with their enemy in their midst in full sight of them, so long as he slept or did not watch them too narrowly.

Finding that blue tits were among the visitors at the back, I hung up some lumps of suet and a cocoa-nut to the twigs of the bushes. The suet was immediately attacked, but judging from the suspicious way in which they regarded the round brown object swinging in the wind, the Bath tits had never before been treated to a cocoa-nut. But though suspicious, it was plain that the singular object greatly excited their curiosity. On the second day they made the discovery that it was a new and delightful dish invented for the benefit of the blue tits, and from that time they were at it at all hours, coming and going from morning till night. There were six of them, and occasionally they were all there at once, each one anxious to secure a place, and never able when he got one to keep it longer than three or four seconds at a time. Looking upon them from an upper window, as they perched against and flitted round and round the suspended cocoa-nut, they looked like a gathering of very large pale-blue flies flitting round and feeding on medlar.

W. H. Hudson
Birds in Town and Village

William Henry Hudson (1841–1922) was born in Argentina, coming to Britain in 1869. He was a naturalist and writer with a particular love of birds.

FIRST SNOW

The wallpaper is falling out of the sky
in tiny bite-sized flakes –
and he wonders what cat
is clawing the clouds.

There's too much here to sweep away.
My dustpan-and-brush that clears up
the torn white underlay between kitchen
and hall (his favourite scratching-post)
would never contain such a blizzard.
This is serious competition
even to his fiercest attack
on the kitchen wall.

He probably wonders why I don't shout
at the miscreant clouds – shake my fist
at the drab sky tipping its load
like an overfilled paper-shredder;

maybe concludes, with the thaw,
that it was all a dream.
That he's the only wallpaper stripper:
king of the heap.

Carolyn King

Carolyn King (1941–) comes from a musical family – her grandfather was a composer and performer, her mother a ballet dancer and her father an instrumentalist. Now resident on the Isle of Wight, she has been writing poetry most of her life. Two of her works have been cast in bronze and placed at Island landmarks. She has published three collections of poems.

WINTER COMES TO THE POND

The pond had in the meanwhile skimmed over in the shadiest and shallowest coves, some days or even weeks before the general freezing. The first ice is especially interesting and perfect, being hard, dark, and transparent, and affords the best opportunity that ever offers for examining the bottom where it is shallow; for you can lie at your length on ice only an inch thick, like a skater insect on the surface of the water, and study the bottom at your leisure, only two or three inches distant, like a picture behind a glass, and the water is necessarily always smooth then. There are many furrows in the sand where some creature has travelled about and doubled on its tracks; and, for wrecks, it is strewn with the cases of caddis-worms made of minute grains of white quartz. Perhaps these have creased it, for you find some of their cases in the furrows, though they are deep and broad for them to make. But the ice itself is the object of most interest, though you must improve the earliest opportunity to study it. If you examine it closely the morning after it freezes, you find that the greater part of the bubbles, which at first appeared to be within it, are against its under surface, and that more are continually rising from the bottom; while the ice is as yet comparatively solid and dark, that is, you see the water through it. These bubbles are from an eightieth to an eighth of an inch in diameter, very clear and beautiful, and you see your face reflected in them through the ice. There may be thirty or forty of them to a square inch. There are also already within the ice narrow oblong perpendicular bubbles about half an inch long, sharp cones with the apex upward; or oftener, if the ice is quite fresh, minute spherical bubbles one directly above another, like a string of beads. But these within the ice are not so numerous nor obvious as those beneath. I sometimes used to cast on stones to try the strength of the ice, and those which broke through carried in air with them, which formed very large and conspicuous white bubbles beneath. One day when I came to the same place forty-eight hours afterward, I found that those large bubbles were still perfect, though an inch more of ice had formed, as I could see distinctly by the seam in the edge of a cake. But as the last two days had been very warm, like an Indian summer, the ice was not now transparent, showing the dark green color of the water, and the bottom, but opaque and whitish or gray, and though twice as thick was hardly stronger than before, for the air bubbles had greatly expanded under this heat and run together, and lost their regularity; they were no longer one directly over another, but often like silvery coins poured from a bag, one overlapping another, or in thin flakes, as if occupying slight cleavages. The beauty of the ice was gone, and it was too late to study the bottom. Being curious to know what position my great bubbles occupied with regard to the new ice, I broke out a cake containing a middling sized one, and turned it bottom upward. The new ice had formed around and under the bubble, so that it was included between the two ices. It was wholly in the lower ice, but close against the upper, and was flattish, or perhaps slightly lenticular, with a rounded edge, a quarter of an inch deep by four inches in diameter; and I was surprised to find that directly under the bubble the ice was melted with great regularity in the form of a saucer reversed, to the height of five eighths of an inch in the middle, leaving a thin partition there between the water and the bubble, hardly an eighth of an inch thick; and in many places the small bubbles in this partition had burst out downward, and probably there was no ice at all under the largest bubbles, which were a foot in diameter. I inferred that the infinite number of minute bubbles which I had first seen against the under surface of the ice were now frozen in likewise, and that each, in its degree, had operated like a burning-glass on the ice beneath to melt and rot it. These are the little air-guns which contribute to make the ice crack and whoop.

At length the winter set in good earnest, just as I had finished plastering, and the wind began to howl around the house as if it had not had permission to do so till then. Night after night the geese came lumbering in the dark with a clangor and a whistling of wings, even after the ground was covered with snow, some to alight in Walden, and some flying low over the woods toward Fair Haven, bound for Mexico. Several times, when returning from the village at ten or eleven o'clock at night, I heard the tread of a flock of geese, or else ducks, on the dry leaves in the woods by a pond-hole behind my dwelling, where they had come up to feed, and the faint honk or quack of their leader as they hurried off. In 1845 Walden froze entirely over for the first time on the night of the 22d of December, Flint's and other shallower ponds and the river having been frozen ten days or more; in '46, the 16th; in '49, about the 31st; and in '50, about the 27th of December; in '52, the 5th of January; in '53, the 31st of December. The snow had already covered the ground since the 25th of November, and surrounded me suddenly with the scenery of winter. I withdrew yet farther into my shell, and endeavored to keep a bright fire both within my house and within my breast. My employment out of doors now was to collect the dead wood in the forest, bringing it in my hands or on my shoulders, or sometimes trailing a dead pine tree under each arm to my shed. An old forest fence which had seen its best days was a great haul for me. I sacrificed it to Vulcan, for it was past serving the god Terminus. How much more interesting an event is that man's supper who has just been forth in the snow to hunt, nay, you might say, steal, the fuel to cook it with! His bread and meat are sweet. There are enough fagots and waste wood of all kinds in the forests of most of our towns to support many fires, but which at present warm none, and, some think, hinder the growth of the young wood. There was also the driftwood of the pond. In the course of the summer I had discovered a raft of pitch pine logs with the bark on, pinned together by the Irish when the railroad was built. This I hauled up partly on the shore. After soaking two years and then lying high six months it was perfectly sound, though waterlogged past drying. I amused myself one winter day with sliding this piecemeal across the pond, nearly half a mile, skating behind with one end of a log fifteen feet long on my shoulder, and the other on the ice; or I tied several logs together with a birch withe, and then, with a longer birch or alder which had a hook at the end, dragged them across. Though completely waterlogged and almost as heavy as lead, they not only burned long, but made a very hot fire; nay, I thought that they burned better for the soaking, as if the pitch, being confined by the water, burned longer, as in a lamp.

Henry Thoreau
Walden

Henry David Thoreau (1817–1862) was an American poet, essayist and lover of nature. For two yeas he lived in a hut he built for himself at Walden Pond, near Concord, Massachusetts. His book about his experiences, *Walden; or, Life in the Woods*, is an American classic.

FARMING IN DECEMBER

Abrode for the raine, when thou canst do no good ;
then go let thy flayles, as the threshers were wood.
Beware they threshe dene, though the lesser they yarne :
and if thou wilt thriue, loke thy selfe to thy barne.

If barne rome will serue, lay thy stoouer vp drye
and eche kinde of strawe, by hitselfe let it lie.
Thy chaffe, housed sweete, kept from pullein and dust :
shall serue well thy horses, when labour they must.

When pasture is gone, and the fildes mier and weate :
then stable thy plough horse, and there giue them meate.
The better thou vse them, in place where they stande :
more strength shall they haue, for to breake vp thy lande.

Giue cattell their fodder, the plot drie and warme :
and count them, for miring or other like harme.
Trust neuer to boyes, if thou trust well to spede :
be serued with those, that may helpe at a nede.

Serue first out thy rie strawe, then wheate & then pease,
then otestrawe then barley, then hay if you please.
But serue them with haye, while thy straw stoouer last,
they loue no more strawe, they had rather to fast.

Kepe neuer such seruantes, as doth thee no good,
for making thy heare, growing thorrough thy hood.
For nestling of verlettes, of brothels and hoores :
make many a rich man, to shet vp his doores.

Get luye and hull, woman deck vp thyne house :
and take this same brawne, for to seeth and to souse.
Prouide vs good chere, for thou knowst the old guise :
olde customes, that good be, let no man dispise.

Thomas Tusser
Five hundred points of good husbandry

Thomas Tusser (?1524–1580) was a poet and farmer. Educated at Eton and Cambridge, he farmed in Suffolk, where he was the first person to grow barley. His poem 'A Hundred Points of Good Husbandry' (1557) tells farmers and gardeners what they should be doing. He later added 'A Hundred Good Points of Housewifery' and before he died the 100 points had grown to 500. The work is a great source of proverbs and sayings.

TAKE THY OLD CLOAK ABOUT THEE

This winters weather itt waxeth cold,
And frost doth freese on every hill,
And Boreas blowes his blasts soe bold,
That all our cattell are like to spill;
Bell my wiffe, who loves noe strife,
She sayd unto me quietlye,
Rise up, and save cow Crumbockes liffe,
Man, put thine old cloake about thee.
He.
O Bell, why dost thou flyte 'and scorne'?
Thou kenst my cloak is very thin:
Itt is soe bare and overworne
A cricke he theron cannot renn:
Then Ile noe longer borrowe nor lend,
'For once Ile new appareld bee,
To-morrow Ile to towne and spend,'
For Ile have a new cloake about mee.
She.
Cow Crumbocke is a very good cowe,
Shee ha beene alwayes true to the payle,
Shee has helpt us to butter and cheese, I trow,
And other things shee will not fayle;
I wold be loth to see her pine,
Good husband, councell take of mee,
It is not for us to go soe fine,
Man, take thine old cloake about thee.

He.

My cloake it was a verry good cloake,
Itt hath been alwayes true to the weare,
But now it is not worth a groat;
I have had it four and forty yeere:
Sometime itt was of cloth in graine,
'Tis now but a sigh clout as you may see,
It will neither hold out winde nor raine;
And Ile have a new cloake about mee.

She.

It is four and fortye yeeres agoe
Since the one of us the other did ken,
And we have had betwixt us towe
Of children either nine or ten;
Wee have brought them up to women and men;
In the feare of God I trow they bee;
And why wilt thou thyselfe misken?
Man, take thine old cloake about thee.

He.

O Bell my wiffe, why dost thou 'floute!'
Now is nowe, and then was then:
Seeke now all the world throughout,
Thou kenst not clownes from gentlemen.
They are cladd in blacke, greene, yellowe, or 'gray',
Soe far above their owne degree:
Once in my life Ile 'doe as they,'
For Ile have a new cloake about mee.

She.

King Stephen was a worthy peere,
His breeches cost him but a crowne,
He held them sixpence all too deere;
Therefore he calld the taylor Lowne.
He was a wight of high renowne,
And thouse but of a low degree:
Itt's pride that putts this countrye downe,
Man, take thine old cloake about thee.

He.

'Bell my wife she loves not strife,

— 40 —

Yet she will lead me if she can;
And oft, to live a quiet life,
I am forced to yield, though Ime good-man:'
Itt's not for a man with a woman to threape,
Unlesse he first give oer the plea:
As wee began wee now will leave,
And Ile take mine old cloake about mee.

Traditional
Percy's Reliques

Percy's *Reliques of Ancient English Poetry* is a collection of early and traditional ballads, based on a seventeenth-century manuscript collected by an antiquarian, Thomas Percy (1729–1811). Published in 1765, the ballads included in *Reliques* have been considerably adapted – but the book helped revive the ballad tradition, and it influenced the Romantic poets.

THE COP AND THE ANTHEM

On his bench in Madison Square Soapy moved uneasily. When wild geese honk high of nights, and when women without sealskin coats grow kind to their husbands, and when Soapy moves uneasily on his bench in the park, you may know that winter is near at hand.

A dead leaf fell in Soapy's lap. That was Jack Frost's card. Jack is kind to the regular denizens of Madison Square, and gives fair warning of his annual call. At the corners of four streets he hands his pasteboard to the North Wind, footman of the mansion of All Outdoors, so that the inhabitants thereof may make ready.

Soapy's mind became cognisant of the fact that the time had come for him to resolve himself into a singular Committee of Ways and Means to provide against the coming rigour. And therefore he moved uneasily on his bench.

The hibernatorial ambitions of Soapy were not of the highest. In them there were no considerations of Mediterranean cruises, of soporific Southern skies drifting in the Vesuvian Bay. Three months on the Island was what his soul craved. Three months of assured board and bed and congenial company, safe from Boreas and bluecoats, seemed to Soapy the essence of things desirable.

For years the hospitable Blackwell's had been his winter quarters. Just as his more fortunate fellow New Yorkers had bought their tickets to Palm Beach and the Riviera each winter, so Soapy had made his humble arrangements for his annual hegira to the Island. And now the time was come. On the previous night three Sabbath newspapers, distributed beneath his coat, about his ankles and over his lap, had failed to repulse the cold as he slept on his bench near the spurting fountain in the ancient square. So the Island loomed big and timely in Soapy's mind. He scorned the provisions made in the name of charity for the city's dependents. In Soapy's opinion the Law was more benign than Philanthropy. There was an endless round of institutions, municipal and eleemosynary, on which he might set out and receive lodging and food accordant with the simple life. But to one of Soapy's proud spirit the gifts of charity are encumbered. If not in coin you must pay in humiliation of spirit for every benefit received at the hands of philanthropy. As Caesar had his Brutus, every bed of charity must have its toll of a bath, every loaf of bread its compensation of a private and personal inquisition. Wherefore it is better to be a guest of the law, which though conducted by rules, does not meddle unduly with a gentleman's private affairs.

Soapy, having decided to go to the Island, at once set about accomplishing his desire. There were many easy ways of doing this. The pleasantest was to dine luxuriously at some expensive restaurant; and then, after declaring insolvency, be handed over quietly and without uproar to a policeman. An accommodating magistrate would do the rest.

Soapy left his bench and strolled out of the square and across the level sea of asphalt, where Broadway and Fifth Avenue flow together. Up Broadway he turned, and halted at a glittering café, where are gathered together nightly the choicest products of the grape, the silkworm and the protoplasm.

Soapy had confidence in himself from the lowest button of his vest upward. He was shaven, and his coat was decent and his neat black, ready-tied four-in-hand had been presented to him by a lady missionary on Thanksgiving Day. If he could reach a table in the restaurant unsuspected success would be his. The portion of him that would show above the table would raise no doubt in the waiter's mind. A roasted mallard duck, thought Soapy, would be about the thing—with a bottle of Chablis, and then Camembert, a demi-tasse and a cigar. One dollar for the cigar would be enough. The total would not be so high as to call forth any supreme manifestation of revenge from the café management; and yet the meat would leave him filled and happy for the journey to his winter refuge.

But as Soapy set foot inside the restaurant door the head waiter's eye fell upon his frayed trousers and decadent shoes. Strong and ready hands turned him about and conveyed him in silence and haste to the sidewalk and averted the ignoble fate of the menaced mallard.

Soapy turned off Broadway. It seemed that his route to the coveted island was not to be an epicurean one. Some other way of entering limbo must be thought of.

At a corner of Sixth Avenue electric lights and cunningly displayed wares behind plate-glass made a shop window conspicuous. Soapy took a cobblestone and dashed it through the glass. People came running around the corner, a policeman in the lead. Soapy stood still, with his hands in his pockets, and smiled at the sight of brass buttons.

"Where's the man that done that?" inquired the officer excitedly.

"Don't you figure out that I might have had something to do with it?" said Soapy, not without sarcasm, but friendly, as one greets good fortune.

The policeman's mind refused to accept Soapy even as a clue. Men who smash windows do not remain to parley with the law's minions. They take to their heels. The policeman saw a man half way down the block running to catch a car. With drawn club he joined in the pursuit. Soapy, with disgust in his heart, loafed along, twice unsuccessful.

On the opposite side of the street was a restaurant of no great pretensions. It catered to large appetites and modest purses. Its crockery and atmosphere were thick; its soup and napery thin. Into this place Soapy took his accusive shoes and telltale trousers without challenge. At a table he sat and consumed beefsteak, flapjacks, doughnuts and pie. And then to the waiter be betrayed the fact that the minutest coin and himself were strangers.

"Now, get busy and call a cop," said Soapy. "And don't keep a gentleman waiting."

"No cop for youse," said the waiter, with a voice like butter cakes and an eye like the cherry in a Manhattan cocktail. "Hey, Con!"

Neatly upon his left ear on the callous pavement two waiters pitched Soapy. He arose, joint by joint, as a carpenter's rule opens, and beat the dust from his clothes. Arrest seemed but a rosy dream. The Island seemed very far away. A policeman who stood before a drug store two doors away laughed and walked down the street.

Five blocks Soapy travelled before his courage permitted him to woo capture again. This time the opportunity presented what he fatuously termed to himself a "cinch." A young woman of a modest and pleasing guise was standing before a show window gazing with sprightly interest at its display of shaving mugs and inkstands, and two yards from the window a large policeman of severe demeanour leaned against a water plug.

It was Soapy's design to assume the role of the despicable and execrated "masher." The refined and elegant appearance of his victim and the contiguity of the conscientious cop encouraged him to believe that he would soon feel the pleasant official clutch upon his arm that would insure his winter quarters on the right little, tight little isle.

Soapy straightened the lady missionary's ready-made tie, dragged his shrinking cuffs into the open, set his hat at a killing cant and sidled toward the young woman. He made eyes at her, was taken with sudden coughs and "hems," smiled, smirked and went brazenly through the impudent and contemptible litany of the "masher." With half an eye Soapy saw that the policeman was watching him fixedly. The young woman moved away a few steps, and again bestowed her absorbed attention upon the shaving mugs. Soapy followed, boldly stepping to her side, raised his hat and said:

"Ah there, Bedelia! Don't you want to come and play in my yard?"

The policeman was still looking. The persecuted young woman had but to beckon a finger and Soapy would be practically en route for his insular haven. Already he imagined he could feel the cozy warmth of the station-house. The young woman faced him and, stretching out a hand, caught Soapy's coat sleeve.

"Sure, Mike," she said joyfully, "if you'll blow me to a pail of suds. I'd have spoke to you sooner, but the cop was watching."

With the young woman playing the clinging ivy to his oak Soapy walked past the policeman overcome with gloom. He seemed doomed to liberty.

At the next corner he shook off his companion and ran. He halted in the district where by night are found the lightest streets, hearts, vows and librettos. Women in furs and men in greatcoats moved gaily in the wintry air. A sudden fear seized Soapy that some dreadful enchantment had rendered him immune to arrest. The thought brought a little of panic upon it, and when he came upon another policeman lounging grandly in front of a transplendent theatre he caught at the immediate straw of "disorderly conduct."

On the sidewalk Soapy began to yell drunken gibberish at the top of his harsh voice. He danced, howled, raved and otherwise disturbed the welkin.

The policeman twirled his club, turned his back to Soapy and remarked to a citizen.

"'Tis one of them Yale lads celebratin' the goose egg they give to the Hartford College. Noisy; but no harm. We've instructions to lave them be."

Disconsolate, Soapy ceased his unavailing racket. Would never a policeman lay hands on him? In his fancy the Island seemed an unattainable Arcadia. He buttoned his thin coat against the chilling wind.

In a cigar store he saw a well-dressed man lighting a cigar at a swinging light. His silk umbrella he had set by the door on entering. Soapy stepped inside, secured the umbrella and sauntered off with it slowly. The man at the cigar light followed hastily.

"My umbrella," he said, sternly.

"Oh, is it?" sneered Soapy, adding insult to petit larceny. "Well, why don't you call a policeman? I took it. Your umbrella! Why don't you call a cop? There stands one on the corner."

The umbrella owner slowed his steps. Soapy did likewise, with a presentiment that luck would again run against him. The policeman looked at the two curiously.

"Of course," said the umbrella man—"that is—well, you know how these mistakes occur—I—if it's your umbrella I hope you'll excuse me—I picked it up this morning in a restaurant—If you recognise it as yours, why—I hope you'll—"

"Of course it's mine," said Soapy, viciously.

The ex-umbrella man retreated. The policeman hurried to assist a tall blonde in an opera cloak across the street in front of a street car that was approaching two blocks away.

Soapy walked eastward through a street damaged by improvements. He hurled the umbrella wrathfully into an excavation. He muttered against the men who wear helmets and carry clubs. Because he wanted to fall into their clutches, they seemed to regard him as a king who could do no wrong.

At length Soapy reached one of the avenues to the east where the glitter and turmoil was but faint. He set his face down this toward Madison Square, for the homing instinct survives even when the home is a park bench.

But on an unusually quiet corner Soapy came to a standstill. Here was an old church, quaint and rambling and gabled. Through one violet-stained window a soft light glowed, where, no doubt, the organist loitered over the keys, making sure of his mastery of the coming Sabbath anthem. For there drifted out to Soapy's ears sweet music that caught and held him transfixed against the convolutions of the iron fence.

The moon was above, lustrous and serene; vehicles and pedestrians were few; sparrows twittered sleepily in the eaves—for a little while the scene might have been a country churchyard. And the anthem that the organist played cemented Soapy to the iron fence, for he had known it well in the days when his life contained such things as mothers and roses and ambitions and friends and immaculate thoughts and collars.

The conjunction of Soapy's receptive state of mind and the influences about the old church wrought a sudden and wonderful change in his soul. He viewed with swift horror the pit into which he had tumbled, the degraded days, unworthy desires, dead hopes, wrecked faculties and base motives that made up his existence.

And also in a moment his heart responded thrillingly to this novel mood. An instantaneous and strong impulse moved him to battle with his desperate fate. He would pull himself out of the mire; he would make a man of himself again; he would conquer the evil that had taken possession of him. There was time; he was comparatively young yet; he would resurrect his old eager ambitions and pursue them without faltering. Those solemn but sweet organ notes had set up a revolution in him. To-morrow he would go into the roaring downtown district and find work. A fur importer had once offered him a place as driver. He would find him to-morrow and ask for the position. He would be somebody in the world. He would—

Soapy felt a hand laid on his arm. He looked quickly around into the broad face of a policeman.

"What are you doin' here?" asked the officer.

"Nothin'," said Soapy.

"Then come along," said the policeman.

"Three months on the Island," said the Magistrate in the Police Court the next morning.

O Henry
The Four Million

O Henry (William Sydney Porter, 1862–1910) started writing short stories in prison, having been jailed for embezzlement from the bank he worked in. After his release he moved to New York (that's Fifth Avenue below, about 1900). His short stories, often containing a surprise ending, became very successful. He was troubled by debts and health problems all his life.

SKATERS

1st December, 1662. Having seen the strange and wonderful dexterity of the sliders on the new canal in St. James's Park, performed before their Majesties by divers gentlemen and others with skates, after the manner of the Hollanders, with what swiftness they pass, how suddenly they stop in full career upon the ice; I went home by water, but not without exceeding difficulty, the Thames being frozen, great flakes of ice encompassing our boat.

John Evelyn
Diary

John Evelyn (1630–1706) kept a diary for most of his life. Although he did not fight in the Civil Wars, Evelyn was a Royalist and an Anglican, and spent some years abroad to avoid living under the Commonwealth. He was one of the first Fellows of the Royal Society and wrote a number of books on scientific and practical matters: one, Fumifugium: or, The Inconvenience of the Air and Smoke of London Dissipated was an early attempt to deal with air pollution in the capital. The authorities did nothing! The painting is by Henry Sandham (1842–1910).

SKATING

And in the frosty season, when the sun
Was set, and visible for many a mile
The cottage windows through the twilight blaz'd,
I heeded not the summons:—happy time
It was, indeed, for all of us; to me
It was a time of rapture: clear and loud
The village clock toll'd six; I wheel'd about,
Proud and exulting, like an untired horse,
That cares not for its home.—All shod with steel,
We hiss'd along the polish'd ice, in games
Confederate, imitative of the chace
And woodland pleasures, the resounding horn,
The Pack loud bellowing, and the hunted hare.
So through the darkness and the cold we flew,
And not a voice was idle; with the din,
Meanwhile, the precipices rang aloud,
The leafless trees, and every icy crag
Tinkled like iron, while the distant hills
Into the tumult sent an alien sound
Of melancholy, not unnoticed, while the stars,
Eastward, were sparkling clear, and in the west
The orange sky of evening died away.

William Wordsworth
The Prelude

William Wordsworth (1770–1850) was a major poet of the nineteenth century, who became Poet Laureate in 1843. This extract comes from *The Prelude*, an enormously long autobiographical poem, published in 13 books after Wordsworth's death. Born in Cumberland, Wordsworth later lived in the Lake District and the beauty of the area and the simple lives of ordinary people are evident in much of his work.

BIRDS AT WINTER NIGHTFALL

Around the house the flakes fly faster,
And all the berries now are gone
From holly and cotoneaster
Around the house. The flakes fly! - faster
Shutting indoors that crumb-outcaster
We used to see upon the lawn
Around the house. The flakes fly faster,
And all the berries now are gone!

Thomas Hardy

Thomas Hardy (1840–1928) trained as an architect, but became famous first for his stories and later his poems. His novels, largely set in his native Dorset, are pessimistic, but his poetry shows a sense of humour and a love of nature.

THE NORTH WIND DOTH BLOW

The north wind doth blow,
And we shall have snow,
And what will the robin do then, poor thing?
He'll sit in a barn,
And keep himself warm,
And hide his head under his wing, poor thing!

Traditional

THE WINTER RETREAT

The next day it was resolved that they should set off with all possible speed, before the enemy had time to collect and occupy the defile. Having got their kit and baggage together, they at once began their march through deep snow with several guides, and, crossing the high pass the same day on which Tiribazus was to have attacked them, got safely into cantonments. From this point they marched three desert stages—fifteen parasangs—to the river Euphrates, and crossed it in water up to the waist. The sources of the river were reported to be at no great distance. From this place they marched through deep snow over a flat country three stages—fifteen parasangs. The last of these marches was trying, with the north wind blowing in their teeth, drying up everything and benumbing the men. Here one of the seers suggested to them to do sacrifice to Boreas, and sacrifice was done. The effect was obvious to all in the diminished fierceness of the blast. But there was six feet of snow, so that many of the baggage animals and slaves were lost, and about thirty of the men themselves.

They spent the whole night in kindling fire; for there was fortunately no dearth of wood at the halting-place; only those who came late into camp had no wood. Accordingly those who had arrived a good while and had kindled fires were not for allowing these late-comers near the fires, unless they would in return give a share of their corn or of any other victuals they might have. Here then a general exchange of goods was set up. Where the fire was kindled the snow melted, and great trenches formed themselves down to the bare earth, and here it was possible to measure the depth of the snow.

Leaving these quarters, they marched the whole of the next day over snow, and many of the men were afflicted with "boulimia" (or hunger-faintness). Xenophon, who was guarding the rear, came upon some men who had dropt down, and he did not know what ailed them; but some one who was experienced in such matters suggested to him that they had evidently got boulimia; and if they got something to eat, they would revive. Then he went the round of the baggage train, and laying an embargo on any eatables he could see, doled out with his own hands, or sent off other able-bodied agents to distribute to the sufferers, who as soon as they had taken a mouthful got on their legs again and continued the march.

On and on they marched, and about dusk Cheirisophus reached a village, and surprised some women and girls who had come from the village to fetch water at the fountain outside the stockade. These asked them who they were. The interpreters answered for them in Persian: "They were on their way from the king to the satrap;" in reply to which the women gave them to understand that the satrap was not at home, but was away a parasang farther on. As it was late they entered with the water-carriers within the stockade to visit the headman of the village. Accordingly Cheirisophus and as many of the troops as were able got into cantonments there, while the rest of the soldiers—those namely who were unable to complete the march—had to spend the night out, without food and without fire; under the circumstances some of the men perished.

On the heels of the army hung perpetually bands of the enemy, snatching away disabled baggage animals and fighting with each other over the carcasses. And in its track not seldom were left to their fate disabled soldiers, struck down with snow-blindness or with toes mortified by frostbite. As to the eyes, it was some alleviation against the snow to march with something black before them; for the feet, the only remedy was to keep in motion without stopping for an instant, and to loose the sandal at night. If they went to sleep with the sandals on, the thong worked into the feet, and the sandals were frozen fast to them. This was partly due to the fact that, since their old sandals had failed, they wore untanned brogues made of newly-flayed ox-hides. It was owing to some such dire necessity that a party of men fell out and were left behind, and seeing a black-looking patch of ground where the snow had evidently disappeared, they conjectured it must have been melted; and this was actually so, owing to a spring of some sort which was to be seen steaming up in a dell close by. To this they had turned aside and sat down, and were loth to go a step further. But Xenophon, with his rearguard, perceived them, and begged and implored them by all manner of means not to be left behind, telling them that the enemy were after them in large packs pursuing; and he ended by growing angry. They merely bade him put a knife to their throats; not one step farther would they stir. Then it seemed best to frighten the pursuing enemy if possible, and prevent their falling upon the invalids. It was already dusk, and the pursuers were advancing with much noise and hubbub, wrangling and disputing over their spoils. Then all of a sudden the rearguard, in the plenitude of health and strength, sprang up out of their lair and run upon the enemy, whilst those weary wights bawled out as loud as their sick throats could sound, and clashed their spears against their shields; and the enemy in terror hurled themselves through the snow into the dell, and not one of them ever uttered a sound again.

Xenophon and his party, telling the sick folk that next day people would come for them, set off, and before they had gone half a mile they fell in with some soldiers who had laid down to rest on the snow with their cloaks wrapped round them, but never a guard was established, and they made them get up. Their explanation was that those in front would not move on. Passing by this group he sent forward the strongest of his light infantry in advance, with orders to find out what the stoppage was. They reported that the whole army lay reposing in such fashion. That being so, Xenophon's men had nothing for it but to bivouac in the open air also, without fire and supperless, merely posting what pickets they could under the circumstances. But as soon as it drew towards day, Xenophon despatched the youngest of his men to the sick folk behind, with orders to make them get up and force them to proceed. Meanwhile Cheirisophus had sent some of his men quartered in the village to enquire how they fared in the rear; they were overjoyed to see them, and handed over the sick folk to them to carry into camp, while they themselves continued their march forward, and ere twenty furlongs were past reached the village in which Cheirisophus was quartered. As soon as the two divisions were met, the resolution was come to that it would be safe to billet the regiments throughout the villages; Cheirisophus remained where he was, while the rest drew lots for the villages in sight, and then, with their several detachments, marched off to their respective destinations.

Xenophon
Anabasis, trans. H. G. Dakyns

Xenophon (*c.* 435–354 BC) was a Greek historian and soldier. With 10,000 Greek soldiers, he went in the year 401 to fight in Persia for Cyrus, who was at war with his brother Artaxerxes, the king of Persia. When Cyrus was killed, the Greeks were more than 1500 km from home. Elected leader of the troops, Xenophon successfully led the men back to the Black Sea. This extraordinary feat is described in his major work, *Anabasis*.

WINTER – A DIRGE

The wintry west extends his blast,
And hail and rain does blaw;
Or the stormy north sends driving forth
The blinding sleet and snaw:
While, tumbling brown, the burn comes down,
And roars frae bank to brae;
And bird and beast in covert rest,
And pass the heartless day.

The sweeping blast, the sky o'ercast,
The joyless winter-day,
Let others fear, to me more dear
Than all the pride of May:
The tempest's howl, it soothes my soul,
My griefs it seems to join;
The leafless trees my fancy please,
Their fate resembles mine!

Thou Pow'r Supreme, whose mighty scheme
These woes of mine fulfil,
Here, firm, I rest, they must be best,
Because they are Thy will!
Then all I want (O, do Thou grant
This one request of mine!)
Since to enjoy Thou dost deny,
Assist me to resign.

Robert Burns

Robert Burns (1759–1796) is regarded as Scotland's national poet. The son of a farmer, he spent a good deal of his life farming, though not always successfully. He published one collection of poems in an effort to raise the money to emigrate to Jamaica. As well as his own poetry he collected – and wrote – many songs. Rural life, animals and Scottish folklore are regular and important themes in his work.

THE COVERLEY HUNT

Those who have searched into human nature observe, that nothing so much shows the nobleness of the soul, as that its felicity consists in action. Every man has such an active principle in him, that he will find out something to employ himself upon, in whatever place or state of life he is posted. I have heard of a gentleman who was under close confinement in the Bastile seven years ; during which time he amused himself in scattering a few small pins about his chamber, gathering them up again, and placing them in different figures on the arm of a great chair. He often told his friends afterwards, that unless he had found out this piece of exercise, he verily believed he should have lost his senses.

After what has been said, I need not inform my readers, that Sir Roger, with whose character I hope they are at present pretty well acquainted, has in his youth gone through the whole course of those rural diversions which the country abounds in ; and which seem to be extremely well suited to that laborious industry a man may observe here in a far greater degree than in towns and cities. I have before hinted at some of my friend's exploits : he has in his youthful days taken forty coveys of partridges in a season; and tired many a salmon with a line consisting but of a single hair. The constant thanks and good wishes of the neighborhood always attended him on account of his remarkable enmity towards foxes ; having destroyed more of those vermin in one year than it was thought the whole country could have produced.

Indeed, the Knight does not scruple to own among his most intimate friends, that in order to establish his reputation this way, he has secretly sent for great numbers of them out of other counties, which he used to turn loose about the country by night, that he might the better signalize himself in their destruction the next day. His hunting horses were the finest and best managed in all these parts : his tenants are still full of the praises of a gray stone horse that unhappily staked himself several years since, and was buried with great solemnity in the orchard.

Sir Koger, being at present too old for fox-hunting, to keep himself in action, has disposed of his beagles and got a pack of stop-hounds. What these want in speed he endeavors to make amends for by the deepness of their mouths and the variety of their notes, which are suited in such manner to each other that the whole cry makes up a complete concert. He is so nice in this particular, that a gentleman having made him a present of a very fine hound the other day, the Knight returned it by the servant with a great many expressions of civility ; but desired him to tell his master that the dog he had sent was indeed a most excellent base, but that at present he only wanted a counter-tenor. Could I believe my friend had ever read Shakespeare I should certainly conclude he had taken the hint from Theseus in the Midsummer Night's Dream : —

> My hounds are bred out of the Spartan kind,
> So flew'd, so sanded ; and their heads are hung
> With ears that sweep away the morning dew;
> Crook-knee'd and dew-lapp'd like Thessalian bulls;
> Slow in pursuit, but match'd in mouth like bells,
> Each under each : a cry more tuneable
> Was never holla'd to, nor cheer'd with horn.

Sir Roger is so keen at this sport that he has been out almost every day since I came down; and upon the chaplain's offering to lend me his easy pad, I was prevailed on yesterday morning to make one of the company. I was extremely pleased, as we rid along, to observe the general benevolence of all the neighborhood towards my friend. The farmers' sons thought themselves happy if they could open a gate for the good old Knight as he passed by; which he generally requited with a nod or a smile, and a kind inquiry after their fathers and uncles.

After we had rid about a mile from home, we came upon a large heath, and the sportsmen began to beat. They had done so for some time, when, as I was at a little distance from the rest of the company, I saw a hare pop out from a small furze-brake almost under my horse's feet. I marked the way she took, which I endeavored to make the company sensible of by extending my arm; but to no purpose, till Sir Roger, who knows that none of my extraordinary motions are insignificant, rode up to me, and asked me if puss was gone that way. Upon my answering " Yes," he immediately called in the dogs and put them upon the scent. As they were going off, I heard one of the country-fellows muttering to his companion that lo 'twas a wonder they had not lost all their sport, for want of the silent gentleman's crying " Stole away ! " This, with my aversion to leaping hedges, made me withdraw to a rising ground, from whence I could have the picture of the whole chase, without the fatigue of keeping in with the hounds. The hare immediately threw them above a mile behind her; but I was pleased to find that instead of running straight forwards, or in hunter's language, " flying the country," as I was afraid she might have done, she wheeled about, and described a sort of circle round the hill where I had taken my station, in such manner as gave me a very distinct view of the sport. I could see her first pass by, and the dogs some time afterwards unravelling the whole track she had made, and following her through all her doubles. I was at the same time delighted in observing that deference which the rest of the pack paid to each particular hound, according to the character he had acquired amongst them: if they were at fault, and an old hound of reputation opened but once, he was immediately followed by the whole cry ; while a raw dog, or one who was a noted liar, might have yelped his heart out, without being taken notice of.

The hare now, after having squatted two or three times, and been put up again as often, came still nearer to the place where she was at first started. The dogs pursued her, and these were followed by the jolly Knight, who rode upon a white gelding, encompassed by his tenants and servants, and cheering his hounds with all the gaiety of five-and-twenty. One of the sportsmen rode up to me, and told me that he was sure the chase was almost at an end, because the old dogs, which had hitherto lain behind, now headed the pack. The fellow was in the right. Our hare took a large field just under us, followed by the full cry, " In view." I must confess the brightness of the weather, the cheerfulness of everything around me, the chiding of the hounds, which was returned upon us in a double echo from two neighboring hills, with the holloaing of the sportsmen and the sounding of the horn, lifted my spirits into a most lively pleasure, which I freely indulged because I was sure it was innocent. If I was under any concern, it was on the account of the poor hare, that was now quite spent, and almost within the reach of her enemies; when the huntsman, getting forward, threw down his pole before the dogs. They were now within eight yards of that game which they had been pursuing for almost as many hours ; yet on the signal before-mentioned they all made a sudden stand, and though they continued opening as much as before, durst not once attempt to pass beyond the pole. At the same time Sir Roger rode forward, and alighting, took up the hare in his arms ; which he soon delivered up to one of his servants with an order, if she could be kept alive, to let her go in his great orchard ; where it seems he has several of these prisoners of war, who live together in a very comfortable captivity. I was highly pleased to see the discipline of the pack, and the good nature of the Knight, who could not find in his heart to murder a creature that had given him so much diversion.

As we were returning home, I remembered that Monsieur Pascal, in his most excellent discourse on the Misery of Man, tells us, that all our endeavors after greatness proceed from nothing but a desire of being surrounded by a multitude of persons and affairs that may hinder us from looking into ourselves, which is a view we cannot bear. He afterwards goes on to show that our love of sports comes from the same reason, and is particularly severe upon hunting. "What" says he, "unless it be to drown thought, can make men throw away so much time and pains upon a silly animal, which they might buy cheaper in the market?" The foregoing reflection is certainly just, when a man suffers his whole mind to be drawn into his sports, and altogether loses himself in the woods ; but does not affect those who propose a far more laudable end for this exercise, I mean the preservation of health, and keeping all the organs of the soul in a condition to execute her orders. Had that incomparable person, whom I last quoted, been a little more indulgent to himself in this point, the world might probably have enjoyed him much longer;

whereas through too great an application to his studies in his youth, he contracted that ill habit of body, which, after a tedious sickness, carried him off in the fortieth year of his age ; and the whole history we have of his life till that time is but one continued account of the behavior of a noble soul struggling under innumerable pains and distempers.

For my own part I intend to hunt twice a week during my stay with Sir Roger; and shall prescribe the moderate use of this exercise to all my country friends, as the best kind of physic for mending a bad constitution, and preserving a good one.

Joseph Addison
The Spectator

Joseph Addison (1672–1719) essayist and politician, wrote articles for the *Tatler*, started in 1709 by his old school friend Richard Steele. In 1711 the friends founded the *Spectator*, and it was in this publication that Sir Roger de Coverley appeared. He was portrayed as a Worcestershire baronet, a typical Tory country gentleman, interested in his land and the activities of his neighbourhood. He was supposed to be the grandson of the man who invented the dance of the same name. Addison portrayed Sir Roger as 'more beloved than esteemed': the comic aspects of this character made him very popular.

THE RUSSIAN WINTER

The whole countrey differeth very much from it self by reason of the yeare: so that a man would marvel to see the great alteration and difference betwixt the winter and the summer Russia. The whole countrey in the winter lieth under snow, which falleth continually, and is sometime of a yard or two thick, but greater towards the North. The rivers and other waters are frozen up a yard or more thick, how swift or broad so ever they be. And this continueth commonly five moneths, viz. from the beginning of November till towards the end of March, what time the snow beginneth to melt. So that it would breed a frost in a man to look abroad at that time, and see the winter face of that countrey. The sharpnesse of the aire you may judge of by this, for that water dropped down, or cast up into the aire, congealeth into Ice before it come to the ground. In the extremitie of winter, if you hold a pewter dish or pot in your hand, or any other metall (except in some chamber where their warm stoves be) your fingers will frieze fast unto it, and draw off the skinne at the parting. When you passe out of a warm room into a cold, you shall sensibly feel your breath to wax stark, and even stifling with the colde, as you draw it in and out. Divers not onely that travel abroad, but in the very markets and streets of their towns are mortally pinched and killed withall: so that you shall see many drop down in the streets, many travellers brought into the towns sitting dead and stiff in their fleds. Divers lose their noses, the tips of their ears, and the balls of their cheeks, their toes, feet, &c. Many times (when the Winter is very hard and extreme) the bears and wolves issue by troups out of the woods driven by hunger, and enter the villages, tearing and ravening all they can find, so that the inhabitants are fain to flee for safeguard of their lives.

Giles Fletcher
Of The Russe Common Wealth

Giles Fletcher (1546–1611) was a poet and diplomat. In 1588 he was sent as ambassador to Moscow, to the court of Tsar Fyodor I, and the book he subsequently wrote, *Of the Russe Commonwealth*, was popular and influential: the most important account of Russia of its time in English. Giles Fletcher was the father of the poets Giles and Phineas Fletcher, and the uncle of John Fletcher the dramatist.

THE RETREAT FROM MOSCOW

But on the 6th of November, the heavens declared against us. Their azure disappeared. The army marched enveloped in cold fogs. These fogs became thicker, and presently an immense cloud descended upon it in large flakes of snow. It seemed as if the very sky was falling, and joining the earth and our enemies to complete our destruction. All objects changed their appearance, and became confounded, and not to be recognised again; we proceeded, without knowing where we were, without perceiving the point to which we were bound; every thing was transformed into an obstacle. While the soldier was struggling with the tempest of wind and snow, the flakes, driven by the storm, lodged and accumulated in every hollow; their surfaces concealed unknown abysses, which perfidiously opened beneath our feet. There the men were engulphed, and the weakest, resigning themselves to their fate, found a grave in these snow-pits.

Those who followed turned aside, but the storm drove into their faces both the snow that was descending from the sky, and that which it raised from the ground: it seemed bent on opposing their progress. The Russian winter, under this new form, attacked them on all sides: it penetrated through their light garments and their torn shoes and boots. Their wet clothes froze upon their bodies; an icy envelope encased them and stiffened all their limbs. A keen and violent wind interrupted respiration: it seized their breath at the moment when they exhaled it, and converted it into icicles, which hung from their beards all round their mouths.

The unfortunate creatures still crawled on, shivering, till the snow, gathering like balls under their feet, or the fragment of some broken article, a branch of a tree, or the body of one of their comrades, caused them to stumble and fall. There they groaned in vain; the snow soon covered them; slight hillocks marked the spot where they lay: such was their only grave! The road was studded with these undulations, like a cemetery: the most intrepid and the most indifferent were affected; they passed on quickly with averted looks. But before them, around them, there was nothing but snow: this immense and dreary uniformity extended farther than the eye could reach; the imagination was astounded; it was like a vast winding-sheet which Nature had thrown over the army. The only objects not enveloped by it, were some gloomy pines, trees of the tombs, with their funeral verdure, the motionless aspect of their gigantic black trunks and their dismal look, which completed the doleful appearance of a general mourning, and of an army dying amidst a nature already dead.

Every thing, even to their very arms, still offensive at Malo-Yaroslawetz, but since then defensive only, now turned against them. These seemed to their frozen limbs insupportably heavy, in the frequent falls which they experienced, they dropped from their hands and were broken or buried in the snow. If they rose again, it was without them; for they did not throw them away; hunger and cold wrested them from their grasp. The fingers of many others were frozen to the musket which they still held, which deprived them of the motion necessary for keeping up some degree of warmth and life.

We soon met with numbers of men belonging to all the corps, sometimes singly, at others in troops. They had not basely deserted their colours; it was cold and inanition which had separated them from their columns. In this general and individual struggle, they had parted from one another, and there they were, disarmed, vanquished, defenceless, without leaders, obeying nothing but the urgent instinct of self-preservation.

Most of them, attracted by the sight of by-paths, dispersed themselves over the country, in hopes of finding bread and shelter for the coming night: but, on their first passage, all had been laid waste to the extent of seven or eight leagues; they met with nothing but Cossacks, and an armed population, which encompassed, wounded, and stripped them naked, and then left them, with ferocious bursts of laughter, to expire on the snow. These people, who had risen at the call of Alexander and Kutusoff, and who had not then learned, as they since have, to avenge nobly a country which they were unable to defend, hovered on both flanks of the army under favour of the woods. Those whom they did not despatch with their pikes and hatchets, they brought back to the fatal and all-devouring high road.

Night then came on—a night of sixteen hours! But on that snow which covered every thing, they knew not where to halt, where to sit, where to lie down, where to find some root or other to eat, and dry wood to kindle a fire! Fatigue, darkness, and repeated orders nevertheless stopped those whom their moral and physical strength and the efforts of their officers had kept together. They strove to establish themselves; but the tempest, still active, dispersed the first preparations for bivouacs. The pines, laden with frost, obstinately resisted the flames; their snow, that from the sky which yet continued to fall fast, and that on the ground, which melted with the efforts of the soldiers, and the effect of the first fires, extinguished those fires, as well as the strength and spirits of the men.

General Count Philip de Ségur
History of the Expedition to Russia

Phillipe Paul, Comte de Ségur, (1780–1873) was a soldier and historian. He came from an aristocratic family that was sympathetic to the French revolution. Joining the cavalry in 1800, he was appointed to Napoleon's personal staff, serving in many of the important campaigns of the first Empire. This included the 1812 Russian campaign, in which an enormous French army of 680,000 men invaded Russia. Attempts to force the Russian army to stand and fight failed, and when the French reached Moscow in mid-September, it was empty. The governor had left a small party of men who set the city on fire: with no food or shelter the French had to retire. However, the Russians had destroyed the land as they fell back in the face of the French advance. The French were faced with moving an army with no sources of food, no extra horses, no shelter, no winter clothes – and through harsh winter weather. It is estimated that 400,00 men were lost during the retreat.

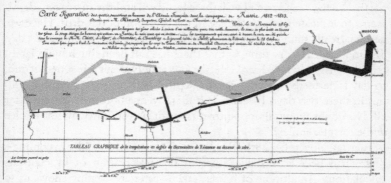

Charles Joseph Minard's diagram shows how the French army diminished during the Russian campaign. The thick line at the top shows the size of the army at the start, getting smaller as it approaches then reaches Moscow. The black line below shows how the dreadful conditions of the Retreat caused the army to dwindle. At the base is a scale of temperatures. (Multiply Réaumur temperatures by 1.25 to get Celsius, e.g. –30 °R = –37.5 °C).

THE NORTHERN LIGHTS
FROM *FRAM*

We looked for pressure with full moon and spring-tide on 23rd of November; but then, and for several days afterwards, the ice was quite quiet. On the afternoon of Saturday, the 25th, however, its distant roar was heard from the south, and we have heard it from the same direction every day since. This morning it was very loud, and came gradually nearer. At nine o'clock it was quite close to us, and this evening we hear it near us again. It seems, however, as if we had now got out of the groove to which the pressure principally confines itself. We were regularly in it before. The ice round us is perfectly quiet. The probability is that the last severe pressure packed it very tight about us, and that the cold since has frozen it into such a thick strong mass that it offers great resistance, while the weaker ice in other places yields to the pressure. The depth of the sea is increasing steadily, and we are drifting north.

This evening Hansen has worked out the observations of the day before yesterday, and finds that we are in 79° 11' north latitude. That is good, and the way we ought to get on. It is the most northern point we have reached yet, and to-day we are in all likelihood still farther north. We have made good way these last days, and the increasing depth seems to indicate a happy change in the direction of our drift. Have we, perhaps, really found the right road at last? We are drifting about 5' a day. The most satisfactory thing is that there has not been much wind lately, especially the two last days; yesterday it was only about 3 feet per second; to-day is perfectly still, and yet the depth has increased 21 fathoms (40 m.) in these two days. It seems as if there were a northerly current after all. No doubt many disappointments await us yet; but why not rejoice while fortune smiles?'

Tuesday, November 28th. The disappointment lost no time in coming-. There had been a mistake either in the observation or in Hansen's calculations. An altitude of Jupiter taken yesterday evening shows us to be in 78° 36' north latitude. The soundings to-day showed 74 fathoms (142 m.) of water, or about the same as yesterday, and the sounding-line indicated a south-westerly drift. However anxious one is to take things philosophically, one can't help feeling a little depressed. I try to find solace in a book; absorb myself in the learning of the Indians: their happy faith in transcendental powers, in the supernatural faculties of the soul, and in a future life. Oh, if one could only get hold of a little supernatural power now, and oblige the winds always to blow from the south!

I went on deck this evening in rather a gloomy frame of mind, but was nailed to the spot the moment I got outside. There is the supernatural for you – the northern lights flashing in matchless power and beauty over the sky in all the colours of the rainbow! Seldom or never have I seen the colours so brilliant. The prevailing one at first was yellow, but that gradually flickered over into green, and then a sparkling ruby-red began to show at the bottom of the rays on the under side of the arch, soon spreading over the whole arch. And now from the far-away western horizon a fiery serpent writhed itself up over the sky, shining brighter and brighter as it came. It split into three, all brilliantly glittering. Then the colours changed. The serpent to the south turned almost ruby-red, with spots of yellow; the one in the middle, yellow; and the one to the north, greenish-white. Sheafs of rays swept along the sides of the serpents, driven through the ether-like waves before a storm-wind. They sway backwards and forwards, now strong, now fainter again. The serpents reached and passed the zenith. Though I was thinly dressed and shivering with cold, I could not tear myself away till the spectacle was over, and only a faintly-glowing fiery serpent, near the western horizon showed where it had begun. When I came on deck later the masses of light had passed northwards, and spread themselves in incomplete arches over the northern sky. If one wants to read mystic meanings into the phenomena of nature, here, surely, is the opportunity.

The observation this afternoon showed us to be in 78° 38' 42" N. lat. This is anything but rapid progress.

Fridtjof Nansen
Farthest North

The Norwegian explorer Fridtjof Nansen (1861–1930) was convinced that there was a current in the Arctic that would allow him to reach the North Pole by sea. In his specially-built ship *Fram*, he and his crew deliberately positioned themselves north of Siberia, where the vessel froze into the ice. The current moved *Fram* to a latitude of 84°4' – at that point Nansen and some of his men left *Fram* and walked to 86° 14', the furthest north anyone had been. It took three years for the *Fram* to work its way through the ice, emerging in the North Atlantic near Greenland. Nansen later won the Nobel Peace Prize for his work with refugees after World War I.

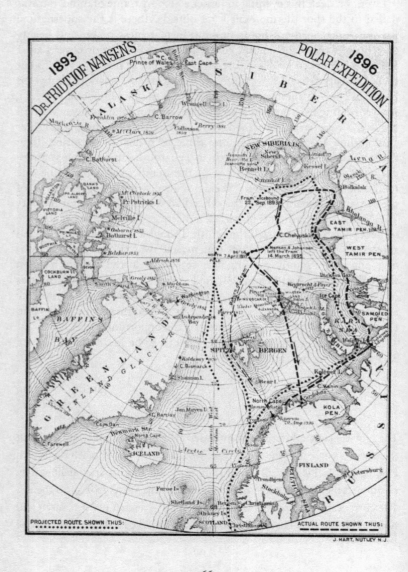

WEST BAY IN WINTER

Landscape of absentees, where nothing
Is on itself, but anticipates
Patiently the next coming.

Landscape of withdrawn teashops, of shut
Pizzerias and doughnutteries,
Lavatories out of order.

Brooding self-absorbed till Easter makes
Sense of immense carparks, hides duckboards
And sandbags for a season.

Showers chase us, and mysterious light
Behind clouds falls on water we can't
Quite see. Gulls alone mark us.

Caravans turn their backs like cattle.
Laked fields lie apathetic. Only
The sea, that old ham, relentlessly
Goes on performing.

U. A. Fanthorpe
Queueing for the Sun

U. A. Fanthorpe (1929–2009) taught English for sixteen years after leaving Oxford, but it was not until she had given up teaching and taken a job as a receptionist in a psychiatric hospital that she began to write poetry. England and English values often inspired her understated and witty work.

REPORT BY SUPERINTENDENT ON DISASTER AT FLANNAN ISLANDS LIGHTHOUSE

On receipt of Captain Harvie's telegram on 26 December 1900 reporting that the three keepers on Flannan Islands, viz James Ducat, Principal, Thomas Marshall, second Assistant, and Donald McArthur, Occasional Keeper (doing duty for William Ross, first Assistant, on sick leave), had disappeared and that they must have been blown over the cliffs or drowned, I made the following arrangements with the Secretary for the temporary working of the Station.

James Ferrier, Principal Keeper was sent from Stornoway Lighthouse to Tiumpan Head Lighthouse and John Milne, Principal Keeper at Tiumpan Head was sent to take temporary charge at Flannan Islands. Donald Jack, the second Assistant Storekeeper was also despatched to Flannan Islands, the intention being that these two men, along with Joseph Moore, the third Assistant at Flannan Islands, who was ashore when the accident took place, should do duty pending permanent arrangements being made. I also proceeded to Flannan Islands where I was landed, along with Milne and Jack, early on the 29th ulto.

After satisfying myself that everything connected with the light was in good order and that the men landed would be able to maintain the light, I proceeded to ascertain, if possible, the cause of the disaster and also took statements from Captain Harvie and Mr McCormack the second mate of the HESPERUS, Joseph Moore, third Assistant keeper, Flannan Islands and Allan MacDonald, Buoymaster and the following is the result of my investigations:-

The HESPERUS arrived at Flannan Islands for the purpose of making the ordinary relief about noon Wednesday, 26 December and, as neither signals were shown, nor any of the usual preparations for landing made, Captain Harvie blew both the steam whistle and the siren to call the attention of the Keepers. As this had no effect, he fired a rocket, which also evoked no response, and a boat was lowered and sent ashore to the East landing with Joseph Moore, Assistant Keeper. When the boat reached the landing there being still no signs of the keepers, the boat was backed into the landing and with some difficulty Moore managed to jump ashore. When he went up to the Station he found the entrance gate and outside doors closed, the clock stopped, no fire lit, and, looking into the bedrooms, he found the beds empty. He became alarmed at this and ran down to the boat and informed Mr McCormack and one of the seamen managed to jump ashore and with Moore made a thorough search of the Station but could discover nothing. They then returned to the ship and informed Captain Harvie who told Moore he would have to return to the Island to keep the light going pending instructions, and called for volunteers from his crew to assist in this.

He met with a ready response and two seamen, Lamont and Campbell, were selected with Mr MacDonald, the Buoymaster, who was on board, also offered his services, which were accepted and Moore, MacDonald and these two seamen were left in charge of the light while Captain Harvie returned to Breasclete and telegraphed an account of the disaster to the Secretary.

The men left on the Island made a thorough search, in the first place, of the Station and found that the last entry on the slate had been made by Mr Ducat, the Principal Keeper on the morning of Saturday, 15 December. The lamp was crimmed, the oil fountains and canteens were filled up and the lens and machinery cleaned, which proved that the work of the 15th had been completed. The pots and pans had been cleaned and the kitchen tidied up, which showed that the man who had been acting as cook had completed his work, which goes to prove that

the men disappeared on the afternoon which was received (after news of the disaster had been published) that Captain Holman had passed the Flannan Islands in the steamer ARCHTOR at midnight on the 15th ulto, and could not observe the light, he felt satisfied that he should have seen it.

On the Thursday and Friday the men made a thorough search over and round the island and I went over the ground with them on Saturday. Everything at the East landing place was in order and the ropes which had been coiled and stored there on the completion of the relief on 7 December were all in their places and the lighthouse buildings and everything at the Stations was in order. Owing to the amount of sea, I could not get down to the landing place, but I got down to the crane platform 70 feet above the sea level. The crane originally erected on this platform was washed away during last winter, and the crane put up this summer was found to be unharmed, the jib lowered and secured to the rock, and the canvas covering the wire rope on the barrel securely lashed round it, and there was no evidence that the men had been doing anything at the crane. The mooring ropes, landing ropes, derrick landing ropes and crane handles, and also a wooden box in which they were kept and which was secured in a crevice in the rocks 70 feet up the tramway from its terminus, and about 40 feet higher than the crane platform, or 110 feet in all above the sea level, had been washed away, and the ropes were strewn in the crevices of the rocks near the crane platform and entangled among the crane legs, but they were all coiled up, no single coil being found unfastened. The iron railings round the crane platform and from the terminus of the tramway to the concrete steps up from the West landing were displaced and twisted. A large block of stone, weighing upwards of 20 cwt, had been dislodged from its position higher up and carried down to and left on the concrete path leading from the terminus of the tramway to the top of the steps.

A life buoy fastened to the railings along this path, to be used in case of emergency had disappeared, and I thought at first that it had been removed for the purpose of being used but, on examining the ropes by which it was fastened, I found that they had not been touched, and as pieces of canvas was adhering to the ropes, it was evident that the force of the sea pouring through the railings had, even at this great height (110 feet above sea level) torn the life buoy off the ropes.

When the accident occurred, Ducat was wearing sea boots and a waterproof, and Marshall sea boots and oilskins, and as Moore assures me that the men only wore those articles when going down to the landings, they must have intended, when they left the Station, either to go down to the landing or the proximity of it.

Robert Muirhead
Northern Lighthouse Board Report

The lighthouse on Eilean Mòr, one of the Flannan Islands in the Outer Hebrides, was the scene of a maritime mystery: the three keepers disappeared in December 1900. Many rumours circulated – murder, sea serpents, foreign spies and a phantom ship full of ghosts were among the suggestions advanced to explain the absence of the men. Robert Muirhead, a superintendent of the Northern Lighthouse Board, conducted the official investigation. His report is somewhat more prosaic!

WINTER

How clearly winter shows
　The beauty of the street;
How pure, how fine he blows
　The unsubstantial sheet
Of half transparent glass
　That is the frosted sky;
How pale he paints the grass
　Where fallen petals like.

Fredegond Shove
Daybreak

Fredegond Shove (1889–1949) wrote poetry throughout her life. She married the anti-Keynsian economist Gerald Shove and lived in Cambridge, but was also associated with the Bloomsbury group. Some of her work was set to music by Ralph Vaughan Williams, whose first wife Adeline Fisher was Fredegond Shove's aunt.

IN A DREAR-NIGHTED DECEMBER

In drear-nighted December,
  Too happy, happy tree,
Thy branches ne'er remember
  Their green felicity—
The north cannot undo them
With a sleety whistle through them
Nor frozen thawings glue them
  From budding at the prime.

In drear-nighted December,
  Too happy, happy brook,
Thy bubblings ne'er remember
  Apollo's summer look;
But with a sweet forgetting,
They stay their crystal fretting,
Never, never petting
  About the frozen time.

Ah! would 'twere so with many
  A gentle girl and boy—
But were there ever any
  Writh'd not of passed joy?
The feel of not to feel it,
When there is none to heal it
Nor numbed sense to steel it,
  Was never said in rhyme.

John Keats

WHITE CLOTHES

Next after fine colors, I like plain white. One of my sorrows, when the summer ends, is that I must put off my cheery and comfortable white clothes and enter for the winter into the depressing captivity of the shapeless and degrading black ones. It is mid-October now, and the weather is growing cold up here in the New Hampshire hills, but it will not succeed in freezing me out of these white garments, for here the neighbors are few, and it is only of crowds that I am afraid. I made a brave experiment, the other night, to see how it would feel to shock a crowd with these unseasonable clothes, and also to see how long it might take the crowd to reconcile itself to them and stop looking astonished and outraged. On a stormy evening I made a talk before a full house, in the village, clothed like a ghost, and looking as conspicuous, all solitary and alone on that platform, as any ghost could have looked; and I found, to my gratification, that it took the house less than ten minutes to forget about the ghost and give its attention to the tidings I had brought. I am nearly seventy-one, and I recognize that my age has given me a good many privileges; valuable privileges; privileges which are not granted to younger persons. Little by little I hope to get together courage enough to wear white clothes all through the winter, in New York. It will be a great satisfaction to me to show off in this way; and perhaps the largest of all the satisfactions will be the knowledge that every scoffer, of my sex, will secretly envy me and wish he dared to follow my lead.

Mark Twain
Autobiography of Mark Twain

Mark Twain (1835–1910) was an American writer, humorist and lecturer. Two of his novels, *The Adventures of Tom Sawyer* and *The Adventures of Huckleberry Finn* – both based on his boyhood memories – became classics. Poor investments led to bankruptcy in 1884. He managed to overcome his difficulties through writing and lecturing, but his later work is darker and less optimistic than that of his earlier years.

SCHOOLBOYS IN WINTER

THE schoolboys still their morning ramble take
To neighboring village school with playing speed,
Loitering with passtime's leisure till they quake,
Oft looking up the wild-geese droves to heed,
Watching the letters which their journeys make;
Or plucking haws on which their fieldfares feed,
And hips and sloes; and on each shallow lake
Making glib slides, where they like shadows go
Till some fresh passtimes in their minds awake.
Then off they start anew and hasty blow
Their numbed and clumpsing fingers till they glow;
Then races with their shadows wildly run
That stride huge giants o'er the shining snow
In the pale splendour of the winter sun.

John Clare

The rural poet John Clare (1793–1864) was devoted to the village
of Helpston in Northamptonshire, where he was born and where he
worked as a farm labourer and gardener. Here he wrote about the life
he knew: farming was changing dramatically as land was enclosed, and
he lamented the old days as well as showing deep concern for the poor of
the neighbourhood. Moving to Northborough, a village three miles from
Helpston in 1832, he became melancholic, and was eventually admitted to
an asylum in Epping. He escaped and walked home, but eventually had to
go into the asylum in Northampton, where he continued to write poetry.

THE SNOW MAN

"It is so delightfully cold," said the Snow Man, "that it makes my whole
body crackle. This is just the kind of wind to blow life into one. How that
great red thing up there is staring at me!" He meant the sun, who was just
setting. "It shall not make me wink. I shall manage to keep the pieces."

He had two triangular pieces of tile in his head, instead of eyes; his mouth was made of an old broken rake, and was, of course, furnished with teeth. He had been brought into existence amidst the joyous shouts of boys, the jingling of sleigh-bells, and the slashing of whips. The sun went down, and the full moon rose, large, round, and clear, shining in the deep blue.

"There it comes again, from the other side," said the Snow Man, who supposed the sun was showing himself once more. "Ah, I have cured him of staring, though; now he may hang up there, and shine, that I may see myself. If I only knew how to manage to move away from this place,—I should so like to move. If I could, I would slide along yonder on the ice, as I have seen the boys do; but I don't understand how; I don't even know how to run."

"Away, away," barked the old yard-dog. He was quite hoarse, and could not pronounce "Bow wow" properly. He had once been an indoor dog, and lay by the fire, and he had been hoarse ever since. "The sun will make you run some day. I saw him, last winter, make your predecessor run, and his predecessor before him. Away, away, they all have to go."

"I don't understand you, comrade," said the Snow Man. "Is that thing up yonder to teach me to run? I saw it running itself a little while ago, and now it has come creeping up from the other side."

"You know nothing at all," replied the yard-dog; "but then, you've only lately been patched up. What you see yonder is the moon, and the one before it was the sun. It will come again to-morrow, and most likely teach you to run down into the ditch by the well; for I think the weather is going to change. I can feel such pricks and stabs in my left leg; I am sure there is going to be a change."

"I don't understand him," said the Snow Man to himself; "but I have a feeling that he is talking of something very disagreeable. The one who stared so just now, and whom he calls the sun, is not my friend; I can feel that too."

"Away, away," barked the yard-dog, and then he turned round three times, and crept into his kennel to sleep.

There was really a change in the weather. Towards morning, a thick fog covered the whole country round, and a keen wind arose, so that the cold seemed to freeze one's bones; but when the sun rose, the sight was splendid. Trees and bushes were covered with hoar frost, and looked like a forest of white coral; while on every twig glittered frozen dew-drops. The many delicate forms concealed in summer by luxuriant foliage, were now clearly defined, and looked like glittering lace-work. From every twig glistened a white radiance. The birch, waving in the wind, looked full of life, like trees in summer; and its appearance was wondrously beautiful. And where the sun shone, how everything glittered and sparkled, as if diamond dust had been strewn about; while the snowy carpet of the earth appeared as if covered with diamonds, from which countless lights gleamed, whiter than even the snow itself.

"This is really beautiful," said a young girl, who had come into the garden with a young man; and they both stood still near the Snow Man, and contemplated the glittering scene. "Summer cannot show a more beautiful sight," she exclaimed, while her eyes sparkled.

"And we can't have such a fellow as this in the summer time," replied the young man, pointing to the Snow Man; "he is capital."

The girl laughed, and nodded at the Snow Man, and then tripped away over the snow with her friend. The snow creaked and crackled beneath her feet, as if she had been treading on starch.

"Who are these two?" asked the Snow Man of the yard-dog. "You have been here longer than I have; do you know them?"

"Of course I know them," replied the yard-dog; "she has stroked my back many times, and he has given me a bone of meat. I never bite those two."

"But what are they?" asked the Snow Man.

"They are lovers," he replied; "they will go and live in the same kennel by-and-by, and gnaw at the same bone. Away, away!"

"Are they the same kind of beings as you and I?" asked the Snow Man.

"Well, they belong to the same master," retorted the yard-dog. "Certainly people who were only born yesterday know very little. I can see that in you. I have age and experience. I know every one here in the house, and I know there was once a time when I did not lie out here in the cold, fastened to a chain. Away, away!"

"The cold is delightful," said the Snow Man; "but do tell me tell me; only you must not clank your chain so; for it jars all through me when you do that."

"Away, away!" barked the yard-dog; "I'll tell you; they said I was a pretty little fellow once; then I used to lie in a velvet-covered chair, up at the master's house, and sit in the mistress's lap. They used to kiss my nose, and wipe my paws with an embroidered handkerchief, and I was called 'Ami, dear Ami, sweet Ami.' But after a while I grew too big for them, and they sent me away to the housekeeper's room; so I came to live on the lower story. You can look into the room from where you stand, and see where I was master once; for I was indeed master to the housekeeper. It was certainly a smaller room than those up stairs; but I was more comfortable; for I was not being continually taken hold of and pulled about by the children as I had been. I received quite as good food, or even better. I had my own cushion, and there was a stove—it is the finest thing in the world at this season of the year. I used to go under the stove, and lie down quite beneath it. Ah, I still dream of that stove. Away, away!"

"Does a stove look beautiful?" asked the Snow Man, "is it at all like me?"

"It is just the reverse of you," said the dog; "it's as black as a crow, and has a long neck and a brass knob; it eats firewood, so that fire spurts out of its mouth. We should keep on one side, or under it, to be comfortable. You can see it through the window, from where you stand."

Then the Snow Man looked, and saw a bright polished thing with a brazen knob, and fire gleaming from the lower part of it. The Snow Man felt quite a strange sensation come over him; it was very odd, he knew not what it meant, and he could not account for it. But there are people who are not men of snow, who understand what it is. "And why did you leave her?" asked the Snow Man, for it seemed to him that the stove must be of the female sex. "How could you give up such a comfortable place?"

"I was obliged," replied the yard-dog. "They turned me out of doors, and chained me up here. I had bitten the youngest of my master's sons in the leg, because he kicked away the bone I was gnawing. 'Bone for bone,' I thought; but they were so angry, and from that time I have been fastened with a chain, and lost my bone. Don't you hear how hoarse I am. Away, away! I can't talk any more like other dogs. Away, away, that is the end of it all."

But the Snow Man was no longer listening. He was looking into the housekeeper's room on the lower storey; where the stove stood on its four iron legs, looking about the same size as the Snow Man himself. "What a strange crackling I feel within me," he said. "Shall I ever get in there? It is an innocent wish, and innocent wishes are sure to be fulfilled. I must go in there and lean against her, even if I have to break the window."

"You must never go in there," said the yard-dog, "for if you approach the stove, you'll melt away, away."

"I might as well go," said the Snow Man, "for I think I am breaking up as it is."

During the whole day the Snow Man stood looking in through the window, and in the twilight hour the room became still more inviting, for from the stove came a gentle glow, not like the sun or the moon; no, only the bright light which gleams from a stove when it has been well fed. When the door of the stove was opened, the flames darted out of its mouth; this is customary with all stoves. The light of the flames fell directly on the face and breast of the Snow Man with a ruddy gleam. "I can endure it no longer," said he; "how beautiful it looks when it stretches out its tongue?"

The night was long, but did not appear so to the Snow Man, who stood there enjoying his own reflections, and crackling with the cold. In the morning, the window-panes of the housekeeper's room were covered with ice. They were the most beautiful ice-flowers any Snow Man could desire, but they concealed the stove. These window-panes would not thaw, and he could see nothing of the stove, which he pictured to himself, as if it had been a lovely human being. The snow crackled and the wind whistled around him; it was just the kind of frosty weather a Snow Man might thoroughly enjoy. But he did not enjoy it; how, indeed, could he enjoy anything when he was "stove sick?"

"That is terrible disease for a Snow Man," said the yard-dog; "I have suffered from it myself, but I got over it. Away, away," he barked and then he added, "the weather is going to change." And the weather did change; it began to thaw. As the warmth increased, the Snow Man decreased. He said nothing and made no complaint, which is a sure sign. One morning he broke, and sunk down altogether; and, behold, where he had stood, something like a broomstick remained sticking up in the ground. It was the pole round which the boys had built him up. "Ah, now I understand why he had such a great longing for the stove," said the yard-dog. "Why, there's the shovel that is used for cleaning out the stove, fastened to the pole." The Snow Man had a stove scraper in his body; that was what moved him so. "But it's all over now. Away, away." And soon the winter passed. "Away, away," barked the hoarse yard-dog. But the girls in the house sang,

> "Come from your fragrant home, green thyme;
> Stretch your soft branches, willow-tree;
> The months are bringing the sweet spring-time,

When the lark in the sky sings joyfully.
Come gentle sun, while the cuckoo sings,
And I'll mock his note in my wanderings."

And nobody thought any more of the Snow Man.

Hans Christian Andersen, trans. H. P. Paull

The Danish writer Hans Christian Andersen (1805–1875) produced poems and satires but is most renowned for his fairy tales, which made him world-famous. Children have loved them, but Andersen maintained that he was writing for all ages.

"The Sun will soon teach you to run"
said the Yard-dog.

THE FROST IN DECEMBER 1784

As the frost in December, 1784, was very extraordinary, you, I trust, will not be displeased to hear the particulars; and especially when I promise to say no more about the severities of winter after I have finished this letter.

The first week in December was very wet, with the barometer very low. On the 7th, with the barometer at 28-five-tenths, came on a vast snow, which continued all that day and the next, and most part of the following night; so that by the morning of the 9th the works of men were quite overwhelmed, the lanes filled so as to be impassable, and the ground covered twelve or fifteen inches without any drifting. In the evening of the 9th the air began to be so very sharp that we thought it would be curious to attend to the motions of a thermometer: we therefore hung out two; one made by Martin and one by Dollond, which soon began to show us what we were to expect; for, by ten o'clock, they fell to 21, and at eleven to 4, when we went to bed. On the 10th, in the morning, the quicksilver of Dollond's glass was down to half a degree below zero; and that of Martin's, which was absurdly graduated only to four degrees above zero, sunk quite into the brass guard of the ball; so that when the weather became most interesting this was useless. On the 10th, at eleven at night, though the air was perfectly still, Dollond's glass went down to one degree below zero! This strange severity of the weather made me very desirous to know what degree of cold there might be in such an exalted and near situation as Newton. We had therefore, on the morning of the 10th, written to Mr. ——, and entreated him to hang out his thermometer, made by Adams; and to pay some attention to it morning and evening; expecting wonderful phaenomena, in so elevated a region, at two hundred feet or more above my house. But, behold! on the 10th, at eleven at night, it was down only to 17, and the next morning at 22, when mine was at 10. We were so disturbed at this unexpected reverse of comparative local cold, that we sent one of my glasses up, thinking that of Mr. —— must, somehow, be wrongly constructed. But, when the instruments came to be confronted, they went exactly together: so that, for one night at least, the cold at Newton was 18 degrees less than at Selborne; and, through the whole frost, 10 or 12 degrees; and indeed, when we came to observe consequences, we could readily credit this; for all my laurustines, bays, ilexes, arbutuses, cypresses, and even my Portugal laurels,* and (which occasions more regret) my fine sloping laurel hedge, were scorched up; while, at Newton, the same trees have not lost a leaf! (* Mr. Miller, in his Gardener's Dictionary, says positively that the Portugal laurels remained untouched in the remarkable frost of 1739 - 40. So that either that accurate observer was much mistaken, or else the frost of December, 1784, was much more severe and destructive than that in the year above mentioned.)

We had steady frost on to the 25th, when the thermometer in the morning was down to 10 with us, and at Newton only to 21. Strong frost continued till the 31st, when some tendency to thaw was observed, and, by January the 3rd, 1785, the thaw was confirmed, and some rain fell.

A circumstance that I must not omit, because it was new to us, is, that on Friday, December the 10th, being bright sun-shine, the air was full of icy spiculae, floating in all directions, like atoms in a sun-beam let into a dark room. We thought them at first particles of the rime falling from my tall hedges; but were soon convinced to the contrary, by making our observations in open places where no rime could reach us.

Were they watery particles of the air frozen as they floated; or were they evaporations from the snow frozen as they mounted ?

We were much obliged to the thermometers for the early information they gave us: and hurried our apples, pears, onions, potatoes, etc., into the cellar, and warm closets; while those who had not, or neglected such warnings, lost all their stores of roots and fruits, and had their very bread and cheese frozen.

I must not omit to tell you that, during those two Siberian days, my parlour-cat was so electric, that had a person stroked her, and been properly insulated, the shock might have been given to a whole circle of people.

I forgot to mention before, that, during the two severe days, two men, who were tracing hares in the snow, had their feet frozen; and two men, who were much better employed, had their fingers so affected by the frost, while they were thrashing in a barn, that a mortification followed, from which they did not recover for many weeks.

This frost killed all the furze and most of the ivy, and in many places stripped the hollies of all their leaves. It came at a very early time of the year, before old November ended; and yet it may be allowed from its effects to have exceeded any since 1739 - 40.

Gilbert White
The Natural History of Selborne: Letter LXIII To The Honourable Daines Barrington

The clergyman and naturalist Gilbert White (1720–1793) was born in Selborne, Hampshire, and lived and worked there all his life. He kept detailed observations of the changes brought by the seasons and of the wildlife in his garden and in the countryside around Selborne: over twenty years he included these observations in letters to friends. The friends eventually persuaded him to publish the letters: *The Natural History of Selborne* is a scientific and literary classic, which has never been out of print.

FROST FAIR 1688

A French writer who visited England during the severe frost in the year 1688, says, (in a small volume which he published in Paris,) "that besides hackney-coaches, a large sledge, or sledges, were then exhibited on the frozen Thames, and that King Charles passed a whole night upon the ice."

The following extract is also an account of this frost by an eye-witness .... He says, "On the 20th of December, 1688, a very violent frost began, which lasted to the 6th of February, in so great extremity, that the pools were frozen 18 inches thick at least, and the Thames was so frozen that a great street from the Temple to Southwark was built with shops, and all manner of things sold. Hackney coaches plied there as in the streets. There were also bull-baiting, and a great many shows and tricks to be seen. This day the frost broke up. In the morning I saw a coach and six horses driven from Whitehall almost to the bridge (London Bridge) yet by three o'clock that day, February the 6th, next to Southwark the ice was gone, so as boats did row to and fro, and the next day all the frost was gone. On Candlemas Day I went to Croydon market, and led my horse over the ice to the Horseferry from Westminster to Lambeth; as I came back I led him from Lambeth upon the middle of the Thames to Whitefriars' stairs, and so led him up by them. And this day an ox was roasted whole, over against Whitehall. King Charles and the Queen ate part of it."

N.B. In 1740, a palace of ice was built by the Empress Anne of Russia, on the banks of the Neva, 52 feet long, which, when illuminated, had a surprising effect.

P. T. W.
The Mirror of Literature, Amusement and Instruction, Vol. 13, No. 355, Feb. 7, 1829

I HEARD A BIRD SING

I heard a bird sing
In the dark of December.
A magical thing
And sweet to remember.

"We are nearer to Spring
Than we were in September,"
I heard a bird sing
In the dark of December.

Oliver Herford

Oliver Herford (1863–1935) was an American, born in Sheffield in Britain, where his father was a Unitarian minister. His family returned to the States when he was twelve. He studied art in London and Paris, then settled in New York in his late twenties. He was a humorist, poet and illustrator, contributing regularly to magazines such as *The Mentor*, *Life* and *Ladies' Home Journal*. He was nicknamed 'the American Oscar Wilde'.

A WINTER'S MORNING

The pale beams of the waning moon still cast a shadow of the cottage, when the labourer rises from his heavy sleep on a winter's morning. Often he huddles on his things and slips his feet into his thick 'water-tights'—which are stiff and hard, having been wet over night—by no other light than this. If the household is comparatively well managed, however, he strikes a match, and his 'dip' shows at the window. But he generally prefers to save a candle, and clatters down the narrow steep stairs in the semi-darkness, takes a piece of bread and cheese, and steps forth into the sharp air. The cabbages in the garden he notes are covered with white frost, so is the grass in the fields, and the footpath is hard under foot. In the furrows is a little ice—white because the water has shrunk from beneath it, leaving it hollow—and on the stile is a crust of rime, cold to the touch, which he brushes off in getting over. Overhead the sky is clear—cloudless but pale—and the stars, though not yet fading, have lost the brilliant glitter of midnight. Then, in all their glory, the idea of their globular shape is easily accepted; but in the morning, just as the dawn is breaking, the absence of glitter comes the impression of flatness—circular rather than globular. But yonder, over the elms, above the cowpens, the great morning star has risen, shining far brighter, in proportion, than the moon; an intensely clear metallic light—like incandescent silver.

The shadows of the trees on the frosted ground are dull. As the footpath winds by the hedge the noise of his footstep startles the blackbird roosting in the bushes, and he bustles out and flies across the field. There is more rime on the posts and rails around the rickyard, and the thatch on the haystack is white with it in places. He draws out the broad hay-knife—a vast blade, wide at the handle, the edge gradually curving to a point—and then searches for the rubber or whetstone, stuck somewhere in the side of the rick. At the first sound of the stone upon the steel the cattle in the adjoining yard and sheds utter a few low 'moos,' and there is a stir among them. Mounting the ladder he forces the knife with both hands into the hay, making a square cut which bends outwards, opening from the main mass till it appears on the point of parting and letting him fall with it to the ground. But long practice has taught him how to balance himself half on the ladder, half on the hay. Presently, with a truss unbound and loose on his head, he enters the yard, and passes from crib to crib, leaving a little here and a little there, for if he fills one first, there will be quarrelling among the cows, and besides, if the crib is too liberally filled, they will pull it out and tread it under foot. The cattle that are in the sheds fattening for Christmas have cake as well, and this must be supplied in just proportion.

The hour of milking, which used to be pretty general everywhere, varies now in different places, to suit the necessities of the milk trade. The milk has, perhaps, to travel three or four miles to the railway station; near great towns, where some of the farmers deliver milk themselves from house to house, the cows are milked soon after noonday. What would their grandfathers have said to that? But where the old customs have not much altered, the milker sits down in the morning to his cow with the stars still visible overhead, punching his hat well into her side—a hat well battered and thickly coated with grease, for the skin of the cow exudes an unctuous substance. This hat he keeps for the purpose. A couple of milking pails—they are of large size—form a heavy load when filled.

The milker, as he walks back to the farmhouse, bends his head under the yoke—whence so many men are round-shouldered—and steps slowly with a peculiar swaying motion of the body, which slight swing prevents it from spilling.

Another man who has to be up while the moon casts a shadow is the carter, who must begin to feed his team very early in order to get them to eat sufficient. If the manger be over-filled they spill and waste it, and at the same time will not eat so much. This is tedious work. Then the lads come and polish up the harness, and so soon as it is well light get out to plough. The custom with the horses is to begin to work as early as possible, but to strike off in the afternoon some time before the other men, the lads riding home astride. The strength of the carthorse has to be husbanded carefully, and the labour performed must be adjusted to it and to the food, i.e. fuel, consumed. To manage a large team of horses, so as to keep them in good condition, with glossy coats and willing step, and yet to get the maximum of work out of them, requires long experience and constant attention. The carter, therefore, is a man of much importance on a farm. If he is up to his duties he is a most valuable servant; if he neglects them he is a costly nuisance, not so much from his pay, but because of the hindrance and disorganisation of the whole farm-work which such neglect entails.

Foggers and milkers, if their cottages are near at hand, having finished the first part of the day's work, can often go back home to breakfast, and, if they have a good woman in the cottage, find a fire and hot tea ready. The carter can rarely leave his horses for that, and, therefore, eats his breakfast in the stable; but then he has the advantage that up to the time of starting forth he is under cover. The fogger and milker, on the other hand, are often exposed to the most violent tempests. A gale of wind, accompanied with heavy rain, often readies its climax just about the dawn. They find the soil saturated, and the step sinks into it—the furrows are full of water; the cow-yard, though drained, is a pool, no drain being capable of carrying it off quick enough. The thatch of the sheds drips continually; the haystack drips; the thatch of the stack, which has to be pulled off before the hay-knife can be used, is wet; the old decaying wood of the rails and gates is wet. They sit on the three-legged milking-stool (whose rude workmanship has taken a dull polish from use) in a puddle; the hair of the cow, against which the head is placed, is wet; the wind blows the rain into the nape of the neck behind, the position being stooping. Staggering under the heavy yoke homewards, the boots sink deep into the slush and mire in the gateways, the weight carried sinking them well in. The teams do not usually work in very wet weather, and most of the out-door work waits; but the cattle must be attended to, Sundays and holidays included. Even in summer it often happens that a thunderstorm bursts about that time of the morning. But in winter, when the rain is driven by a furious wind, when the lantern is blown out, and the fogger stumbles in pitchy darkness through mud and water, it would be difficult to imagine a condition of things which concentrates more discomfort.

If, as often happens, the man is far from home—perhaps he has walked a mile or two to work—of course he cannot change his clothes, or get near a fire, unless in the farmer's kitchen. In some places the kitchen is open to the men, and on Sundays, at all events, they get a breakfast free. But the kindly old habits are dying out before the hard-and-fast money system and the abiding effects of Unionism, which, even when not prominently displayed, causes a silent, sullen estrangement.

Shepherds, too, sometimes visit the fold very early in the morning, and in the lambing season may be said to be about both day and night. They come, however, under a different category to the rest of the men, because they have no regular hours, but are guided solely by the season and the work. A shepherd often takes his ease when other men are busily labouring. On the other hand, he is frequently anxiously engaged when they are sleeping. His sheep rule his life, and he has little to do with the artificial divisions of time.

Hedgers and ditchers often work by the piece, and so take their own time for meals; the ash woods, which are cut in the winter, are also usually thrown by the piece. Hedging and ditching, if done properly, is hard work, especially if there is any grubbing. Though the arms get warm from swinging the grub-axe or billhook, or cleaning out the ditch and plastering and smoothing the side of the mound with the spade, yet feet and ankles are chilled by the water in the ditch. This is often dammed up and so kept back partially, but it generally forces its way through. The ditcher has a board to stand on; there is a hole through it, and a projecting stick attached, with which to drag it into position. But the soft soil allows the board to sink, and he often throws it aside as more encumbrance than use. He has some small perquisites: he is allowed to carry home a bundle of wood or a log every night, and may gather up the remnants after the faggoting is finished. On the other hand, he cannot work in bad weather.

Other men come to the farm buildings to commence work about the time the carter has got his horses fed, groomed, and harnessed, and after the fogger and milker have completed their early duties. If it is a frosty morning and the ground firm, so as to bear up a cart without poaching the soil too much, the manure is carried out into the fields. This is plain, straightforward labour, and cannot be looked upon as hard work. If the cattle want no further attention, the foggers and milkers turn their hands after breakfast to whatever may be going on. Some considerable time is taken up in slicing roots with the machine, or chaff-cutting—monotonous work of a simple character, and chiefly consisting in turning a handle.

The general hands—those who come on when the carter is ready, and who are usually young men, not yet settled down to any particular branch—seem to get the best end of the stick. They do not begin so early in the morning by some time as the fogger, milker, carter, or shepherd; consequently, if the cottage arrangements are tolerable, they can get a comfortable breakfast first. They have no anxieties or trouble whatever; the work may be hard in itself, but there is no particular hurry (in their estimation) and they do not distress themselves. They receive nearly the same wages as the others who have the care of valuable flocks, herds, and horses; the difference is but a shilling or two, and, to make up for that, they do not work on Sundays. Now, the fogger must feed his cows, the carter his horse, the shepherd look to his sheep every day; consequently their extra wages are thoroughly well earned. The young labourer—who is simply a labourer, and professes no special branch—is, therefore, in a certain sense, the best off. He is rarely hired by the year—he prefers to be free, so that when harvest comes he may go where wages chance to be highest. He is an independent person, and full of youth, strength, and with little experience of life, is apt to be rough in his manners and not overcivil. His wages too often go in liquor, but if such a young man keeps steady (and there are a few that do keep steady) he does very well indeed, having no family to maintain.

A set of men who work very hard are those who go with the steam-ploughing tackle. Their pay is so arranged as to depend in a measure on the number of acres they plough. They get the steam up as early as possible in the morning, and continue as late as they can at night. Just after the harvest, when the days are long, and, indeed, it is still summer, they work for extremely long hours. Their great difficulty lies in getting water. This must be continually fetched in carts, and, of course, requires a horse and man. These are not always forthcoming in the early morning, but they begin as soon as they can get water for the boiler, and do not stop till the field be finished or it is dark.

The women do not find much work in the fields during the winter. Now and then comes a day's employment with the threshing-machine when the farmer wants a rick of corn threshed out. In pasture or dairy districts some of them go out into the meadows and spread the manure. They wear gaiters, and sometimes a kind of hood for the head. If done carefully, it is hard work for the arms—knocking the manure into small pieces by striking it with a fork swung to and fro smartly.

In the spring, when the great heaps of roots are opened—having been protected all the winter by a layer of straw and earth—it is necessary to trim them before they are used. This is often done by a woman. She has a stool or log of wood to sit on, and arranges a couple of sacks or something of the kind, so as to form a screen and keep off the bitter winds which are then so common—colder than those of the winter proper. With a screen one side, the heap of roots the other, and the hedge on the third, she is in some sense sheltered, and, taking her food with her, may stay there the whole day long, quite alone in the solitude of the broad, open, arable fields.

From a variety of causes, the number of women working in the fields is much less than was formerly the case; thus presenting precisely the reverse state of things to that complained of in towns, where the clerks, &c., say that they are undersold by female labour. The contrast is rather curious. The price of women's labour has, too, risen; and there does not appear to be any repugnance on their part to field-work. Whether the conclusion is to be accepted that there has been a diminution in the actual number of women living in rural places, it is impossible to decide with any accuracy. But there are signs that female labour has drifted to the towns quite as much as male—especially the younger girls. In some places it seems rare to see a young girl working in the field (meaning in winter)—those that are to be found are generally women well advanced in life. Spring and summer work brings forth more, but not nearly so many as used to be the case.

Although the work of the farm begins so soon in the morning, it is, on the other hand, in the cold months, over early. 'The night cometh when no man can work' was, one would think, originally meant in reference to agricultural labour. It grows dusk before half-past four on a dull winter's day, and by five is almost, if not quite, dark. Lanterns may be moving in the cowyards and stables; but elsewhere all is quiet—the hedger and ditcher cannot see to strike his blow, the ploughs have ceased to move for some time, the labourer's workshop—the field—is not lighted by gas as the rooms of cities.

The shortness of the winter day is one of the primary reasons why, in accordance with ancient custom, wages are lowered at that time. In summer, on the contrary, the hours are long, and the pay high—which more than makes up for the winter reduction. A labourer who has any prudence can, in fact, do very well by putting by a portion of his extra summer wages for the winter; if he does not choose to exercise common sense, he cannot expect the farmer (or any manufacturer) to pay the same price for a little work and short time as for much work and long hours. Reviewing the work the labourer actually does in winter, it seems fair and just to state that the foggers, or milkers, i.e. the men who attend on cattle, the carters, and the shepherds, work hard, continuously, and often in the face of the most inclement weather. The mere labourers, who, as previously remarked, are usually younger and single men, do not work so hard, nor so long. And when they are at it—whether turning the handle of a winnowing machine in a barn, cutting a hedge, spreading manure, or digging—it must be said that they do not put the energy into it of which their brawny arms are capable.

'The least work and the most money,' however, is a maxim not confined to the agricultural labourer. Recently I had occasion to pass through a busy London street in the West-end where the macadam of the roadway was being picked up by some score of men, and, being full of the subject of labour, I watched the process. Using the right hand as a fulcrum and keeping it stationary, each navvy slowly lifted his pick with the left half-way up, about on a level with his waistcoat, when the point of the pick was barely two feet above the ground. He then let it fall—simply by its own weight—producing a tiny indentation such as might be caused by the kick of one's heel It required about three such strokes, if they could so called strokes, to detach one single small stone. After that exhausting labor the man stood at ease for a few minutes, so that there were often three or four at once staring about them, while several others lounged against the wooden railing placed to keep vehicles back.

A more irritating spectacle it would be hard to imagine. Idle as much agricultural labour is, it is rarely so lazy as that. How contractors get their work done, if that is a sample, it is a puzzle to understand. The complaint of the poor character of the work performed by the agricultural labourer seems also true of other departments, where labour—pure and simple labour of thews and sinews—is concerned. The rich city merchant, who goes to his office daily, positively works harder, in spite of all his money. So do the shopmen and assistants behind their counters; so do the girls in drapers' shops, standing the whole day and far into the evening when, as just observed, the fields have been dark for hours; so, indeed, do most men and women who earn their bread by any other means than mere bodily strength.

But the cattle-men, carters, and shepherds, men with families and settled, often seem to take an interest in their charges, in the cows, horses, or sheep; some of them are really industrious, deserving men. The worst feature of unionism is the lumping of all together, for where one man is hardly worth his salt, another is a good workman. It is strange that such men as this should choose to throw in their lot with so many who are idle—whom they must know to be idle—thus jeopardising their own position for the sake of those who are not worth one-fifth the sacrifice the agricultural cottager must be called upon to make in a strike. The hard-working carter or cattle-man, according to the union theory, is to lose his pay, his cottage, his garden, and get into bad odour with his employer, who previously trusted him, and was willing to give him assistance, in order that the day labourer who has no responsibilities either of his own or his master's, and who has already the best end of the stick, should enjoy still further opportunities for idleness.

Richard Jefferies
Hodge and his Master

Richard Jefferies (1848–1887) was a journalist and novelist. He was brought up on a farm in north Wiltshire, and his knowledge of and love for the countryside of southern England are major features of his work. His work is written in a plain, unsentimental style. Jefferies' detailed descriptions of wildlife and the countryside in books such as the semi-autobiographical *Wood Magic* and *Bevis, the Story of a Boy* are considered by some to have had an influence on Kenneth Grahame.

THE SNOW STORM

Announced by all the trumpets of the sky,
Arrives the snow, and, driving o'er the fields,
Seems nowhere to alight: the whited air
Hides hills and woods, the river, and the heaven,
And veils the farmhouse at the garden's end.
The sled and traveler stopped, the courier's feet
Delayed, all friends shut out, the housemates sit
Around the radiant fireplace, enclosed
In a tumultuous privacy of storm.

Come see the north wind's masonry.
Out of an unseen quarry evermore
Furnished with tile, the fierce artificer
Curves his white bastions with projected roof
Round every windward stake, or tree, or door.
Speeding, the myriad-handed, his wild work
So fanciful, so savage, nought cares he
For number or proportion. Mockingly,
On coop or kennel he hangs Parian wreaths;
A swan-like form invests the hidden thorn;
Fills up the farmer's lane from wall to wall,
Maugre the farmer's sighs; and, at the gate,
A tapering turret overtops the work.
And when his hours are numbered, and the world
Is all his own, retiring, as he were not,
Leaves, when the sun appears, astonished Art
To mimic in slow structures, stone by stone,
Built in an age, the mad wind's night-work,
The frolic architecture of the snow.

Ralph Waldo Emerson

The son of a Unitarian minister in Boston, Massachusetts, Ralph Waldo Emerson (1803–1882) was himself a Unitarian minister for some years, but resigned because of his controversial views. Travelling to Europe, he met many literary figures, becoming a close friend of the philosopher and historian Thomas Carlyle. Back in America, he started lecturing, especially on religious and philosophical subjects. He believed that human thoughts and actions derived from nature and that no intermediary was necessary to reach the Divine. He kept journals, published his lectures, and wrote much-acclaimed poetry and essays.

TO THE RESCUE

The sun rose in the sky with every appearance of a fine day, and we grew warmer as we toiled through the soft snow. Ahead of us lay the ridges and spurs of a range of mountains, the transverse range that we had noticed from the bay. We were travelling over a gently rising plateau, and at the end of an hour we found ourselves growing uncomfortably hot. Years before, on an earlier expedition, I had declared that I would never again growl at the heat of the sun, and my resolution had been strengthened during the boat journey. I called it to mind as the sun beat fiercely on the blinding white snow-slope. After passing an area of crevasses we paused for our first meal. We dug a hole in the snow about three feet deep with the adze and put the Primus into it. There was no wind at the moment, but a gust might come suddenly. A hot hoosh was soon eaten and we plodded on towards a sharp ridge between two of the peaks already mentioned. By 11 a.m. we were almost at the crest. The slope had become precipitous and it was necessary to cut steps as we advanced. The adze proved an excellent instrument for this purpose, a blow sufficing to provide a foothold. Anxiously but hopefully I cut the last few steps and stood upon the razor-back, while the other men held the rope and waited for my news. The outlook was disappointing. I looked down a sheer precipice to a chaos of crumpled ice 1500 ft. below. There was no way down for us. The country to the east was a great snow upland, sloping upwards for a distance of seven or eight miles to a height of over 4000 ft. To the north it fell away steeply in glaciers into the bays, and to the south it was broken by huge outfalls from the inland ice-sheet. Our path lay between the glaciers and the outfalls, but first we had to descend from the ridge on which we stood. Cutting steps with the adze, we moved in a lateral direction round the base of a dolomite, which blocked our view to the north. The same precipice confronted us. Away to the north-east there appeared to be a snow-slope that might give a path to the lower country, and so we retraced our steps down the long slope that had taken us three hours to climb. We were at the bottom in an hour. We were now feeling the strain of the unaccustomed marching. We had done little walking since January and our muscles were out of tune. Skirting the base of the mountain above us, we came to a gigantic bergschrund, a mile and a half long and 1000 ft. deep. This tremendous gully, cut in the snow and ice by the fierce winds blowing round the mountain, was semicircular in form, and it ended in a gentle incline. We passed through it, under the towering precipice of ice, and at the far end we had another meal and a short rest. This was at 12:30 p.m. Half a pot of steaming Bovril ration warmed us up, and when we marched again ice-inclines at angles of 45 degrees did not look quite as formidable as before.

Once more we started for the crest. After another weary climb we reached the top. The snow lay thinly on blue ice at the ridge, and we had to cut steps over the last fifty yards. The same precipice lay below, and my eyes searched vainly for a way down. The hot sun had loosened the snow, which was now in a treacherous condition, and we had to pick our way carefully. Looking back, we could see that a fog was rolling up behind us and meeting in the valleys a fog that was coming up from the east. The creeping grey clouds were a plain warning that we must get down to lower levels before becoming enveloped.

The ridge was studded with peaks, which prevented us getting a clear view either to the right or to the left. The situation in this respect seemed no better at other points within our reach, and I had to decide that our course lay back the way we had come. The afternoon was wearing on and the fog was rolling up ominously from the west. It was of the utmost importance for us to get down into the next valley before dark. We were now up 4500 ft. and the night temperature at that elevation would be very low. We had no tent and no sleeping-bags, and our clothes had endured much rough usage and had weathered many storms during the last ten months. In the distance, down the valley below us, we could see tussock-grass close to the shore, and if we could get down it might be possible to dig out a hole in one of the lower snow-banks, line it with dry grass, and make ourselves fairly comfortable for the night. Back we went, and after a detour we reached the top of another ridge in the fading light. After a glance over the top I turned to the anxious faces of the two men behind me and said, "Come on, boys." Within a minute they stood beside me on the ice-ridge. The surface fell away at a sharp incline in front of us, but it merged into a snow-slope. We could not see the bottom clearly owing to mist and bad light, and the possibility of the slope ending in a sheer fall occurred to us; but the fog that was creeping up behind allowed no time for hesitation. We descended slowly at first, cutting steps in the snow; then the surface became softer, indicating that the gradient was less severe. There could be no turning back now, so we unroped and slid in the fashion of youthful days. When we stopped on a snow-bank at the foot of the slope we found that we had descended at least 900 ft. in two or three minutes. We looked back and saw the grey fingers of the fog appearing on the ridge, as though reaching after the intruders into untrodden wilds. But we had escaped.

The country to the east was an ascending snow upland dividing the glaciers of the north coast from the outfalls of the south. We had seen from the top that our course lay between two huge masses of crevasses, and we thought that the road ahead lay clear. This belief and the increasing cold made us abandon the idea of camping. We had another meal at 6 p.m. A little breeze made cooking difficult in spite of the shelter provided for the cooker by a hole. Crean was the cook, and Worsley and I lay on the snow to windward of the lamp so as to break the wind with our bodies. The meal over, we started up the long, gentle ascent. Night was upon us, and for an hour we plodded along in almost complete darkness, watching warily for signs of crevasses. Then about 8 p.m. a glow which we had seen behind the jagged peaks resolved itself into the full moon, which rose ahead of us and made a silver pathway for our feet. Along that pathway in the wake of the moon we advanced in safety, with the shadows cast by the edges of crevasses showing black on either side of us. Onwards and upwards through soft snow we marched, resting now and then on hard patches which had revealed themselves by glittering ahead of us in the white light. By midnight we were again at an elevation of about 4000 ft. Still we were following the light, for as the moon swung round towards the north-east, our path curved in that direction. The friendly moon seemed to pilot our weary feet. We could have had no better guide. If in bright daylight we had made that march we would have followed the course that was traced for us that night.

Midnight found us approaching the edge of a great snowfield, pierced by isolated nunataks which cast long shadows like black rivers across the white expanse. A gentle slope to the north-east lured our all-too-willing feet in that direction. We thought that at the base of the slope lay Stromness Bay. After we had descended about 300 ft. a thin wind began to attack us. We had now been on the march for over twenty hours, only halting for our occasional meals. Wisps of cloud drove over the high peaks to the southward, warning us that wind and snow were likely to come. After 1 a.m. we cut a pit in the snow, piled up loose snow around it, and started the Primus again. The hot food gave us another renewal of energy. Worsley and Crean sang their old songs when the Primus was

going merrily. Laughter was in our hearts, though not on our parched and cracked lips.

We were up and away again within half an hour, still downward to the coast. We felt almost sure now that we were above Stromness Bay. A dark object down at the foot of the slope looked like Mutton Island, which lies off Husvik. I suppose our desires were giving wings to our fancies, for we pointed out joyfully various landmarks revealed by the now vagrant light of the moon, whose friendly face was cloud-swept. Our high hopes were soon shattered. Crevasses warned us that we were on another glacier, and soon we looked down almost to the seaward edge of the great riven ice-mass. I knew there was no glacier in Stromness and realized that this must be Fortuna Glacier. The disappointment was severe. Back we turned and tramped up the glacier again, not directly tracing our steps but working at a tangent to the south-east. We were very tired.

At 5 a.m. we were at the foot of the rocky spurs of the range. We were tired, and wind that blew down from the heights was chilling us. We decided to get down under the lee of a rock for a rest. We put our sticks and the adze on the snow, sat down on them as close to one another as possible, and put our arms round each other. The wind was bringing a little drift with it and the white dust lay on our clothes. I thought that we might be able to keep warm and have half an hour's rest this way. Within a minute my two companions were fast asleep. I realized that it would be disastrous if we all slumbered together, for sleep under such conditions merges into death. After five minutes I shook them into consciousness again, told them that they had slept for half an hour, and gave the word for a fresh start. We were so stiff that for the first two or three hundred yards we marched with our knees bent. A jagged line of peaks with a gap like a broken tooth confronted us. This was the ridge that runs in a southerly direction from Fortuna Bay, and our course eastward to Stromness lay across it. A very steep slope led up to the ridge and an icy wind burst through the gap.

We went through the gap at 6 a.m. with anxious hearts as well as weary bodies. If the farther slope had proved impassable our situation would have been almost desperate; but the worst was turning to the best for us. The twisted, wave-like rock formations of Husvik Harbour appeared right ahead in the opening of dawn. Without a word we shook hands with one another. To our minds the journey was over, though as a matter of fact twelve miles of difficult country had still to be traversed. A gentle snow-slope descended at our feet towards a valley that separated our ridge from the hills immediately behind Husvik, and as we stood gazing Worsley said solemnly, "Boss, it looks too good to be true!" Down we went, to be checked presently by the sight of water 2500 ft. below. We could see the little wave-ripples on the black beach, penguins strutting to and fro, and dark objects that looked like seals lolling lazily on the sand. This was an eastern arm of Fortuna Bay, separated by the ridge from the arm we had seen below us during the night. The slope we were traversing appeared to end in a precipice above this beach. But our revived spirits were not to be damped by difficulties on the last stage of the journey, and we camped cheerfully for breakfast. Whilst Worsley and Crean were digging a hole for the lamp and starting the cooker I climbed a ridge above us, cutting steps with the adze, in order to secure an extended view of the country below. At 6.30 a.m. I thought I heard the sound of a steam-whistle. I dared not be certain, but I knew that the men at the whaling-station would be called from their beds about that time. Descending to the camp I told the others, and in intense excitement we watched the chronometer for seven o'clock, when the whalers would be summoned to work. Right to the minute the steam-whistle came to us, borne clearly on the wind across the intervening miles of rock and snow. Never had any one of us heard sweeter music. It was the first sound created by outside human agency that had come to our ears since we left Stromness Bay in December 1914. That whistle told us that men were living near, that ships were ready, and that within a few hours we should be on our way back to Elephant Island to the rescue of the men waiting there under the watch and ward of Wild. It was a moment hard to describe. Pain and ache, boat journeys, marches, hunger and fatigue seemed to belong to the limbo of forgotten things, and there remained only the perfect contentment that comes of work accomplished.

My examination of the country from a higher point had not provided definite information, and after descending I put the situation before Worsley and Crean. Our obvious course lay down a snow-slope in the direction of Husvik. "Boys," I said, "this snow-slope seems to end in a precipice, but perhaps there is no precipice. If we don't go down we shall have to make a detour of at least five miles before we reach level going What shall it be?" They both replied at once, "Try the slope." So we started away again downwards. We abandoned the Primus lamp, now empty, at the breakfast camp and carried with us one ration and a biscuit each. The deepest snow we had yet encountered clogged our feet, but we plodded downward, and after descending about 500 ft., reducing our altitude to 2000 ft. above sea-level, we thought we saw the way clear ahead. A steep gradient of blue ice was the next obstacle. Worsley and Crean got a firm footing in a hole excavated with the adze and then lowered me as I cut steps until the full 50 ft. of our alpine rope was out. Then I made a hole big enough for the three of us, and the other two men came down the steps. My end of the rope was anchored to the adze and I had settled myself in the hole braced for a strain in case they slipped. When we all stood in the second hole I went down again to make more steps, and in this laborious fashion we spent two hours descending about 500 ft. Halfway down we had to strike away diagonally to the left, for we noticed that the fragments of ice loosened by the adze were taking a leap into space at the bottom of the slope. Eventually we got off the steep ice, very gratefully, at a point where some rocks protruded, and we could see then that there was a perilous precipice directly below the point where we had started to cut steps. A slide down a slippery slope, with the adze and our cooker going ahead, completed this descent, and incidentally did considerable damage to our much-tried trousers.

When we picked ourselves up at the bottom we were not more than 1500 ft. above the sea. The slope was comparatively easy. Water was running beneath the snow, making "pockets" between the rocks that protruded above the white surface. The shells of snow over these pockets were traps for our feet; but we scrambled down, and presently came to patches of tussock. A few minutes later we reached the sandy beach. The tracks of some animals were to be seen, and we were puzzled until I remembered that reindeer, brought from Norway, had been placed on the island and now ranged along the lower land of the eastern coast. We did not pause to investigate. Our minds were set upon reaching the haunts of man, and at our best speed we went along the beach to another rising ridge of tussock. Here we saw the first evidence of the proximity of man, whose work, as is so often the ease, was one of destruction. A recently killed seal was lying there, and presently we saw several other bodies bearing the marks of bullet-wounds. I learned later that men from the whaling-station at Stromness sometimes go round to Fortuna Bay by boat to shoot seals.

Noon found us well up the slope on the other side of the bay working east-south-east, and half an hour later we were on a flat plateau, with one more ridge to cross before we descended into Husvik. I was leading the way over this plateau when I suddenly found myself up to my knees in water and quickly sinking deeper through the snow-crust. I flung myself down and called to the others to do the same, so as to distribute our weight on the treacherous surface. We were on top of a small lake, snow-covered. After lying still for a few moments we got to our feet and walked delicately, like Agag, for 200 yds., until a rise in the surface showed us that we were clear of the lake.

At 1.30 p.m. we climbed round a final ridge and saw a little steamer, a whaling-boat, entering the bay 2500 ft, below. A few moments later, as we hurried forward, the masts of a sailing-ship lying at a wharf came in sight. Minute figures moving to and fro about the boats caught our gaze, and then we saw the sheds and factory of Stromness whaling-station. We paused and shook hands, a form of mutual congratulation that had seemed necessary on four other occasions in the course of the expedition. The first time was when we landed on Elephant Island, the second when we reached South Georgia, and the third when we reached the ridge and saw the snow-slope stretching below on the first day of the overland journey, then when we saw Husvik rocks.

Cautiously we started down the slope that led to warmth and comfort. The last lap of the journey proved extraordinarily difficult. Vainly we searched for a safe, or a reasonably safe, way down the steep ice-clad mountain-side. The sole possible pathway seemed to be a channel cut by water running from the upland. Down through icy water we followed the course of this stream. We were wet to the waist, shivering, cold, and tired. Presently our ears detected an unwelcome sound that might have been musical under other conditions. It was the splashing of a waterfall, and we were at the wrong end. When we reached the top of this fall we peered over cautiously and discovered that there was a drop of 25 or 30 ft., with impassable ice-cliffs on both sides. To go up again was scarcely thinkable in our utterly wearied condition. The way down was through the waterfall itself. We made fast one end of our rope to a boulder with some difficulty, due to the fact that the rocks had been worn smooth by the running water. Then Worsley and I lowered Crean, who was the heaviest man. He disappeared altogether in the falling water and came out gasping at the bottom. I went next, sliding down the rope, and Worsley, who was the lightest and most nimble member of the party, came last. At the bottom of the fall we were able to stand again on dry land. The rope could not be recovered. We had flung down the adze from the top of the fall and also the logbook and the cooker wrapped in one of our blouses. That was all, except our wet clothes, that we brought out of the Antarctic, which we had entered a year and a half before with well-found ship, full equipment, and high hopes. That was all of tangible things; but in memories we were rich. We had pierced the veneer of outside things. We had "suffered, starved, and triumphed, grovelled down yet grasped at glory, grown bigger in the bigness of the whole." We had seen God in His splendours, heard the text that Nature renders. We had reached the naked soul of man.

Shivering with cold, yet with hearts light and happy, we set off towards the whaling-station, now not more than a mile and a half distant. The difficulties of the journey lay behind us. We tried to straighten ourselves up a bit, for the thought that there might be women at the station made us painfully conscious of our uncivilized appearance. Our beards were long and our hair was matted. We were unwashed and the garments that we had worn for nearly a year without a change were tattered and stained. Three more unpleasant-looking ruffians could hardly have been imagined. Worsley produced several safety-pins from some corner of his garments and effected some temporary repairs that really emphasized his general disrepair. Down we hurried, and when quite close to the station we met two small boys ten or twelve years of age. I asked these lads where the manager's house was situated. They did not answer. They gave us one look—a comprehensive look that did not need to be repeated. Then they ran from us as fast as their legs would carry them. We reached the outskirts of the station and passed through the "digesting-house," which was dark inside. Emerging at the other end, we met an old man, who started as if he had seen the Devil himself and gave us no time to ask any question. He hurried away. This greeting was not friendly. Then we came to the wharf, where the man in charge stuck to his station. I asked him if Mr. Sorlle (the manager) was in the house.

"Yes," he said as he stared at us.

"We would like to see him," said I.

"Who are you?" he asked.

"We have lost our ship and come over the island," I replied.

"You have come over the island?" he said in a tone of entire disbelief.

The man went towards the manager's house and we followed him. I learned afterwards that he said to Mr. Sorlle: "There are three funny-looking men outside, who say they have come over the island and they know you. I have left them outside." A very necessary precaution from his point of view.

Mr. Sorlle came out to the door and said, "Well?"

"Don't you know me?" I said.

"I know your voice," he replied doubtfully. "You're the mate of the *Daisy*."

"My name is Shackleton," I said.

Immediately he put out his hand and said, "Come in. Come in."

"Tell me, when was the war over?" I asked.

"The war is not over," he answered. "Millions are being killed. Europe is mad. The world is mad."

Mr. Sorlle's hospitality had no bounds. He would scarcely let us wait to remove our freezing boots before he took us into his house and gave us seats in a warm and comfortable room. We were in no condition to sit in anybody's house until we had washed and got into clean clothes, but the kindness of the station-manager was proof even against the unpleasantness of being in a room with us. He gave us coffee and cakes in the Norwegian fashion, and then showed us upstairs to the bathroom, where we shed our rags and scrubbed ourselves luxuriously.

Mr. Sorlle's kindness did not end with his personal care for the three wayfarers who had come to his door. While we were washing he gave orders for one of the whaling-vessels to be prepared at once in order that it might leave that night for the other side of the island and pick up the three men there. The whalers knew King Haakon Bay, though they never worked on that side of the island. Soon we were clean again. Then we put on delightful new clothes supplied from the station stores and got rid of our superfluous hair. Within an hour or two we had ceased to be savages and had become civilized men again. Then came a splendid meal, while Mr. Sorlle told us of the arrangements he had made and we discussed plans for the rescue of the main party on Elephant Island.

I arranged that Worsley should go with the relief ship to show the exact spot where the carpenter and his two companions were camped, while I started to prepare for the relief of the party on Elephant Island. The whaling-vessel that was going round to King Haakon Bay was expected back on the Monday morning, and was to call at Grytviken Harbour, the port from which we had sailed in December 1914, in order that the magistrate resident there might be informed of the fate of the Endurance.

It was possible that letters were awaiting us there. Worsley went aboard the whaler at ten o'clock that night and turned in. The next day the relief ship entered King Haakon Bay and he reached Peggotty Camp in a boat. The three men were delighted beyond measure to know that we had made the crossing in safety and that their wait under the upturned James Caird was ended. Curiously enough, they did not recognize Worsley, who had left them a hairy, dirty ruffian and had returned his spruce and shaven self. They thought he was one of the whalers. When one of them asked why no member of the party had come round with the relief, Worsley said, "What do you mean?" "We thought the Boss or one of the others would come round," they explained. "What's the matter with you?" said Worsley. Then it suddenly dawned upon them that they were talking to the man who had been their close companion for a year and a half. Within a few minutes the whalers had moved our bits of gear into their boat. They towed off the James Caird and hoisted her to the deck of their ship. Then they started on the return voyage. Just at dusk on Monday afternoon they entered Stromness Bay, where the men of the whaling-station mustered on the beach to receive the rescued party and to examine with professional interest the boat we had navigated across 800 miles of the stormy ocean they knew so well.

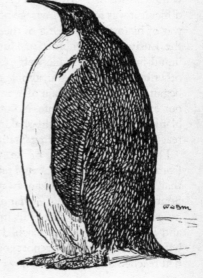

When I look back at those days I have no doubt that Providence guided us, not only across those snowfields, but across the storm-white sea that separated Elephant Island from our landing-place on South Georgia. I know that during that long and racking march of thirty-six hours over the unnamed mountains and glaciers of South Georgia it seemed to me often that we were four, not three. I said nothing to my companions on the point, but afterwards Worsley said to me, "Boss, I had a curious feeling on the march that there was another person with us." Crean confessed to the same idea. One feels "the dearth of human words, the roughness of mortal speech" in trying to describe things intangible, but a record of our journeys would be incomplete without a reference to a subject very near to our hearts.

Our first night at the whaling-station was blissful. Crean and I shared a beautiful room in Mr. Sorlle's house, with electric light and two beds, warm and soft. We were so comfortable that we were unable to sleep. Late at night a steward brought us tea, bread and butter and cakes, and we lay in bed, revelling in the luxury of it all. Outside a dense snow-storm, which started two hours after our arrival and lasted until the following day, was swirling and driving about the mountain-slopes. We were thankful indeed that we had made a place of safety, for it would have gone hard with us if we had been out on the mountains that night. Deep snow lay everywhere when we got up the following morning.

After breakfast Mr. Sorlle took us round to Husvik in a motor-launch. We were listening avidly to his account of the war and of all that had happened while we were out of the world of men. We were like men arisen from the dead to a world gone mad. Our minds accustomed themselves gradually to the tales of nations in arms, of deathless courage and unimagined slaughter, of a world-conflict that had grown beyond all conceptions, of vast red battlefields in grimmest contrast with the frigid whiteness we had left behind us. The reader may not realize quite how difficult it was for us to envisage nearly two years of the most stupendous war of history. The locking of the armies in the trenches, the sinking of the Lusitania, the murder of Nurse Cavell, the use of poison-gas and liquid fire, the submarine warfare, the Gallipoli campaign, the hundred other incidents of the war, almost stunned us at first, and then our minds began to compass the train of events and develop a perspective. I suppose our experience was unique. No other civilized men could have been as blankly ignorant of world-shaking happenings as we were when we reached Stromness Whaling Station.

I heard the first rumour of the Aurora's misadventures in the Ross Sea from Mr. Sorlle. Our host could tell me very little. He had been informed that the Aurora had broken away from winter quarters in McMurdo Sound and reached New Zealand after a long drift, and that there was no news of the shore party. His information was indefinite as to details, and I had to wait until I reached the Falkland Islands some time later before getting a definite report concerning the Aurora. The rumour that had reached South Georgia, however, made it more than ever important that I should bring out the rest of the Weddell Sea party quickly, so as to free myself for whatever effort was required on the Ross Sea side.

When we reached Husvik that Sunday morning we were warmly greeted by the magistrate (Mr. Bernsten), whom I knew of old, and the other members of the little community. Moored in the harbour was one of the largest of the whalers, the Southern Sky, owned by an English company but now laid up for the winter. I had no means of getting into communication with the owners without dangerous delay, and on my accepting all responsibility Mr. Bernsten made arrangements for me to take this ship down to Elephant Island. I wrote out an agreement with Lloyd's for the insurance of the ship. Captain Thom, an old friend of the Expedition, happened to be in Husvik with his ship, the Orwell, loading oil for use in Britain's munition works, and he at once volunteered to come with us in any capacity. I asked him to come as captain of the Southern Sky. There was no difficulty about getting a crew. The whalers were eager to assist in the rescue of men in distress. They started work that Sunday to prepare and stow the ship. Parts of the engines were ashore, but willing hands made light labour. I purchased from the station stores all the stores and equipment required, including special comforts for the men we hoped to rescue, and by Tuesday morning the Southern Sky was ready to sail. I feel it is my duty as well as my pleasure to thank here the Norwegian whalers of South Georgia for the sympathetic hands they stretched out to us in our need. Among memories of kindness received in many lands sundered by the seas, the recollection of the hospitality and help given to me in South Georgia ranks high. There is a brotherhood of the sea. The men who go down to the sea in ships, serving and suffering, fighting their endless battle against the caprice of wind and ocean, bring into their own horizons the perils and troubles of their brother sailormen.

The Southern Sky was ready on Tuesday morning, and at nine o'clock we steamed out of the bay, while the whistles of the whaling-station sounded a friendly farewell. We had forgathered aboard Captain Thom's ship on the Monday night with several whaling captains who were bringing up their sons to their own profession. They were "old stagers" with faces lined and seamed by the storms of half a century, and they were even more interested in the story of our voyage from Elephant Island than the younger generation was. They congratulated us on having accomplished a remarkable boat journey. I do not wish to belittle our success with the pride that apes humility. Under Providence we had overcome great difficulties and dangers, and it was pleasant to tell the tale to men who knew those sullen and treacherous southern seas.

McCarthy, McNeish, and Vincent had been landed on the Monday afternoon. They were already showing some signs of increasing strength under a regime of warm quarters and abundant food. The carpenter looked woefully thin after he had emerged from a bath. He must have worn a lot of clothes when he landed from the boat, and I did not realize how he had wasted till I saw him washed and changed. He was a man over fifty years of age, and the strain had told upon him more than upon the rest of us. The rescue came just in time for him.

The early part of the voyage down to Elephant Island in the Southern Sky was uneventful. At noon on Tuesday, May 23, we were at sea and steaming at ten knots on a south-westerly course. We made good progress, but the temperature fell very low, and the signs gave me some cause for anxiety as to the probability of encountering ice. On the third night out the sea seemed to grow silent. I looked over the side and saw a thin film of ice. The sea was freezing around us and the ice gradually grew thicker, reducing our speed to about five knots. Then lumps of old pack began to appear among the new ice. I realized that an advance through pack-ice was out of the question. The Southern Sky was a steel-built steamer, and her structure, while strong to resist the waves, would not endure the blows of masses of ice. So I took the ship north, and at daylight on Friday we got clear of the pancake-ice. We skirted westward, awaiting favourable conditions. The morning of the 28th was dull and overcast, with little wind. Again the ship's head was turned to the south-west, but at 3 p.m. a definite line of pack showed up on the horizon. We were about 70 miles from Elephant Island, but there was no possibility of taking the steamer through the ice that barred the way. North-west again we turned. We were directly north of the island on the following day, and I made another move south. Heavy pack formed an impenetrable barrier.

To admit failure at this stage was hard, but the facts had to be faced. The Southern Sky could not enter ice of even moderate thickness. The season was late, and we could not be sure that the ice would open for many months, though my opinion was that the pack would not become fast in that quarter even in the winter, owing to the strong winds and currents. The Southern Sky could carry coal for ten days only, and we had been out six days. We were 500 miles from the Falkland Islands and about 600 miles from South Georgia. So I determined that, since we could not wait about for an opening, I would proceed to the Falklands, get a more suitable vessel either locally or from England, and make a second attempt to reach Elephant Island from that point.

We encountered very bad weather on the way up, but in the early afternoon of May 31 we arrived at Port Stanley, where the cable provided a link with the outer world. The harbour-master came out to meet us, and after we had dropped anchor I went ashore and met the Governor, Mr. Douglas Young. He offered me his assistance at once. He telephoned to Mr. Harding, the manager of the Falkland Islands station, and I learned, to my keen regret, that no ship of the type required was available at the islands. That evening I cabled to London a message to His Majesty the King, the first account of the loss of the Endurance and the subsequent adventures of the Expedition. The next day I received the following message from the King:

"Rejoice to hear of your safe arrival in the Falkland Islands and trust your comrades on Elephant Island may soon be rescued.

"GEORGE R.I."

The events of the days that followed our arrival at the Falkland Islands I will not attempt to describe in detail. My mind was bent upon the rescue of the party on Elephant Island at the earliest possible moment. Winter was advancing, and I was fully conscious that the lives of some of my comrades might be the price of unnecessary delay. A proposal had been made to send a relief ship from England, but she could not reach the southern seas for many weeks. In the meantime I got into communication with the Governments of the South American Republics by wireless and cable and asked if they had any suitable ship I could use for a rescue. I wanted a wooden ship capable of pushing into loose ice, with fair speed and a reasonable coal capacity. Messages of congratulation and goodwill were reaching me from all parts of the world, and the kindness of hundreds of friends in many lands was a very real comfort in a time of anxiety and stress.

The British Admiralty informed me that no suitable vessel was available in England and that no relief could be expected before October. I replied that October would be too late. Then the British Minister in Montevideo telegraphed me regarding a trawler named *Instituto de Pesca* No. 1, belonging to the Uruguayan Government. She was a stout little vessel, and the Government had generously offered to equip her with coal, provisions, clothing, etc., and send her across to the Falkland Islands for me to take down to Elephant Island. I accepted this offer gladly, and the trawler was in Port Stanley on June 10. We started south at once.

The weather was bad but the trawler made good progress, steaming steadily at about six knots, and in the bright, clear dawn of the third day we sighted the peaks of Elephant Island. Hope ran high; but our ancient enemy the pack was lying in wait, and within twenty miles of the island the trawler was stopped by an impenetrable barrier of ice. The pack lay in the form of a crescent, with a horn to the west of the ship stretching north. Steaming north-east, we reached another horn and saw that the pack, heavy and dense, then trended away to the east. We made an attempt to push into the ice, but it was so heavy that the trawler was held up at once and began to grind in the small thick floes, so we cautiously backed out. The propeller, going slowly, was not damaged, though any moment I feared we might strip the blades. The island lay on our starboard quarter, but there was no possibility of approaching it. The Uruguayan engineer reported to me that he had three days' coal left, and I had to give the order to turn back. A screen of fog hid the lower slopes of the island, and the men watching from the camp on the beach could not have seen the ship. Northward we steamed again, with the engines knocking badly, and after encountering a new gale, made Port Stanley with the bunkers nearly empty and the engines almost broken down. H.M.S. *Glasgow*

was in the port, and the British sailors gave us a hearty welcome as we steamed in.

The Uruguayan Government offered to send the trawler to Punta Arenas and have her dry-docked there and made ready for another effort. One of the troubles on the voyage was that according to estimate the trawler could do ten knots on six tons of coal a day, which would have given us a good margin to allow for lying off the ice; but in reality, owing to the fact that she had not been in dock for a year, she only developed a speed of six knots on a consumption of ten tons a day. Time was precious and these preparations would have taken too long. I thanked the Government then for its very generous offer, and I want to say now that the kindness of the Uruguayans at this time earned my warmest gratitude. I ought to mention also the assistance given me by Lieut. Ryan, a Naval Reserve officer who navigated the trawler to the Falklands and came south on the attempt at relief. The Instituto de Pesca went off to Montevideo and I looked around for another ship.

A British mail-boat, the *Orita* called at Port Stanley opportunely, and I boarded her with Worsley and Crean and crossed to Punta Arenas in the Magellan Straits. The reception we received there was heartening. The members of the British Association of Magellanes took us to their hearts. Mr. Allan McDonald was especially prominent in his untiring efforts to assist in the rescue of our twenty-two companions on Elephant Island. He worked day and night, and it was mainly due to him that within three days they had raised a sum of £1500 amongst themselves, chartered the schooner Emma and equipped her for our use. She was a forty-year-old oak schooner, strong and seaworthy, with an auxiliary oil-engine.

Out of the complement of ten men all told who were manning the ship, there were eight different nationalities; but they were all good fellows and understood perfectly what was wanted. The Chilian Government lent us a small steamer, the *Yelcho*, to tow us part of the way. She could not touch ice, though, as she was built of steel. However, on July 12 we passed her our tow-rope and proceeded on our way. In bad weather we anchored next day, and although the wind increased to a gale I could delay no longer, so we hove up anchor in the early morning of the 14th. The strain on the tow-rope was too great. With the crack of a gun the rope broke. Next day the gale continued, and I will quote from the log of the Emma, which Worsley kept as navigating officer.

"9 a.m.—Fresh, increasing gale; very rough, lumpy sea. 10 a.m.—Tow-rope parted. 12 noon. Similar weather. 1 p.m.—Tow-rope parted again. Set foresail and forestay-sail and steered south-east by south. 3 p.m.—Yelcho hailed us and said that the ship's bilges were full of water (so were our decks) and they were short of coal. Sir Ernest told them that they could return to harbour. After this the Yelcho steamed into San Sebastian Bay."

After three days of continuous bad weather we were left alone to attempt once more to rescue the twenty-two men on Elephant Island, for whom by this time I entertained very grave fears.

At dawn of Friday, July 21, we were within a hundred miles of the island, and we encountered the ice in the half-light. I waited for the full day and then tried to push through. The little craft was tossing in the heavy swell, and before she had been in the pack for ten minutes she came down on a cake of ice and broke the bobstay. Then the water-inlet of the motor choked with ice. The schooner was tossing like a cork in the swell, and I saw after a few bumps that she was actually lighter than the fragments of ice around her. Progress under such conditions was out of the question. I worked the schooner out of the pack and stood to the east. I ran her through a line of pack towards the south that night, but was forced to turn to the north-east, for the ice trended in that direction as far as I could see. We hove to for the night, which was now sixteen hours long. The winter was well advanced and the weather conditions were thoroughly bad. The ice to the southward was moving north rapidly. The motor-engine had broken down and we were entirely dependent on the sails. We managed to make a little southing during the next day, but noon found us 108 miles from the island. That night we lay off the ice in a gale, hove to, and morning found the schooner iced up. The ropes, cased in frozen spray, were as thick as a man's arm, and if the wind had increased much we would have had to cut away the sails, since there was no possibility of lowering them. Some members of the scratch crew were played out by the cold and the violent tossing. The schooner was about seventy feet long, and she responded to the motions of the storm-racked sea in a manner that might have disconcerted the most seasoned sailors.

I took the schooner south at every chance, but always the line of ice blocked the way. The engineer, who happened to be an American, did things to the engines occasionally, but he could not keep them running, and, the persistent south winds were dead ahead. It was hard to turn back a third time, but I realized we could not reach the island under those conditions, and we must turn north in order to clear the ship of heavy masses of ice. So we set a northerly course, and after a tempestuous passage reached Port Stanley once more. This was the third reverse, but I did not abandon my belief that the ice would not remain fast around Elephant Island during the winter, whatever the arm-chair experts at home might say. We reached Port Stanley in the schooner on August 8, and I learned there that the ship Discovery was to leave England at once and would be at the Falkland Islands about the middle of September. My good friend the Governor said I could settle down at Port Stanley and take things quietly for a few weeks. The street of that port is about a mile and a half long. It has the slaughter-house at one end and the graveyard at the other. The chief distraction is to walk from the slaughter-house to the graveyard. For a change one may walk from the graveyard to the slaughter-house. Ellaline Terriss was born at Port Stanley—a fact not forgotten by the residents, but she has not lived there much since. I could not content myself to wait for six or seven weeks, knowing that six hundred miles away my comrades were in dire need. I asked the Chilian Government to send the Yelcho, the steamer that had towed us before, to take the schooner across to Punta Arenas, and they consented promptly, as they had done to every other request of mine. So in a north-west gale we went across, narrowly escaping disaster on the way, and reached Punta Arenas on August 14.

There was no suitable ship to be obtained. The weather was showing some signs of improvement, and I begged the Chilian Government to let me have the *Yelcho* for a last attempt to reach the island. She was a small steel-built steamer, quite unsuitable for work in the pack, but I promised that I would not touch the ice. The Government was willing to give me another chance, and on August 25 I started south on the fourth attempt at relief. This time Providence favoured us. The little steamer made a quick run down in comparatively fine weather, and I found as we neared Elephant Island that the ice was open. A southerly gale had sent it northward temporarily, and the Yelcho had her chance to slip through. We approached the island in a thick fog. I did not dare to wait for this to clear, and at 10 a.m. on August 30 we passed some stranded bergs. Then we saw the sea breaking on a reef, and I knew that we were just outside the island. It was an anxious moment, for we had still to locate the camp and the pack could not be trusted to allow time for a prolonged search in thick weather; but presently the fog lifted and revealed the cliffs and glaciers of Elephant Island. I proceeded to the east, and at 11.40 a.m. Worsley's keen eyes detected the camp, almost invisible under its covering of snow. The men ashore saw us at the same time, and we saw tiny black figures hurry to the beach and wave signals to us. We were about a mile and a half away from the camp. I turned the Yelcho in, and within half an hour reached the beach with Crean and some of the Chilian sailors. I saw a little figure on a surf-beaten rock and recognized Wild. As I came nearer I called out, "Are you all well?" and he answered, "We are all well, boss," and then I heard three cheers. As I drew close to the rock I flung packets of cigarettes ashore; they fell on them like hungry tigers, for well I knew that for months tobacco was dreamed of and talked of. Some of the hands were in a rather bad way, but Wild had held the party together and kept hope alive in their hearts. There was no time then to exchange news or congratulations. I did not even go up the beach to see the camp, which Wild assured me had been much improved. A heavy sea was running and a change of wind might bring the ice back at any time. I hurried the party aboard with all possible speed, taking also the records of the Expedition and essential portions of equipment. Everybody was aboard the *Yelcho* within an hour, and we steamed north at the little steamer's best speed. The ice was open still, and nothing worse than an expanse of stormy ocean separated us from the South American coast.

During the run up to Punta Arenas I heard Wild's story, and blessed again the cheerfulness and resource that had served the party so well during four and a half months of privation. The twenty-two men on Elephant Island were just at the end of their resources when the *Yelcho* reached them. Wild had husbanded the scanty stock of food as far as possible and had fought off the devils of despondency and despair on that little sand-spit, where the party had a precarious foothold between the grim ice-fields and the treacherous, ice-strewn sea. The pack had opened occasionally, but much of the time the way to the north had been barred. The Yelcho had arrived at the right moment. Two days earlier she could not have reached the island, and a few hours later the pack may have been impenetrable again. Wild had reckoned that help would come in August, and every morning he had packed his kit, in cheerful anticipation that proved infectious, as I have no doubt it was meant to be. One of the party to whom I had said "Well, you all were packed up ready," replied, "You see, boss, Wild never gave up hope, and whenever the sea was at all clear of ice he rolled up his sleeping-bag and said to all hands, 'Roll up your sleeping-bags, boys; the boss may come to-day.'" And so it came to pass that we suddenly came out of the fog, and, from a black outlook, in an hour all were in safety homeward bound. The food was eked out with seal and penguin meat, limpets, and seaweed. Seals had been scarce, but the supply of penguins had held out fairly well during the first three months. The men were down to the last Bovril ration, the only form of hot drink they had, and had scarcely four days' food in hand at the time of the rescue. The camp was in constant danger of being buried by the snow, which drifted heavily from the heights behind, and the men moved the accumulations with what implements they could provide. There was danger that the camp would become completely invisible from the sea, so that a rescue party might look for it in vain.

"It had been arranged that a gun should be fired from the relief ship when she got near the island," said Wild. "Many times when the glaciers were 'calving,' and chunks fell off with a report like a gun, we thought that it was the real thing, and after a time we got to distrust these signals. As a matter of fact, we saw the *Yelcho* before we heard any gun. It was an occasion one will not easily forget. We were just assembling for lunch to the call of 'Lunch O!' and I was serving out the soup, which was particularly good that day, consisting of boiled seal's backbone, limpets, and seaweed, when there was another hail from Marston of 'Ship O!' Some of the men thought it was 'Lunch O!' over again, but when there was another yell from Marston lunch had no further attractions. The ship was about a mile and a half away and steaming past us. A smoke-signal was the agreed sign from the shore, and, catching up somebody's coat that was lying about, I struck a pick into a tin of kerosene kept for the purpose, poured it over the coat, and set it alight. It flared instead of smoking; but that didn't matter, for you had already recognized the spot where you had left us and the *Yelcho* was turning in."

We encountered bad weather on the way back to Punta Arenas, and the little Yelcho laboured heavily; but she had light hearts aboard. We entered the Straits of Magellan on September 3 and reached Rio Secco at 8 a.m. I went ashore, found a telephone, and told the Governor and my friends at Punta Arenas that the men were safe. Two hours later we were at Punta Arenas, where we were given a welcome none of us is likely to forget. The

Chilian people were no less enthusiastic than the British residents. The police had been instructed to spread the news that the Yelcho was coming with the rescued men, and lest the message should fail to reach some people, the fire-alarm had been rung. The whole populace appeared to be in the streets. It was a great reception, and with the strain of long, anxious months lifted at last, we were in a mood to enjoy it.

The next few weeks were crowded ones, but I will not attempt here to record their history in detail. I received congratulations and messages of friendship and good cheer from all over the world, and my heart went out to the good people who had remembered my men and myself in the press of terrible events on the battlefields. The Chilian Government placed the *Yelcho* at my disposal to take the men up to Valparaiso and Santiago. We reached Valparaiso on September 27. Everything that could swim in the way of a boat was out to meet us, the crews of Chilian warships were lined up, and at least thirty thousand thronged the streets. I lectured in Santiago on the following evening for the British Red Cross and a Chilian naval charity. The Chilian flag and the Union Jack were draped together, the band played the Chilian national anthem, "God Save the King," and the "Marseillaise," and the Chilian Minister for Foreign Affairs spoke from the platform and pinned an Order on my coat. I saw the President and thanked him for the help that he had given a British expedition. His Government had spent £4000 on coal alone. In reply he recalled the part that British sailors had taken in the making of the Chilian Navy.

The Chilian Railway Department provided a special train to take us across the Andes, and I proceeded to Montevideo in order to thank personally the President and Government of Uruguay for the help they had given generously in the earlier relief voyages. We were entertained royally at various spots en route. We went also to Buenos Ayres on a brief call. Then we crossed the Andes again. I had made arrangements by this time for the men and the staff to go to England. All hands were keen to take their places in the Empire's fighting forces. My own immediate task was the relief of the marooned Ross Sea party, for news had come to me of the Aurora's long drift in the Ross Sea and of her return in a damaged condition to New Zealand. Worsley was to come with me. We hurried northwards via Panama, steamship and train companies giving us everywhere the most cordial and generous assistance, and caught at San Francisco a steamer that would get us to New Zealand at the end of November. I had been informed that the New Zealand Government was making arrangements for the relief of the Ross Sea party, but my information was incomplete, and I was very anxious to be on the spot myself as quickly as possible.

Ernest Shackleton
South!

The Irishman Sir Ernest Henry Shackleton (1874–1922) was a junior member of Sir Robert Scott's Antarctic expedition of 1901–1903. Shackleton himself led an expedition in 1909 which nearly reached the South Pole. His next expedition, the Imperial Trans-Antarctic Expedition, started in 1914, with the aim of crossing Antarctica from sea to sea. However, his ship, the *Endurance*, was trapped and crushed in pack ice in 1915. It had to be abandoned, and the crew used the lifeboats to reach Elephant Island, where they set up camp. Shackleton, with a small crew, then travelled for fifteen days in hurricane-force winds 720 nautical miles across the sea to South Georgia to get help. This extraordinary feat has only recently been fully appreciated: at the time it was overshadowed by Scott's last Antarctic expedition, in which everyone died.

POEM XII

Now winter nights enlarge
  The number of their houres,
And clouds their stormes discharge
  Upon the ayrie towres;
Let now the chimneys blaze
  And cups o'erflow with wine,
Let well-tun'd words amaze
  With harmonie divine.
Now yellow waxen lights
  Shall waite on hunny Love
While youthful Revels, Masks, and Courtly sights
  Sleepes leaden spels remove.

This time doth well dispence
  With lovers long discourse;
Much speech hath some defence,
  Though beauty no remorse.
All doe not all things well:
  Some measures comely tread,
Some knotted Ridles tell,
  Some Poems smoothly read.
The Summer hath his joyes,
  And Winter his delights;
Though Love and all his pleasures are but toyes,
  They shorten tedious nights.

Thomas Campion
The Third Booke of Ayres

Thomas Campion (1567–1620) studied at Cambridge, then law at Gray's Inn and medicine in France, later practising as a doctor in London. However, he is remembered as a poet and musician – he composed and published songs of all kinds. He also wrote masques.

DREADFUL ACCIDENT ON THE TAY BRIDGE

Loss of Passenger Train
Dundee, Sunday Midnight

To-night a heavy gale swept over Dundee and a portion of the Tay bridge was blown down while a train from Edinburgh due at 7.15 was passing. It is believed that the train is in the water, but the gale is still so strong that a steamboat has not yet been able to reach the bridge. The train was duly signalled from Fife as having entered the bridge at 7.14. It was seen running along the rails, and then suddenly was observed a flash of fire. The opinion was that the train left the rails, and went over the bridge. Those who saw the incident repaired immediately to the Tay-bridge station at Dundee and informed the station master of what they had seen. He immediately put himself in communication with the man in charge of the signal-box at the north end of the bridge. The telegraph wires are stretched across the bridge, but when the instrument was tried it was soon seen that the wires were broken.

Mr. Smith, the station-master and Mr. Roberts, locomotive superintendent, determined, notwithstanding the fierce gale, to walk across the bridge as far as possible from the north side, with the view of ascertaining the extent of the disaster. They were able to get out a considerable distance, and the first thing that caught their eye was the water spurting from a pipe which was laid

across the bridge for the supply of Newport, a village on the south side, from the Dundee reservoirs. Going a little further, they could distinctly see by the aid of the strong moonlight that there was a large gap in the bridge caused by the fall, so far as they could discern, of two or three of the largest spars. They thought, however, that they observed a red light on the south part of the bridge, and were of the opinion that the train had been brought to a standstill on the driver noticing the accident. This conjecture has, unfortunately, been proved incorrect. At Broughtyferry, four miles from the bridge, several mail bags have come ashore, and there is no doubt that the train is in the river. No precise information as to the number of passengers can be obtained, but it is variously estimated at from 150 to 200.

The Provost and a number of leading citizens of Dundee started at half-past 10 o'clock in a steam-boat for the bridge, the gale being moderated; but they have not yet returned.

Monday, 1.30 A.M.

The scene at the Tay-bridge station to-night is simply appalling. Many thousand persons are congregated around the buildings, and strong men and women are wringing their hands in despair. On the 2d of October 1877, while the bridge was in course of construction, one of the girders was blown down during a gale similar to that of to-day, but the only one of the workmen lost his life. The return of the steamboat is anxiously awaited.

The Times, 29th December 1879

The Tay Bridge Disaster on 28 December 1879 was one of the worst railway accidents to occur in Britain. The train from Edinburgh to Dundee tried to cross a new bridge over the river Tay during a fierce storm with hurricane-force winds, measuring 10 or 11 on the Beaufort scale, blowing at right angles to the bridge. Quite what happened is still not completely known, but there were no survivors from an estimated seventy-five passengers and crew. A subsequent enquiry found many problems, including the use of poor-quality iron in the construction of the bridge, and the engineer Sir Thomas Bouch's failure to allow for the force of wind. Bizarrely the engine was recovered, and continued to work on the North British Railway until1908. The stone piers that carried the bridge can still be seen. The disaster is particularly well-known because of a dreadful poem written about it by William McGonagall.

A PRAYER

From winter, plague and pestilence, good Lord deliver us!

Thomas Nashe
Summer's Last Will and Testament

Summer's Last Will and Testament was a satirical masque written in 1592 by Thomas Nashe (1567–1601). Thomas Nashe was known as a satirist, having already attacked such targets as plagiarism, artificially romantic literature and Puritans. He also wrote plays: his lost work *The Isle of Dogs* exposed such state corruption that the Privy Council condemned the play as lewd and seditious, the theatre was closed, and Nashe himself was thrown into prison.

CHRISTMAS,
SACRED AND SECULAR

MIDWINTER FIRE

If the heathen of ancient Europe celebrated, as we have good reason to believe, the season of Midsummer with a great festival of fire, of which the traces have survived in many places down to our own time, it is natural to suppose that they should have observed with similar rites the corresponding season of Midwinter; for Midsummer and Midwinter, or, in more technical language, the summer solstice and the winter solstice, are the two great turning-points in the sun's apparent course through the sky, and from the standpoint of primitive man nothing might seem more appropriate than to kindle fires on earth at the two moments when the fire and heat of the great luminary in heaven begin to wane or to wax.

In modern Christendom the ancient fire-festival of the winter solstice appears to survive, or to have survived down to recent years, in the old custom of the Yule log, clog, or block, as it was variously called in England. ... In England ... on the night of Christmas Eve, says the antiquary John Brand, "our ancestors were wont to light up candles of an uncommon size, called Christmas Candles, and lay a log of wood upon the fire, called a Yule-clog or Christmas-block, to illuminate the house, and, as it were, to turn night into day." The old custom was to light the Yule log with a fragment of its predecessor, which had been kept throughout the year for the purpose; where it was so kept, the fiend could do no mischief. The remains of the log were also supposed to guard the house against fire and lightning.

Sir James Frazer
The Golden Bough

Sir James Frazer (1854–1941) was a Scottish social anthropologist and classical scholar. His great work, the twelve-volume *The Golden Bough*, looked at the religions of the primitive world: Frazer proposed that magic came before religion, and religion was followed by science. Frazer is considered as one of the founding fathers of modern anthropology.

NATIVITY CELEBRATIONS

The Christian festival of the Nativity, with which these ancient celebrations have been incorporated, appears to have been appointed at a very early period after the establishment of the new religion. Its first positive footsteps are met with in the second century, during the reign of the Emperor Concordius; but the decretal epistles furnish us with traces of it more remote. At whatever period, however, its formal institution is to be placed, there can be no doubt that an event so striking in its manner and so important in itself would be annually commemorated amongst Christians from the days of the first apostles, who survived our Lord's resurrection. As to the actual year of the birth of Christ, as well as the period of the year at which it took place, great uncertainty seems to exist, and many controversies have been maintained. One of the theories on the subject, held to be amongst the most probable, places that event upwards of five years earlier than the vulgar era, which latter, however, both as regards the year and season of the year, was a tradition of the primitive Church. In the first ages of that Church, and up till the Council of Nice, the celebration of the Nativity and that of the Epiphany were united on the 25th of December, from a belief that the birth of Christ was simultaneous with the appearance of the star in the East which revealed it to the Gentiles. The time of the year at which the Nativity fell has been placed, by contending opinions, at the period of the Jewish Feast of Tabernacles, at that of the Passover, and again at that of the Feast of the Expiation, whose date corresponds with the close of our September. Clemens Alexandrinus informs us that it was kept by many Christians in April, and by others in the Egyptian month Pachon, which answers to our May. Amongst the arguments which have been produced against the theory that places its occurrence in the depth of winter, one has been gathered from that passage in the sacred history of the event which states that "there were shepherds abiding in the field, keeping watch over their flocks by night." It is an argument, however, which does not seem very conclusive in a pastoral country and Eastern climate. Besides the employment which this question has afforded to the learned, it has, in times of religious excitement, been debated with much Puritanical virulence and sectarian rancor. For the purposes of commemoration, however, it is unimportant whether the celebration shall fall or not at the precise anniversary period of the event commemorated; and the arrangement which assigns to it its place in our calendar fixes it at a season when men have leisure for a lengthened festivity, and when their minds are otherwise wholesomely acted upon by many touching thoughts and solemn considerations.

From the first introduction of Christianity into these islands, the period of the Nativity seems to have been kept as a season of festival, and its observance recognized as a matter of state. The Wittenagemots of our Saxon ancestors were held under the solemn sanctions and beneficent influences of the time; and the series of high festivities established by the Anglo-Saxon kings appear to have been continued, with yearly increasing splendor and multiplied ceremonies, under the monarchs of the Norman race. From the court the spirit of revelry descended by all its thousand arteries throughout the universal frame of society, visiting its furthest extremities and most obscure recesses, and everywhere exhibiting its action, as by so many pulses, upon the traditions and superstitions and customs which were common to all or peculiar to each. The pomp and ceremonial of the royal observance were imitated in the splendid establishments of the more wealthy nobles, and more faintly reflected from the diminished state of the petty baron. The revelries of the baronial castle found echoes in the hall of the old manor-house; and these were, again, repeated in the tapestried chamber of the country magistrate or from the sanded parlor of the village inn. Merriment was everywhere a matter of public concernment; and the spirit which assembles men in families now congregated them by districts then.

Neither, however, were the feelings wanting which connected the superstitions of the season with the tutelage of the roof-tree, and mingled its ceremonies with the sanctities of home. Men might meet in crowds to feast beneath the banner of the baron, but the mistletoe hung over each man's own door. The black-jacks might go round in the hall of the lord of the manor; but they who could had a wassail-bowl of their own. The pageantries and high observances of the time might draw men to common centres or be performed on a common account, but the flame of the Yule-log roared up all the individual chimneys of the land. Old Father Christmas, at the head of his numerous and uproarious family, might ride his goat through the streets of the city and the lanes of the village, but he dismounted to sit for some few moments by each man's hearth; while some one or another of his merry sons would break away, to visit the remote farm-houses or show their laughing faces at many a poor man's door. For be it observed, this worthy old gentleman and his kind-hearted children were no respecters of persons. Though trained to courts, they had ever a taste for a country life. Though accustomed in those days to the tables of princes, they sat freely down at the poor man's board. Though welcomed by the peer, they showed no signs of superciliousness when they found themselves cheek-by-jowl with the pauper. Nay, they appear even to have preferred the less exalted society, and to have felt themselves more at ease in the country mansion of the private gentleman than in the halls of kings. Their reception in those high places was accompanied, as royal receptions are apt to be, by a degree of state repugnant to their frank natures; and they seem never to have been so happy as when they found themselves amongst a set of free and easy spirits,—whether in town or country,—unrestrained by the punctilios of etiquette, who had the privilege of laughing just when it struck them to do so, without inquiring wherefore, or caring how loud.

Then, what a festival they created! The land rang with their joyous voices, and the frosty air steamed with the incense of the good things provided for their entertainment. Everybody kept holiday but the cooks; and all sounds known to the human ear seemed mingled in the merry pagan, save the gobble of the turkeys. There were no turkeys.

Thomas K. Hervey
The Book of Christmas

Thomas Hervey (1799–1859) was a poet and critic. In *The Book of Christmas*, he collected up information about every aspect of Christmas celebrations, exploring their meaning and history. The extension to the title is clear – 'descriptive of the customs, ceremonies, traditions, superstitions, fun, feeling and festivities of the Christmas season'.

A PURITAN CHRISTMAS

3rd December, 1654. Advent Sunday. There being no Office at the church but extemporary prayers after the Presbyterian way, for now all forms were prohibited, and most of the preachers were usurpers, I seldom went to church upon solemn feasts; but, either went to London, where some of the orthodox sequestered divines did privately use the Common Prayer, administer sacraments, or else I procured one to officiate in my house; wherefore, on the 10th, Dr. Richard Owen, the sequestered minister of Eltham, preached to my family in my library, and gave us the Holy Communion.

25th December, 1654. Christmas day. No public offices in churches, but penalties on observers, so as I was constrained to celebrate it at home.

John Evelyn
Diary

The Puritans wanted to take out of Christianity anything that they thought was unbiblical – or indeed pagan. So when it was pointed out to Parliament that in 1644 Christmas ('a popish festival with no biblical justification', and 'an occasion of wasteful and immoral behaviour') would fall on the last Wednesday of December – a fast day – they took prompt action, issuing an Ordinance in favour of the fast. Another Ordinance was issued in 1647, banning not just Christmas but all so-called Holy Days. The Puritans believed that 'Those for whom all days are holy can have no holiday.' Barebone's Parliament issued a further Ordinance on 24 December 1652: That no Observation shall be had on the 25th Day of December, commonly called Christmas Day, nor any Solemnity used or exercised in Churches, upon that Day. There was another attempt to stop the celebration of Christmas in 1657. Ultimately all this legislation failed.

Old Father Christmas on Trial

Gentlemen,

To Mr. Anthony Skinner and Mr. John Block his Brother, Merchants in Plymouth. Just now is come into the harbour, the good Ship called the Thankful Remembrance; the Master of her is called Old Christmas, she is

Laden with Hospitality, a Commodity that is very scarce; she could hardly escape Naufrage. The Euroclydon winds and waves conspired against her to dash her in pieces against the black rocks of Oblivion, where she had perished, had she not born up to the Cape of Good Hope. And although M. Starve-mouse, and Mr. Cold-kitching repine at his Landing, yet I know that both you wil congratulate the Master for his safe arrival;

> And speedily to him resort,
> And bid him welcome in your Port.

Yours, J. K.

To my good Friend Mr. Philip Pearce of Modbury.

Sir, Here I present you with a New-no-thing for a New-years gift, I am ashamed of it, but I cannot now prevent it; I have been told that there have some been displeased with the former part, and I am sorry that I have offended my weak Brethren; let them forgive me this, and I will never trouble them with such a Toy any more.

> And for your part you may me justly blame,
> Unto this worthless piece to set your name.
> But if there ought be here that like you do,
> I pray fall to't, and much good do you too.

J. K.

The Afternoon Tryal of CHRISTMAS

To omit the various discourse which the Judges, Sheriffs, and Justices had a Dinner; when they were returned, and had taken their places on the Bench, they commanded to bring Old Christmas to the Bar; who when he came look't so smug and pleasant, his cherry cheeks appeared through his thin milk white locks, like lushing Roses vail'd with snow white Tiffany; or like the Lilly matcht with the Carnation, the true Emblem of Joy and Innocence; which the Judges having taken notice of, said, Methinks you put a good face upon't Old Man.

Chr. An unstain'd Conscience of the Rack can smile, And makes a better face than wine or oil.

Come, come said the Judges, are the Jury agreed? With that Sir Hica told the Judge, that one Mr. Blind-zeal, a man that had the greatest Estate in the Country, with Captain Capons-face, and Mrs. All-tongue his Sister did desire their Evidence might be taken in the behalf of the Commonwealth; and also requested the Judge; that such as were well- affected as they, might have the benefit of a Council as their Antagonist had.

Judge. I will give all liberty and freedom for a Legal proceeding, and will take all pains that may be to give all parties, if possible, satisfaction; and to this purpose Sir Hica chuse your Counsellor, and let the witnesses be call'd on both parts that have not yet appeared: And you Jury, give your best attention, for it concerns the life of the Old man.

With that Sir Hica busie, delivered a Fee to one Counsellour Verjuce, a sowre look't fellow; but Counsellour Crab seemed not dismaid at his Pig-looks, but looked Pig-again: in the mean time there stood up a Country fellow, and called to the Judge and said, My Lord, if your Honour be at Put, it is stop game, for there be two Knaves a-board; meaning the two Counsellors: to whom the Judge replyed;

Judge. Sirrah, sirrah, be silent, or you shall be put, where you shall neither see light, nor Sun this sennight.

Country fell. Then goodnight Sir. Then there was a List delivered to the Clerke, of those that had not yet appeared against the Old man in the forenoon; then the Judge commanded they should be called.

Cler. Cryer, Call Mr. Blind-zeal.

Cry. O yes, Mr. Blind-zeal.

Coun. Crab. Zeal it is blind, if knowledge doth not guide;
Knowledge is lame, if not by zeal supply'd.

Judge. Where is the Witness that was call'd? Cannot he find the way in? Is there never a Scholar to help lead him?

Crab. No, as for such, he wish them hang'd and dead;
The furious fool, will not be taught nor led.
To rost an Egg he as much fire doth make,
As judgment for to roast an Ox doth take.

Judge. Come friend, what can you say?

Blinz. My Lord, this Old wretch Christmas at the Bar, I hate him with an inveterate hatred, he hath been an utter undoer of many a good friend of mine; my Lord it's great pity that the Cockatrice had not been crusht in the shell, then had the life of many a Creature been saved, for he hath been a Murtherer from the beginning; at his coming scarce an house in the Countrey, but there is one or other dead in it; he hath a younger brother called Mr. Lent, he hath always hated his bloudy practises, and openly by Proclamation hath detested them, and Enacted penalties by a Law to be levied on those that follow any of his rioutous courses; yet this milde Gentlemen, Mr. Lent, hath been long sick, and we fear he will hardly recover; but if he do die, I will swear this Old man hath been the death of him. Therefore, my good Lord, let Justice be executed upon him as a Murtherer.

Coun. Crab. Away blind fool, do'st thou not life regard,
To hang him first, and judge him afterward?

Coun. Verj. I would have you know Crab that this Gentlemen that last exprest himself, is as virtuous and Religious as you are profane and base, and were it not in this honourable presence, I could kick you below scorn, as once I raised you above your expectation.

Coun. Crab. You Vinegar face. Your mothers bottle, and the Ink-mans barrell were Couzen germans.

Coun. Verj. Sirrah do not quarrel.

Judge. What Witnesses are there more?

Cler. Cryer, call Captain Capons-face.

Cry. O yes, Captain Capons-face.

Judge. Captain, what can you say in the behalf of the Common-wealth against the Prisoner at the bar?

Coun. Crab. I'le cut his coxcomb by and by.

Capt Capons-face. My Lord I was told that in the forenoon he stood upon his justification, and denied that ever he was the Author of Sedition. Now, my Lord, I can prove that at the Town of Stomach, in the County of Corps, he hath been the chief cause of Mutiny and Insurection; for when Captain Hot, and Lieutenant Cold, Collonel Roast, and Major Boild, Ensign Fish and Serjeant Fowle, and Corporal Flesh, with other Common Souldiers meet [text blanked] the guard, there must needs be a [text blanked] to the great detriment of the C [text blanked] wealth of Nature. And furthermore, my Lord he causeth men to dig their own graves with their Teeth: He makes the Drunkard sing whilst the drink is sighing. And thus in short is that I can say.

Coun. Crab. This was that Bountiful Gentleman, my Lord, that promised his Souldiers, that whosoever did kill the Lion, he would give him the skin for his Labour; I never heard that ever he was so forward as any of his Company, except once at a Rout, and then he out-ran them all.

And I commend his men, 'twas wisely done,
To give their Captain the first place to run.
And when his Worship pleased to run away,
'Tis breach of Discipline for them to stay.
And he unto that Market seldom goes,
 Where there is nothing to be sold but blows:
And when he to his over-match doth came,
He hath his handful, yet goes empty home.

Coun. Verj. You are a base reviling Rabsheka Rascal, it is not thy black-mouthed Envy, nor Toad-coloured Malice, shall any way obscure the splendour and renown of this Captains fame.

Judge. Silence, I will have no more of this: What other Witnesses are there?

Cler. Cryer, call Mrs. All-tongue. Cr. O yes, Mrs. All-tongue.

Judge. Come woman, where dwell you?

All-tongue. My Lord, I dwell at the Town of Tattle in the County of Prate, my Maiden name is All tongue, but I have since been married to one Mark Makebate, by whom I had two Daughters, the one called Tel-tale, the other Back-bite; my Daughter Back-bite is but a sneaking wench; but my Daughter Tel-tale is a bold wench, she hath indeed committed a fault, she hath had a Bastard by an old Rogue, the brat is called Lying, yet neverthelesse, she is much made of at every house she comes at, and brings away with her in her lap abundance of Belly Timbr: And her chief practice is, to get the Mistress or Maids into a corner, and there she sweetly drops her rare inventions into the dripping pans of their ears, and her conclusion is alwayes this, Be sure you do not tell who told you.

Judge. Woman, surely thou art not unfitly named: this is nothing to the purpose, What canst thou say against the Old man at the Bar?

All-tongue: My Lord, When first I began to see the vanity of all humane Ordinances, I took especiall notice of the notirious and vile miscarriages of this Pharisaicall Old Christmas, who strives to colour all his beastiality with the paint of Charity. Me thought I loved him when he was a youth, he was a pretty plum pleasant boy; but his friends (as Parents use to do) doted too much on him, and that spoil'd him. They put him to a Tutor called Mr. Sense, one of the Fellows of the College of Pleasure, and all the Lectures ever he read to him were Epicurean, he brought him up only to sing and Play, Dance, Carrose and Complement, One time my Lord, I came along with the Carrier (and indeed I am seldome out of his company) and standing under this Christmasses Chamber window to hearken, as I commonly do at every bodies house, there I heard him playing and singing this profane Song to his Instrument:

> Let us eat, drink and play;
> And freely injoy,
> Whatsoever our natures desire;
> Whil'st we live on the Earth.
> Let our hearts stew in Mirth,
> Sweetly, over Concupiscense fire.

By this you may perceive, what a precious blade he is, my Lord. Nay one thing more, may it please your Honour, I had almost forgotten, that he comes ten dayes into the Netherlands before he comes hither, and in the time of the Wars, there he drank healths with the Drunken Dutchmen, to the confusion of the English; My Lord, let your pity and compassion, banish him out of our Nation.

Coun. Crab. Sir, I tell your Honour what this Woman is, one Mr. Earle, that was well acquainted with her, gave me a Character of her, in which he told me that she did think her Purity consisted much in clean linnen: And that because she hath heard the Rag of Rome, she thinks it a very sluttish Religion, and rails at the Whore of Babylon for a very naughty woman; she left her Virginity as a Relique of Popery: she has no room for Charity, and understands no good works, but what are wrought on the Sampler; nothing angers her so much, as that Woman cannot preach: but what she cannot do at church she does at the Table, till a Capons sing silence her.

> But now I'le cease, lest I your patience wrong.
> Or thought to be a Kins-man to All-tongue.

Coun.Verj. Your Sirrah, Crab, I knew when you were but a Hedger; my Lord, there is no credit to be given to what he hath spoken, for he will lie as cheap as a beggar, and as loud as a Clock.

Judge. Christmas, Canst thou say nothing for thy self? Thou hast heard what hath been Evidenced against thee.

Christmas. My Lord, their Allegations are too vain, I conceive them not worth answering: but only to Mrs. All-tongues accusation for being in the Netherlands. My Lord, if plain truth may be believed, I shall need no Atturney in that cause; it was my hap to come thither when the Councel was held at Dort, where the most learned and Eminent Divines in Christendome were assembled, amongst t'whom I was courteously entertained, joyfully received and piously approved, which they conspicuously demonstrated, and by their charity to the poor manifested; and by divers other General Councels, I have been lovingly embraced, and of the necessity of my observation, they have testified, as that of Generall Councells approving Christmas. Nice. Armenia. Antioch. Carthage. Chalcedon. Orleance. Constantinople. Ferraria. Constance. Basil.

Captain Capons-face. My Lord, This was he that in the forenoon complained of his memory; I warrant your Honour, if he were searcht, we should find a worse Diary about him, than was found in B Lauds pocket.

Judge. Search him then.

Counf. Crab. Go Pick-pockets, doe, doe. With that the Captain runs to him, and pulls out a paper, and cryes out, Here 'tis, here 'tis.

Judge. Give it to the Clerk to read. The Clerk having received it, read it out audibly. The contents were these;

> Good people if I live or die,
> Be sure you follow Charity;
> For its power it is no lesse,
> Than to make Heaven to Earth depresse.
> And again, it earth can make
> A flight above the Star's to take.
> 'Twas that made immortalitie,
> To become mortal, and t'di.
> Charity, is that which say,
> Come ye blessed, come away.
> Its power is such, that it can make
> The dumb to speak, the dead to wake.
> And whether I do live or die,
> Be sure remember Charity.

With that there was a great shout, and many came in running with distracted looks, and told the Judge that all the Town was up in Arms, to come rescue the Old man; and before they made an end of speaking, in came half a dozen resolved Blades, and delivered a paper to the Judge, in which was this written;

We who unto this paper doe subscribe,
Not mov'd by Faction, nor expect no bribe.
But do unto your Lordship thus declare,
That the Old man that now is at the Bar;
Unless he be with honour quickly freed,
We tell you what you must expect with speed.
Those that endeavour Christmas to undo,
Will quickly down with Law and Judges too.

Hereupon Sir Leonard Love-Peace, the High-Sheriff, was ordered to take care for the Security of the Court, and the Prisoner, to suppress Routs, Riots and Tumults, and if he thought necessary to raise the Power of the County for that purpose.

Mr. Sheriff. My Lord, I have already taken necessary care for the Prevention and Supression of such Disorders; These were only a few unruly Apprentices, that came to shew their good-will to the Prisoner, because he was ever a Friend to them, and us'd to replenish the Exchequor of their Box; a remedy which they must certainly lose, if the Old-man mis-carry.

Coun. Verj. My Lord, here are two more substantial witnesses we desire may be heard against the Prisoner, the learned Sir Musty Make-bate, and the worshipful Squire Flant of Mock-beggars Hall.

Cry. Sir Musty Make-bake, and Squire Flant come into the Court, make room there, I think in my Conscience the Door is too little for the Squire's new Pantaloons.

Judge. Well, Sir Musty, what can you say against the Prisoner?

Sir Musty. My Lord, I have been a great Reader in my time, and have searcht narrowly into the Prisoners Pedigree, and find that he is a meer Counterfeit; for my Lord whereas he pretends the 25th of December to be his Day, the true Christmas happened a great deal sooner, even about the latter end of September, or beginning of October, as I have several Books affirm; and ought then to be observed; therefore I cannot but disown this Pretender, and conceive he deserves to suffer the Justice of the Court, for thus boldly personating another.

Coun. Crab. A shrewd Objection 'tis, but hold Beloved, 'Tis roundly said, but not so squarely proved; This Man reads Books, and loves it as his life, If ought he meet with many encourage strive. Judg. Come Squire Flant, what have you to say?

Flant. My Lord, I say this Christmas is a pitiful mechanick, gutling

Fellow, Company for none but Plow-men, and Carters, and regarded only by a few Yeoman of Kent, or here and there an out-of-fashion'd Gentleman, that loves to walk in the dull ways of his Fore- fathers, and live at the same rate his great Grandsires did, in the days of Queen Dick; whereas the true bred Gallant and man of Quality, in this our refined Age, manages his Affairs at another strain. He has something else to do with his money, than to keep open house for pampering the Paunches of a parcel of lubberly Clowns, and have the Pavement of his Hall spoiled with the dancing of their Hobnails; and therefore when this troublesom Fellow comes abroad cannot endure the Country for him, but as soon as ever Michaelmas Rent is received, to avoid his Impertinences, flips up to London in a Stage-Coach, and there lodges privately till his Jury of Cormorants, call'd the Twelve Days, are past, to save charges.

Coun. Crab. Rare Husbandry indeed: What heretofore

Was spent on Tenant, and the Neighbouring Poor,

Is now consum'd in private on a whore.

My Lord, The prosecutors have now gone through their whole Evidence, your Lordship has heard them with patience; Their Allegations are so weak, frivolous and impertinent,

that I shall not abuse your Lordship's time by going about to refute them, but submit the Innocense of my Clients Cause wholly to the Integrity of the Jury, and your Lordships Justice.

Whereupon the Jury without stirring from the Bar, affirmed their former Verdict and pronounced Old Father Christmas in wise guilty of the Indictment he stood charged with.

Which Verdict streight was welcom'd with the loud Shouts and Applauses of the joyful Crowd.

Then the Judge arose and delivered his final determination.

The Judge's Sentence and Directions to Father Christmas.

You, the Prisoner at the Bar; since upon a fair Tryal you have been acquitted by your Country, I do here publickly declare you Innocent, and set you free from your Confinement. But for avoiding all such Scandals as here have been cast upon you, for the future, do not think fit to admonish you; that you remember your Office is not so much to feast the Body, as to refresh the Soul, by thankful and pious Meditations, on that wonderful Art of Divine Love, in the Sacred Incarnation which you annually commemorate: And that therefore as you are to promote mutual Love and Hospitality amongst Neighbours, and Charity to the Poor, so you are strictly to avoid and banish all Gluttony, Drunkenness, Wantonness and Prophaness; lest you turn the Festival of the Holy Jesus into a Sacrifice to Bacchus; and instead of keeping his Day, dishonour and crucifie the Lord afresh by whole name you are called. And lastly, that as you use Sobriety, so likewise use Prudence in your Entertainments, every one according to his Quality and Abilities,

> For though on Christmas something may be spend,
> Yet not to make the whole year after Lent.
> Observing these directions you will recover,
> Your Ancient dignity and Primitive Honour.

And put to silence the Fanatical Clamors of such ignorant Zealots, and foolish men, as have this day shown themselves your Adversaries.

The jolly Old Father Bow'd his Reverent Head very respectfully to the Court, thanking them not so much for his Acquital (for in that they did but serve their own Justice) as for this wholsom advice, which he declared himself resolv'd henceforth religiously to observe. And so the Court broke up.

> And Christmas streight was courted far and near,
> To each good house to taste their plenteous chear.

FINIS.

Josiah King
The Examination and Tryal of Old Father Christmas

Puritan attempts to ban Christmas and its related festivities on the grounds that they were Papist led to Royalists defending them as a symbol of 'the good old days' of feasting and good cheer. Several pamphlets appeared, mocking the Puritan viewpoint. In Josiah King's pamphlet of 1658, we see Father Christmas, a white-haired old man, on trial for his life. The evidence against him comes from the Commonwealth. This extract covers half of his trial. King's use of the name 'Father Christmas' is the earliest citation given by the Oxford English Dictionary.

THE FARMER'S CHRISTMAS

At Christmas be mery, and thanke god of all :
and feast thy pore neighbours, the great with the small.
yea al the yere long, haue an eie to the poore :
and god shall sende luck, to kepe open thy doore.

Good fruite and good plenty, doth well in thy loft :
then lay for an orcharde, and cherishe it oft.
The profet is mickell, the pleasure is mutch ;
at pleasure with profet, few wise men will grutch.

For plantes and for stockes, lay afore hand to cast :
but set or remoue them, while twelue tide doe last.
Set one from another, full twenty fote square :
the better and greater, they yerely will bare.

Thomas Tusser
Five Hundred Points of Good Husbandry

YET IF HIS MAJESTY OUR SOVEREIGN LORD

Yet if his majesty our sovereign lord
Should of his own accord
Friendly himself invite,
And say "I'll be your guest to-morrow night."
How should we stir ourselves, call and command
All hands to work! "Let no man idle stand.

Set me fine Spanish tables in the hall,
See they be fitted all;
Let there be room to eat,
And order taken that there want no meat.
See every sconce and candlestick made bright,
That without tapers they may give a light.

Look to the presence: are the carpets spread,
The dazie o'er the head,
The cushions in the chairs,
And all the candles lighted on the stairs?
Perfume the chambers, and in any case
Let each man give attendance in his place."

Thus if the king were coming would we do,
And 'twere good reason too;
For 'tis a duteous thing
To show all honour to an earthly king,
And after all our travail and our cost,
So he be pleas'd, to think no labour lost.

But at the coming of the King of Heaven
All's set at six and seven:
We wallow in our sin,
Christ cannot find a chamber in the inn.
We entertain him always like a stranger,
And as at first still lodge him in the manger.

Thomas Ford

Best known as a musician, Thomas Ford (?1580 – 1648) was a composer, lutenist, and viol player, as well as a poet. He worked for Prince Henry, James I's eldest son (below), who died in 1612, and then for Henry's brother Charles until the Civil War broke out in 1642. This poem, which appeared anonymously and with no title, is attributed to Ford.

THE SHEPHERDS

From far away we come to you,
  The snow in the street, and the wind on the door,
To tell of great tidings strange and true,
  Minstrels and maids stand forth on the floor.
 From far away we come to you,
To tell of great tidings strange and true.

For as we wandered far and wide,
  The snow in the street and the wind on the door,
What hap do you deem there should us betide?
  Minstrels and maids stand forth on the floor.
    From far away we come to you,
To tell of great tidings strange and true.

Under a bent when tho night was deep,
   The snow in the street and the wind on the door,
There lay three shepherds tending their sheep,
   Minstrels and maids stand forth on the floor.
From far away we come to you,
    To tell of great tidings strange and true.

"O ye shepherds, what have ye seen,
  The snow in the street and the wind on the door,
To slay your sorrow and heal your teen?"
  Minstrels and maids stand forth on the floor.
From far away we come to you,
To tell of great tidings strange and true.

"In an ox stall this night we saw,
  The snow in the street and the wind on the door
 A Babe and a Maid without a flaw,
  Minstrels and maids stand forth on the floor.
From far away we come to you.
To tell of great tidings strange and true.

There was an old man there beside;
  The snow in the street and the wind on the door,
  His hair was white, and his hood was wide,
  Minstrels and maids stand forth on the floor.

From far away we come to you,
To tell of great tidings strange and true.

And as we gazed this thing upon,
  The snow in the street and the wind on the door,
Those twain knelt down to the little One,
  Minstrels and maids stand forth on the floor.
    From far away we come to you,
To tell of great tidings strange and true.

And a marvellous song we straight did hear,
  The snow in the street and the wind on the door,
That slew our sorrow and healed our care,"
  Minstrels and maids stand forth on the floor.
    From far away we come to you,
To tell of great tidings strange and true.

News of a fair and a marvellous thing,
  The snow in the street and the wind on the door,
Nowell, Nowell, Nowell, we sing!
  Minstrels and maids stand forth on the floor.
From far away we come to you,
To tell of great tidings strange and true.

William Morris

William Morris (1834–1896) studied for the church, but gave this up for the study of architecture. He became a painter, then started designing furniture and fabrics for homes. He thought mediaeval crafts were being destroyed by mass production, and that, plus capitalism, turned him into a Socialist. His first venture into literature was a book of poems. Several more followed, then a verse translation of Icelandic sagas, *Sigurd the Volsung and the Fall of the Niblungs*. Morris's interest in mythology influenced W B Yeats, J R R Tolkien and C S Lewis.

EDDI'S SERVICE

Eddi, priest of St. Wilfrid
In his chapel at Manhood End,
 Ordered a midnight service
For such as cared to attend.

But the Saxons were keeping Christmas,
And the night was stormy as well.
Nobody came to service,
Though Eddi rang the bell.

"'Wicked weather for walking,"
Said Eddi of Manhood End.
"But I must go on with the service
For such as care to attend."

" The altar-lamps were lighted, --
An old marsh-donkey came,
Bold as a guest invited,
And stared at the guttering flame.

The storm beat on at the windows,
The water splashed on the floor,
And a wet, yoke-weary bullock
Pushed in through the open door.

"How do I know what is greatest,
How do I know what is least?
That is My Father's business,"
Said Eddi, Wilfrid's priest.

"But – three are gathered together –
Listen to me and attend.
 I bring good news, my brethren!"
Said Eddi of Manhood End.

And he told the Ox of a Manger
And a Stall in Bethlehem,
And he spoke to the Ass of a Rider,
That rode to Jerusalem.

They steamed and dripped in the chancel,
They listened and never stirred,
While, just as though they were Bishops,
Eddi preached them The Word,

Till the gale blew off on the marshes
And the windows showed the day,
And the Ox and the Ass together
Wheeled and clattered away.

And when the Saxons mocked him,
Said Eddi of Manhood End,
"I dare not shut His chapel
On such as care to attend."

Rudyard Kipling
'The Conversion of St. Wilfrid': Rewards and Fairies

Rudyard Kipling (1865–1936) started his writing career as a journalist in India, where he had been born. His short stories and poems quickly became popular, as did his later work for children (these books are now classics). In 1907 he won the Nobel Prize for Literature. He turned down the chance to be Poet Laureate and the offer of a knighthood.

NO CHRISTMAS SERVICE

5th December, 1655. There was no more notice taken of Christmas-day in churches.

I went to London, where Dr. Wild preached the funeral sermon of Preaching, this being the last day; after which Cromwell's proclamation was to take place, that none of the Church of England should dare either to preach, or administer Sacraments, teach schools, etc., on pain of imprisonment, or exile. So this was the most mournful day that in my life I had seen, or the Church of England herself, since the Reformation; to the great rejoicing of both Papist and Presbyter. So pathetic was his discourse, that it drew many tears from the auditory. Myself, wife, and some of our family, received the Communion, God make me thankful, who hath hitherto provided for us the food of our souls as well as bodies! The Lord Jesus pity our distressed Church, and bring back the captivity of Zion!

John Evelyn
Diary

DULCE DOMUM

The sheep ran huddling together against the hurdles, blowing out thin nostrils and stamping with delicate fore-feet, their heads thrown back and a light steam rising from the crowded sheep-pen into the frosty air, as the two animals hastened by in high spirits, with much chatter and laughter. They were returning across country after a long day's outing with Otter, hunting and exploring on the wide uplands where certain streams tributary to their own River had their first small beginnings; and the shades of the short winter day were closing in on them, and they had still some distance to go. Plodding at random across the plough, they had heard the sheep and had made for them; and now, leading from the sheep-pen, they found a beaten track that made walking a lighter business, and responded, moreover, to that small inquiring something which all animals carry inside them, saying unmistakably, 'Yes, quite right; THIS leads home!'

'It looks as if we were coming to a village,' said the Mole somewhat dubiously, slackening his pace, as the track, that had in time become a path and then had developed into a lane, now handed them over to the charge of a well-metalled road. The animals did not hold with villages, and their own highways, thickly frequented as they were, took an independent course, regardless of church, post office, or public-house.

'Oh, never mind!' said the Rat. 'At this season of the year they're all safe indoors by this time, sitting round the fire; men, women, and children, dogs and cats and all. We shall slip through all right, without any bother or unpleasantness, and we can have a look at them through their windows if you like, and see what they're doing.'

The rapid nightfall of mid-December had quite beset the little village as they approached it on soft feet over a first thin fall of powdery snow. Little was visible but squares of a dusky orange-red on either side of the street, where the firelight or lamplight of each cottage overflowed through the casements into the dark world without. Most of the low latticed windows were innocent of blinds, and to the lookers-in from outside, the inmates, gathered round the tea-table, absorbed in handiwork, or talking with laughter and gesture, had each that happy grace which is the last thing the skilled actor shall capture—the natural grace which goes with perfect unconsciousness of observation. Moving at will from one theatre to another, the two spectators, so far from home themselves, had something of wistfulness in their eyes as they watched a cat being stroked, a sleepy child picked up and huddled off to bed, or a tired man stretch and knock out his pipe on the end of a smouldering log.

But it was from one little window, with its blind drawn down, a mere blank transparency on the night, that the sense of home and the little curtained world within walls—the larger stressful world of outside Nature shut out and forgotten—most pulsated. Close against the white blind hung a bird-cage, clearly silhouetted, every wire, perch, and appurtenance distinct and recognisable, even to yesterday's dull-edged lump of sugar. On the middle perch the fluffy occupant, head tucked well into feathers, seemed so near to them as to be easily stroked, had they tried; even the delicate tips of his plumped-out plumage pencilled plainly on the illuminated screen. As they looked, the sleepy little fellow stirred uneasily, woke, shook himself, and raised his head. They could see the gape of his tiny beak as he yawned in a bored sort of way, looked round, and then settled his head into his back again, while the ruffled feathers gradually subsided into perfect stillness. Then a gust of bitter wind took them in the back of the neck, a small sting of frozen sleet on the skin woke them as from a dream, and they knew their toes to be cold and their legs tired, and their own home distant a weary way.

Once beyond the village, where the cottages ceased abruptly, on either side of the road they could smell through the darkness the friendly fields again; and they braced themselves for the last long stretch, the home stretch, the stretch that we know is bound to end, some time, in the rattle of the door-latch, the sudden firelight, and the sight of familiar things greeting us as long-absent travellers from far over-sea. They plodded along steadily and silently, each of them thinking his own thoughts. The Mole's ran a good deal on supper, as it was pitch-dark, and it was all a strange country for him as far as he knew, and he was following obediently in the wake of the Rat, leaving the guidance entirely to him. As for the Rat, he was walking a little way ahead, as his habit was, his shoulders humped, his eyes fixed on the straight grey road in front of him; so he did not notice poor Mole when suddenly the summons reached him, and took him like an electric shock.

We others, who have long lost the more subtle of the physical senses, have not even proper terms to express an animal's inter-communications with his surroundings, living or otherwise, and have only the word 'smell,' for instance, to include the whole range of delicate thrills which murmur in the nose of the animal night and day, summoning, warning, inciting, repelling. It was one of these mysterious fairy calls from out the void that suddenly reached Mole in the darkness, making him tingle through and through with its very familiar appeal, even while yet he could not clearly remember what it was. He stopped dead in his tracks, his nose searching hither and thither in its efforts to recapture the fine filament, the telegraphic current, that had so strongly moved him. A moment, and he had caught it again; and with it this time came recollection in fullest flood.

Home! That was what they meant, those caressing appeals, those soft touches wafted through the air, those invisible little hands pulling and tugging, all one way! Why, it must be quite close by him at that moment, his old home that he had hurriedly forsaken and never sought again, that day when he first found the river! And now it was sending out its scouts and its messengers to capture him and bring him in. Since his escape on that bright morning he had hardly given it a thought, so absorbed had he been in his new life, in all its pleasures, its surprises, its fresh and captivating experiences. Now, with a rush of old memories, how clearly it stood up before him, in the darkness! Shabby indeed, and small and poorly furnished, and yet his, the home he had made for himself, the home he had been so happy to get back to after his day's work. And the home had been happy with him, too, evidently, and was missing him, and wanted him back, and was telling him so, through his nose, sorrowfully, reproachfully, but with no bitterness or anger; only with plaintive reminder that it was there, and wanted him.

The call was clear, the summons was plain. He must obey it instantly, and go. 'Ratty!' he called, full of joyful excitement, 'hold on! Come back! I want you, quick!'

'Oh, COME along, Mole, do!' replied the Rat cheerfully, still plodding along.

'PLEASE stop, Ratty!' pleaded the poor Mole, in anguish of heart. 'You don't understand! It's my home, my old home! I've just come across the smell of it, and it's close by here, really quite close. And I MUST go to it, I must, I must! Oh, come back, Ratty! Please, please come back!'

The Rat was by this time very far ahead, too far to hear clearly what the Mole was calling, too far to catch the sharp note of painful appeal in his voice. And he was much taken up with the weather, for he too could smell something—something suspiciously like approaching snow.

'Mole, we mustn't stop now, really!' he called back. 'We'll come for it to-morrow, whatever it is you've found. But I daren't stop now—it's late, and the snow's coming on again, and I'm not sure of the way! And I want your nose, Mole, so come on quick, there's a good fellow!' And the Rat pressed forward on his way without waiting for an answer.

Poor Mole stood alone in the road, his heart torn asunder, and a big sob gathering, gathering, somewhere low down inside him, to leap up to the surface presently, he knew, in passionate escape. But even under such a test as this his loyalty to his friend stood firm. Never for a moment did he dream of abandoning him. Meanwhile, the wafts from his old home pleaded, whispered, conjured, and finally claimed him imperiously. He dared not tarry longer within their magic circle. With a wrench that tore his very heartstrings he set his face down the road and followed submissively in the track of the Rat, while faint, thin little smells, still dogging his retreating nose, reproached him for his new friendship and his callous forgetfulness.

With an effort he caught up to the unsuspecting Rat, who began chattering cheerfully about what they would do when they got back, and how jolly a fire of logs in the parlour would be, and what a supper he meant to eat; never noticing his companion's silence and distressful state of mind. At last, however, when they had gone some considerable way further, and were passing some tree-stumps at the edge of a copse that bordered the road, he stopped and said kindly, 'Look here, Mole old chap, you seem dead tired. No talk left in you, and your feet dragging like lead. We'll sit down here for a minute and rest. The snow has held off so far, and the best part of our journey is over.'

The Mole subsided forlornly on a tree-stump and tried to control himself, for he felt it surely coming. The sob he had fought with so long refused to be beaten. Up and up, it forced its way to the air, and then another, and another, and others thick and fast; till poor Mole at last gave up the struggle, and cried freely and helplessly and openly, now that he knew it was all over and he had lost what he could hardly be said to have found.

The Rat, astonished and dismayed at the violence of Mole's paroxysm of grief, did not dare to speak for a while. At last he said, very quietly and sympathetically, 'What is it, old fellow? Whatever can be the matter? Tell us your trouble, and let me see what I can do.'

Poor Mole found it difficult to get any words out between the upheavals of his chest that followed one upon another so quickly and held back speech and choked it as it came. 'I know it's a—shabby, dingy little place,' he sobbed forth at last, brokenly: 'not like—your cosy quarters—or Toad's beautiful hall—or Badger's great house—but it was my own little home—and I was fond of it—and I went away and forgot all about it—and then I smelt it suddenly—on the road, when I called and you wouldn't listen, Rat—and everything came back to me with a rush—and I WANTED it!—O dear, O dear!—and when you WOULDN'T turn back, Ratty—and I had to leave it, though I was smelling it all the time—I thought my heart would break.—We might have just gone and had one look at it, Ratty—only one look—it was close by—but you wouldn't turn back, Ratty, you wouldn't turn back! O dear, O dear!'

Recollection brought fresh waves of sorrow, and sobs again took full charge of him, preventing further speech.

The Rat stared straight in front of him, saying nothing, only patting Mole gently on the shoulder. After a time he muttered gloomily, 'I see it all now! What a PIG I have been! A pig—that's me! Just a pig—a plain pig!'

He waited till Mole's sobs became gradually less stormy and more rhythmical; he waited till at last sniffs were frequent and sobs only intermittent. Then he rose from his seat, and, remarking carelessly, 'Well, now we'd really better be getting on, old chap!' set off up the road again, over the toilsome way they had come.

'Wherever are you (hic) going to (hic), Ratty?' cried the tearful Mole, looking up in alarm.

'We're going to find that home of yours, old fellow,' replied the Rat pleasantly; 'so you had better come along, for it will take some finding, and we shall want your nose.'

'Oh, come back, Ratty, do!' cried the Mole, getting up and hurrying after him. 'It's no good, I tell you! It's too late, and too dark, and the place is too far off, and the snow's coming! And—and I never meant to let you know I was feeling that way about it—it was all an accident and a mistake! And think of River Bank, and your supper!'

'Hang River Bank, and supper too!' said the Rat heartily. 'I tell you, I'm going to find this place now, if I stay out all night. So cheer up, old chap, and take my arm, and we'll very soon be back there again.'

Still snuffling, pleading, and reluctant, Mole suffered himself to be dragged back along the road by his imperious companion, who by a flow of cheerful talk and anecdote endeavoured to beguile his spirits back and make the weary way seem shorter. When at last it seemed to the Rat that they must be nearing that part of the road where the Mole had been 'held up,' he said, 'Now, no more talking. Business! Use your nose, and give your mind to it.'

They moved on in silence for some little way, when suddenly the Rat was conscious, through his arm that was linked in Mole's, of a faint sort of electric thrill that was passing down that animal's body. Instantly he disengaged himself, fell back a pace, and waited, all attention.

The signals were coming through!

Mole stood a moment rigid, while his uplifted nose, quivering slightly, felt the air.

Then a short, quick run forward—a fault—a check—a try back; and then a slow, steady, confident advance.

The Rat, much excited, kept close to his heels as the Mole, with something of the air of a sleep-walker, crossed a dry ditch, scrambled through a hedge, and nosed his way over a field open and trackless and bare in the faint starlight.

Suddenly, without giving warning, he dived; but the Rat was on the alert, and promptly followed him down the tunnel to which his unerring nose had faithfully led him.

It was close and airless, and the earthy smell was strong, and it seemed a long time to Rat ere the passage ended and he could stand erect and stretch and shake himself. The Mole struck a match, and by its light the Rat saw that they were standing in an open space, neatly swept and sanded underfoot, and directly facing them was Mole's little front door, with 'Mole End' painted, in Gothic lettering, over the bell-pull at the side.

Mole reached down a lantern from a nail on the wall and lit it... and the Rat, looking round him, saw that they were in a sort of fore-court. A garden-seat stood on one side of the door, and on the other a roller; for the Mole, who was a tidy animal when at home, could not stand having his ground kicked up by other animals into little runs that ended in earth-heaps. On the walls hung wire baskets with ferns in them, alternating with brackets carrying plaster statuary—Garibaldi, and the infant Samuel, and Queen Victoria, and other heroes of modern Italy. Down on one side of the forecourt ran a skittle-alley, with benches along it and little wooden tables marked with rings that hinted at beer-mugs. In the middle was a small round pond containing gold-fish and surrounded by a cockle-shell border. Out of the centre of the pond rose a fanciful erection clothed in more cockle-shells and topped by a large silvered glass ball that reflected everything all wrong and had a very pleasing effect.

Mole's face-beamed at the sight of all these objects so dear to him, and he hurried Rat through the door, lit a lamp in the hall, and took one glance round his old home. He saw the dust lying thick on everything, saw the cheerless, deserted look of the long-neglected house, and its narrow, meagre dimensions, its worn and shabby contents—and collapsed again on a hall-chair, his nose to his paws. 'O Ratty!' he cried dismally, 'why ever did I do it? Why did I bring you to this poor, cold little place, on a night like this, when you might have been at River Bank by this time, toasting your toes before a blazing fire, with all your own nice things about you!'

The Rat paid no heed to his doleful self-reproaches. He was running here and there, opening doors, inspecting rooms and cupboards, and lighting lamps and candles and sticking them, up everywhere. 'What a capital little house this is!' he called out cheerily. 'So compact! So well planned! Everything here and everything in its place! We'll make a jolly night of it. The first thing we want is a good fire; I'll see to that—I always know where to find things. So this is the parlour? Splendid! Your own idea, those little sleeping-bunks in the wall? Capital! Now, I'll fetch the wood and the coals, and you get a duster, Mole—you'll find one in the drawer of the kitchen table—and try and smarten things up a bit. Bustle about, old chap!'

Encouraged by his inspiriting companion, the Mole roused himself and dusted and polished with energy and heartiness, while the Rat, running to and fro with armfuls of fuel, soon had a cheerful blaze roaring up the chimney. He hailed the Mole to come and warm himself; but Mole promptly had another fit of the blues, dropping down on a couch in dark despair and burying his face in his duster. 'Rat,' he moaned, 'how about your supper, you poor, cold, hungry, weary animal? I've nothing to give you—nothing—not a crumb!'

'What a fellow you are for giving in!' said the Rat reproachfully. 'Why, only just now I saw a sardine-opener on the kitchen dresser, quite distinctly; and everybody knows that means there are sardines about somewhere in the neighbourhood. Rouse yourself! pull yourself together, and come with me and forage.'

They went and foraged accordingly, hunting through every cupboard and turning out every drawer. The result was not so very depressing after all, though of course it might have been better; a tin of sardines—a box of captain's biscuits, nearly full—and a German sausage encased in silver paper.

'There's a banquet for you!' observed the Rat, as he arranged the table. 'I know some animals who would give their ears to be sitting down to supper with us to-night!'

'No bread!' groaned the Mole dolorously; 'no butter, no——'

'No pate de foie gras, no champagne!' continued the Rat, grinning. 'And that reminds me—what's that little door at the end of the passage? Your cellar, of course! Every luxury in this house! Just you wait a minute.'

He made for the cellar-door, and presently reappeared, somewhat dusty, with a bottle of beer in each paw and another under each arm, 'Self-indulgent beggar you seem to be, Mole,' he observed. 'Deny yourself nothing. This is really the jolliest little place I ever was in. Now, wherever did you pick up those prints? Make the place look so home-like, they do.

No wonder you're so fond of it, Mole. Tell us all about it, and how you came to make it what it is.'

Then, while the Rat busied himself fetching plates, and knives and forks, and mustard which he mixed in an egg-cup, the Mole, his bosom still heaving with the stress of his recent emotion, related—somewhat shyly at first, but with more freedom as he warmed to his subject—how this was planned, and how that was thought out, and how this was got through a windfall from an aunt, and that was a wonderful find and a bargain, and this other thing was bought out of laborious savings and a certain amount of 'going without.' His spirits finally quite restored, he must needs go and caress his possessions, and take a lamp and show off their points to his visitor and expatiate on them, quite forgetful of the supper they both so much needed; Rat, who was desperately hungry but strove to conceal it, nodding seriously, examining with a puckered brow, and saying, 'wonderful,' and 'most remarkable,' at intervals, when the chance for an observation was given him.

At last the Rat succeeded in decoying him to the table, and had just got seriously to work with the sardine-opener when sounds were heard from the fore-court without—sounds like the scuffling of small feet in the gravel and a confused murmur of tiny voices, while broken sentences reached them—'Now, all in a line—hold the lantern up a bit, Tommy—clear your throats first—no coughing after I say one, two, three.—Where's young Bill?—Here, come on, do, we're all a-waiting——'

'What's up?' inquired the Rat, pausing in his labours.

'I think it must be the field-mice,' replied the Mole, with a touch of pride in his manner. 'They go round carol-singing regularly at this time of the year. They're quite an institution in these parts. And they never pass me over—they come to Mole End last of all; and I used to give them hot drinks, and supper too sometimes, when I could afford it. It will be like old times to hear them again.'

'Let's have a look at them!' cried the Rat, jumping up and running to the door.

It was a pretty sight, and a seasonable one, that met their eyes when they flung the door open. In the fore-court, lit by the dim rays of a horn lantern, some eight or ten little fieldmice stood in a semicircle, red worsted comforters round their throats, their fore-paws thrust deep into their pockets, their feet jigging for warmth. With bright beady eyes they glanced shyly at each other, sniggering a little, sniffing and applying coat-sleeves a good deal. As the door opened, one of the elder ones that carried the lantern was just saying, 'Now then, one, two, three!' and forthwith their shrill little voices uprose on the air, singing one of the old-time carols that their forefathers composed in fields that were fallow and held by frost, or when snow-bound in chimney corners, and handed down to be sung in the miry street to lamp-lit windows at Yule-time.

CAROL

Villagers all, this frosty tide,
Let your doors swing open wide,
Though wind may follow, and snow beside,
Yet draw us in by your fire to bide;
Joy shall be yours in the morning!

Here we stand in the cold and the sleet,
Blowing fingers and stamping feet,
Come from far away you to greet—
You by the fire and we in the street—
Bidding you joy in the morning!

For ere one half of the night was gone,
Sudden a star has led us on,
Raining bliss and benison—
Bliss to-morrow and more anon,
Joy for every morning!

Goodman Joseph toiled through the snow—
Saw the star o'er a stable low;
Mary she might not further go—
Welcome thatch, and litter below!
Joy was hers in the morning!

And then they heard the angels tell
'Who were the first to cry NOWELL?
Animals all, as it befell,
In the stable where they did dwell!
Joy shall be theirs in the morning!'

The voices ceased, the singers, bashful but smiling, exchanged sidelong glances, and silence succeeded—but for a moment only. Then, from up above and far away, down the tunnel they had so lately travelled was borne to their ears in a faint musical hum the sound of distant bells ringing a joyful and clangorous peal.

'Very well sung, boys!' cried the Rat heartily. 'And now come along in, all of you, and warm yourselves by the fire, and have something hot!'

'Yes, come along, field-mice,' cried the Mole eagerly. 'This is quite like old times! Shut the door after you. Pull up that settle to the fire. Now, you just wait a minute, while we—O, Ratty!' he cried in despair, plumping down on a seat, with tears impending. 'Whatever are we doing? We've nothing to give them!'

'You leave all that to me,' said the masterful Rat. 'Here, you with the lantern! Come over this way. I want to talk to you. Now, tell me, are there any shops open at this hour of the night?'

'Why, certainly, sir,' replied the field-mouse respectfully. 'At this time of the year our shops keep open to all sorts of hours.'

'Then look here!' said the Rat. 'You go off at once, you and your lantern, and you get me——'

Here much muttered conversation ensued, and the Mole only heard bits of it, such as—'Fresh, mind!—no, a pound of that will do—see you get Buggins's, for I won't have any other—no, only the best—if you can't get it there, try somewhere else—yes, of course, home-made, no tinned stuff—well then, do the best you can!' Finally, there was a chink of coin passing from paw to paw, the field-mouse was provided with an ample basket for his purchases, and off he hurried, he and his lantern.

The rest of the field-mice, perched in a row on the settle, their small legs swinging, gave themselves up to enjoyment of the fire, and toasted their chilblains till they tingled; while the Mole, failing to draw them into easy conversation, plunged into family history and made each of them recite the names of his numerous brothers, who were too young, it appeared, to be allowed to go out a-carolling this year, but looked forward very shortly to winning the parental consent.

The Rat, meanwhile, was busy examining the label on one of the beer-bottles. 'I perceive this to be Old Burton,' he remarked approvingly. 'SENSIBLE Mole! The very thing! Now we shall be able to mull some ale! Get the things ready, Mole, while I draw the corks.'

It did not take long to prepare the brew and thrust the tin heater well into the red heart of the fire; and soon every field-mouse was sipping and coughing and choking (for a little mulled ale goes a long way) and wiping his eyes and laughing and forgetting he had ever been cold in all his life.

'They act plays too, these fellows,' the Mole explained to the Rat. 'Make them up all by themselves, and act them afterwards. And very well they do it, too! They gave us a capital one last year, about a field-mouse who was captured at sea by a Barbary corsair, and made to row in a galley; and when he escaped and got home again, his lady-love had gone into a convent. Here, YOU! You were in it, I remember. Get up and recite a bit.'

The field-mouse addressed got up on his legs, giggled shyly, looked round the room, and remained absolutely tongue-tied. His comrades cheered him on, Mole coaxed and encouraged him, and the Rat went so far as to take him by the shoulders and shake him; but nothing could overcome his stage-fright. They were all busily engaged on him like watermen applying the Royal Humane Society's regulations to a case of long submersion, when the latch clicked, the door opened, and the field-mouse with the lantern reappeared, staggering under the weight of his basket.

There was no more talk of play-acting once the very real and solid contents of the basket had been tumbled out on the table. Under the generalship of Rat, everybody was set to do something or to fetch something. In a very few minutes supper was ready, and Mole, as he took the head of the table in a sort of a dream, saw a lately barren board set thick with savoury comforts; saw his little friends' faces brighten and beam as they fell to without delay; and then let himself loose—for he was famished indeed—on the provender so magically provided, thinking what a happy home-coming this had turned out, after all. As they ate, they talked of old times, and the field-mice gave him the local gossip up to date, and answered as well as they could the hundred questions he had to ask them. The Rat said little or nothing, only taking care that each guest had what he wanted, and plenty of it, and that Mole had no trouble or anxiety about anything.

They clattered off at last, very grateful and showering wishes of the season, with their jacket pockets stuffed with remembrances for the small brothers and sisters at home. When the door had closed on the last of them and the chink of the lanterns had died away, Mole and Rat kicked the fire up, drew their chairs in, brewed themselves a last nightcap of mulled ale, and discussed the events of the long day. At last the Rat, with a tremendous yawn, said, 'Mole, old chap, I'm ready to drop. Sleepy is simply not the word. That your own bunk over on that side? Very well, then, I'll take this. What a ripping little house this is! Everything so handy!'

He clambered into his bunk and rolled himself well up in the blankets, and slumber gathered him forthwith, as a swathe of barley is folded into the arms of the reaping machine.

The weary Mole also was glad to turn in without delay, and soon had his head on his pillow, in great joy and contentment. But ere he closed his eyes he let them wander round his old room, mellow in the glow of the firelight that played or rested on familiar and friendly things which had long been unconsciously a part of him, and now smilingly received him back, without rancour. He was now in just the frame of mind that the tactful Rat had quietly worked to bring about in him. He saw clearly how plain and simple—how narrow, even—it all was; but clearly, too, how much it all meant to him, and the special value of some such anchorage in one's existence. He did not at all want to abandon the new life and its splendid spaces, to turn his back on sun and air and all they offered him and creep home and stay there; the upper world was all too strong, it called to him still, even down there, and he knew he must return to the larger stage. But it was good to think he had this to come back to; this place which was all his own, these things which were so glad to see him again and could always be counted upon for the same simple welcome.

Kenneth Grahame
The Wind in the Willows

Kenneth Grahame (1859–1932) worked at the Bank of England, becoming secretary in 1898, After a curious incident in which he was shot at three times, he retired from the bank on the grounds of ill health. *The Wind in the Willows*, from which this tale comes, started as stories and a series of letters he wrote to his son Alastair, nicknamed 'Mouse'. Now a classic, the book was rejected by several publishers, but once it came out it quickly became popular.

THE FIRST CRIB

Now three years before his death it befell that he was minded, at the town of Greccio, to celebrate the memory of the birth of the child Jesus, with all the added solemnity that he might, for the kindling of devotion. That this might not seem an innovation, he sought and obtained licence from the Supreme Pontiff, and then made ready a manger, and bade hay, together with an ox and an ass, be brought unto the place. The Brethren were called together, the folk assembled, the wood echoed with their voices and that august night was made radiant and solemn with many bright lights, and with tuneful and sonorous praises. The man of God, filled with tender love, stood before the manger, bathed in tears, and overflowing with joy. Solemn masses were celebrated over the manger, Francis, the Levite of Christ, chanting the Holy Gospel. Then he preached unto the folk standing round the Birth of the King in poverty, calling Him, when he wished to name Him, the Child of Bethlehem, by reason of his tender love for Him. A certain knight, valorous and true, Messer John of Greccio, who for the love of Christ had left the secular army, and was bound by closest friendship unto the man of God, declared that he beheld a little Child right fair to see sleeping in that manger, Who seemed to be awakened from sleep when the blessed Father Francis embraced him in both arms.

St Bonaventure
Life of St Francis of Assisi

St Francis of Assisi is thought to have created the first nativity scene in the twelfth century, in a cave at Greccio. He wanted people to think about the birth of Jesus, rather than feasting and gift-giving. St Francis used a real manger and real animals, and this form of a Christmas nativity is stlll popular. However models of all the characters in the Nativity story, in a range of sizes, have also been used, and are regularly displayed all around the world before Christmas in locations including cathedrals and churches, public buildings and private homes.

A CAROL

Our Lord Who did the Ox command
  To kneel to Judah's King,
He binds His frost upon the land
  To ripen it for Spring --
To ripen it for Spring, good sirs,
  According to His Word.
Which well must be as ye can see --
  And who shall judge the Lord?

When we poor fenmen skate the ice
  Or shiver on the wold,
We hear the cry of a single tree
  That breaks her heart in the cold --
That breaks her heart in the cold, good sirs,
  And rendeth by the board.
Which well must be as ye can see --
  And who shall judge the Lord?

Her wood is crazed and little worth
  Excepting as to burn,
That we may warm and make our mirth
  Until the Spring return --
Until the Spring return, good sirs,
  When Christians walk abroad;
When well must be as ye can see --
  And who shall judge the Lord?

God bless the master of this house,
  And all who sleep therein!
And guard the fens from pirate folk,
  And keep us all from sin,
To walk in honesty, good sirs,
  Of thought and deed and word!
Which shall befriend our latter end....
  And who shall judge the Lord?

Rudyard Kipling
'The Tree Of Justice': Rewards And Fairies

ON CHRISTMAS EVE

Come bring the noise,
My merry, merry boys,
The Christmas log to the firing;
While my good dame, she
Bids ye all be free,
And drink to your heart's desiring.

With the last year's brand
 Light the new block, and
For good success in his spending,
On your psalteries play,
That sweet luck may
Come while the log is a teending.

Drink now the strong beer,
Cut the white loaf here,
The while the meat is a shredding
 For the rare mince-pie
And the plums standing by,
To fill the paste that's a kneeding.

Robert Herrick

Robert Herrick (1591–1674) first trained as a goldsmith. He was a friend of the playwright Ben Jonson, and began to write before he became a clergyman in 1623. Charles I gave him a parish, Dean Prior, in the diocese of Exeter, but as a royalist he was ejected from it under the Commonwealth. After the Restoration of the monarchy, in 1662 he regained his parish and lived there until he died. Herrick wrote about 2500 poems: his biggest collection, numbering 1200, was entitled *Hesperides* and came out in 1648, the year after he was ejected.

DANCING DAN'S CHRISTMAS

Now one time it comes on Christmas, and in fact it is the evening before Christmas, and I am in Good Time Charley Bernstein's little speakeasy in West Forty-seventh Street, wishing Charley a Merry Christmas and having a few hot Tom and Jerrys with him.

This hot Tom and Jerry is an old-time drink that is once used by one and all in this country to celebrate Christmas with, and in fact it is once so popular that many people think Christmas is invented only to furnish an excuse for hot Tom and Jerry, although of course this is by no means true.

But anybody will tell you that there is nothing that brings out the true holiday spirit like hot Tom and Jerry, and I hear that since Tom and Jerry goes out of style in the United States, the holiday spirit is never quite the same.

The reason hot Tom and Jerry goes out of style is because it is necessary to use rum and one thing and another in making Tom and Jerry, and naturally when rum becomes illegal in this country Tom and Jerry is also against the law, because rum is something that is very hard to get around town these days.

For a while some people try making hot Tom and Jerry without putting rum in it, but somehow it never has the same old holiday spirit, so nearly everybody finally gives up in disgust, and this is not surprising, as making Tom and Jerry is by no means child's play. In fact, it takes quite an expert to make good Tom and Jerry, and in the days when it is not illegal a good hot Tom and Jerry maker commands good wages and many friends.

Now of course Good Time Charley and I are not using rum in the Tom and Jerry we are making, as we do not wish to do anything illegal. What we are using is rye whisky that Good Time Charley gets on a doctor's prescription from a drug store, as we are personally drinking this hot Tom and Jerry and naturally we are not foolish enough to use any of Good Time Charley's own rye in it.

The prescription for the rye whisky comes from old Doc Moggs, who prescribes it for Good Time Charley's rheumatism in case Charley happens to get any rheumatism, as Doc Maggs says there is nothing better for rheumatism than rye whisky, especially if it is made up in a hot Tom and Jerry. In fact, old Doc Moggs comes around and has a few seidels of hot Tom and Jerry with us for his own rheumatism.

He comes around during the afternoon, for Good Time Charley and I start making this Tom and Jerry early in the day, so as to be sure to have enough to last us over Christmas, and it is now along towards six o'clock, and our holiday spirit is practically one hundred per cent.

Well, as Good Time Charley and I are expressing our holiday sentiments to each other over our hot Tom and Jerry, and I am trying to think up the poem about the night before Christmas and all through the house, which I know will interest Charley no little, all of a sudden there is a big knock at the front door, and when Charley opens the door who comes in carrying a large package under one arm but a guy by the name of Dancing Dan.

This Dancing Dan is a good-looking young guy, who always seems well-dressed, and he is called by the name of Dancing Dan because he is a great hand for dancing around and about with dolls in night clubs, and other spots where there is any dancing. In fact, Dan never seems to be doing anything else, although I hear rumours that when he is not dancing he is carrying on in a most illegal manner at one thing and another. But of course you can always hear rumours in this town about anybody, and personally I am rather fond of Dancing Dan as he always seems to be getting a great belt out of life.

Anybody in town will tell you that Dancing Dan is a guy with no Barnaby whatever in him, and in fact he has about as much gizzard as anybody around, although I wish to say I always question his judgment in dancing so much with Miss Muriel O'Neill, who works in the Half Moon night club. And the reason I question his judgment in this respect is because everybody knows that Miss Muriel O'Neill is a doll who is very well thought of by Heine Schmitz, and Heine Schmitz is not such a guy as will take kindly to anybody dancing more than once and a half with a doll that he thinks well of.

This Heine Schmitz is a very influential citizen of Harlem, where he has large interests in beer, and other business enterprises, and it is by no means violating any confidence to tell you that Heine Schmitz will just as soon blow your brains out as look at you. In fact, I hear sooner. Anyway, he is not a guy to monkey with and many citizens take the trouble to advise Dancing Dan that he is not only away out of line in dancing with Miss Muriel O'Neill, but that he is knocking his own price down to where he is no price at all.

But Dancing Dan only laughs ha-ha, and goes on dancing with Miss Muriel O'Neill any time he gets a chance, and Good Time Charley says he does not blame him, at that, as Miss Muriel O'Neill is so beautiful that he will be dancing with her himself no matter what, if he is five years younger and can get a Roscoe out as fast as in the days when he runs with Paddy the Link and other fast guys.

Well, anyway, as Dancing Dan comes in he weighs up the joint in one quick peek, and then he tosses the package he is carrying into a corner where it goes plunk, as if there is something very heavy in it, and then he steps up to the bar alongside of Charley and me and wishes to know what we are drinking.

Naturally we start boosting hot Tom and Jerry to Dancing Dan, and he says he will take a crack at it with us, and after one crack, Dancing Dan says he will have another crack, and Merry Christmas to us with it, and the first thing anybody knows it is a couple of hours later and we are still having cracks at the hot Tom and Jerry with Dancing Dan, and Dan says he never drinks anything so soothing in his life. In fact, Dancing Dan says he will recommend Tom and Jerry to everybody he knows, only he does not know anybody good enough for Tom and Jerry, except maybe Miss Muriel O'Neill, and she does not drink anything with drugstore rye in it.

Well, several times while we are drinking this Tom and Jerry, customers come to the door of Good Time Charley's little speakeasy and knock, but by now Charley is commencing to be afraid they will wish Tom and Jerry, too, and he does not feel we will have enough for ourselves, so he hangs out a sign which says 'Closed on Account of Christmas,' and the only one he will let in is a guy by the name of Ooky, who is nothing but an old rum-dum, and who is going around all week dressed like Santa Claus and carrying a sign advertising Moe Lewinsky's clothing joint around in Sixth Avenue.

This Ooky is still wearing his Santa Claus outfit when Charley lets him in, and the reason Charley permits such a character as Ooky in his joint is because Ooky does the porter work for Charley when he is not Santa Claus for Moe Lewinsky, such as sweeping out, and washing the glasses, and one thing and another.

Well, it is about nine-thirty when Ooky comes in, and his puppies are aching, and he is all petered out generally from walking up and down and here and there with his sign, for any time a guy is Santa Claus for Moe Lewinsky he must earn his dough. In fact, Ooky is so fatigued, and his puppies hurt him so much, that Dancing Dan and Good Time Charley and I all feel very sorry for him, and invite him to have a few mugs of hot Tom and Jerry with us, and wish him plenty of Merry Christmas.

But old Ooky is not accustomed to Tom and Jerry, and after about the fifth mug he folds up in a chair, and goes right to sleep on us. He is wearing a pretty good Santa Claus make-up, what with a nice red suit trimmed with white cotton, and a wig, and false nose, and long white whiskers, and a big sack stuffed with excelsior on his back, and if I do not know Santa Claus is not apt to be such a guy as will snore loud enough to rattle the windows, I will think Ooky is Santa Claus sure enough.

Well, we forget Ooky and let him sleep, and go on with our hot Tom and Jerry, and in the meantime we try to think up a few songs appropriate to Christmas, and Dancing Dan finally renders My Dad's Dinner Pail in a nice baritone and very loud, while I do first-rate with Will You Love Me in December As You Do in May? But personally I always think Good Time Charley Bernstein is a little out of line trying to sing a hymn in Jewish on such an occasion, and it causes words between us.

While we are singing many customers come to the door and knock, and then they read Charley's sign, and this seems to cause some unrest among them, and some of them stand outside saying it is a great outrage, until Charley sticks his noggin out the door and threatens to bust somebody's beezer if they do not go on about their business and stop disturbing peaceful citizens.

Naturally the customers go away, as they do not wish their beezers busted, and Dancing Dan and Charley and I continue drinking our hot Tom and Jerry, and with each Tom and Jerry we are wishing one another a very Merry Christmas, and sometimes a very Happy New Year, although of course this does not go for Good Time Charley as yet, because Charley has his New Year separate from Dancing Dan and me.

By and by we take to waking Ooky up in his Santa Claus outfit and offering him more hot Tom and Jerry, and wishing him Merry Christmas, but Ooky only gets sore and calls us names, so we can see he does not have the right holiday spirit in him, and let him alone until along about midnight when Dancing Dan wishes to see how he looks as Santa Claus.

So Good Time Charley and I help Dancing Dan pull off Ooky's outfit and put it on Dan, and this is easy as Ooky only has this Santa Claus outfit on over his ordinary clothes, and he does not even wake up when we are undressing him of the Santa Claus uniform.

Well, I wish to say I see many a Santa Claus in my time, but I never see a better-looking Santa Claus than Dancing Dan, especially after he gets the wig and white whiskers fixed just right, and we put a sofa pillow that Good Time Charley happens to have around the joint for the cat to sleep on down his pants to give Dancing Dan a nice fat stomach such as Santa Claus is bound to have.

In fact, after Dancing Dan looks at himself in a mirror awhile he is greatly pleased with his appearance, while Good Time Charley is practically hysterical, although personally I am commencing to resent Charley's interest in Santa Claus, and Christmas generally, as he by no means has any claim on these matters. But then I remember Charley furnishes the hot Tom and Jerry, so I am more tolerant towards him.

'Well,' Charley finally says, 'it is a great pity we do not know where there are some stockings hung up somewhere, because then,' he says, 'you can go around and stuff things in these stockings, as I always hear this is the main idea of a Santa Claus. But,' Charley says, 'I do not suppose anybody in this section has any stockings hung up, or if they have,' he says, 'the chances are they are so full of holes they will not hold anything. Anyway,' Charley says, 'even if there are any stockings hung up we do not have anything to stuff in them, although personally,' he says, 'I will gladly donate a few pints of Scotch.'

Well, I am pointing out that we have no reindeer and that a Santa Claus is bound to look like a terrible sap if he goes around without any reindeer, but Charley's remarks seem to give Dancing Dan an idea, for all of a sudden he speaks as follows:

'Why,' Dancing Dan says, 'I know where a stocking is hung up. It is hung up at Miss Muriel O'Neill's flat over here in West Forty-ninth Street. This stocking is hung up by nobody but a party by the name of Gammer O'Neill, who is Miss Muriel O'Neill's grandmamma,' Dancing Dan says. 'Gammer O'Neill is going on ninety-odd,' he says, 'and Miss Muriel O'Neill tells me she cannot hold out much longer, what with one thing and another, including being a little childish in spots.

'Now,' Dancing Dan says, 'I remember Miss Muriel O'Neill is telling me just the other night how Gammer O'Neill hangs up her stocking on Christmas Eve all her life, and,' he says, 'I judge from what Miss Muriel O'Neill says that the old doll always believes Santa Claus will come along some Christmas and fill the stocking full of beautiful gifts. But,' Dancing Dan says, 'Miss Muriel O'Neill tells me Santa Claus never does this, although Miss Muriel O'Neill personally always takes a few gifts home and pops them into the stocking to make Gammer O'Neill feel better.

'But, of course,' Dancing Dan says, 'these gifts are nothing much because Miss Muriel O'Neill is very poor, and proud, and also good, and will not take a dime off of anybody, and I can lick the guy who says she will, although,' Dancing Dan says, 'between me, and Heine Schmitz, and a raft of other guys I can mention, Miss Muriel O'Neill can take plenty.'

Well, I know that what Dancing Dan states about Miss Muriel O'Neill is quite true, and in fact it is a matter that is often discussed on Broadway, because Miss Muriel O'Neill cannot get more than twenty bobs per week working in the Half Moon, and it is well known to one and all that this is no kind of dough for a doll as beautiful as Miss Muriel O'Neill.

'Now,' Dancing Dan goes on, 'it seems that while Gammer O'Neill is very happy to get whatever she finds in her stocking on Christmas morning, she does not understand why Santa Claus is not more liberal, and,' he says, 'Miss Muriel O'Neill is saying to me that she only wishes she can give Gammer O'Neill one real big Christmas before the old doll puts her checks back in the rack.

'So,' Dancing Dan states, 'here is a job for us. Miss Muriel O'Neill and her grandmamma live all alone in this flat over in West Forty-ninth Street, and,' he says, 'at such an hour as this Miss Muriel O'Neill is bound to be working, and the chances are Gammer O'Neill is sound asleep, and we will just hop over there and Santa Claus will fill up her stocking with beautiful gifts.'

Well, I say, I do not see where we are going to get any beautiful gifts at this time of night, what with all the stores being closed, unless we dash into an all-night drug store and buy a few bottles of perfume and a bum toilet set as guys always do when they forget about their everloving wives until after store hours on Christmas Eve, but Dancing Dan says never mind about this, but let us have a few more Tom and Jerrys first.

So we have a few more Tom and Jerrys, and then Dancing Dan picks up the package he heaves into the corner, and dumps most of the excelsior out of Ooky's Santa Claus sack, and puts the bundle in, and Good Time Charley turns out all the lights but one, and leaves a bottle of Scotch on the table in front of Ooky for a Christmas gift, and away we go.

Personally, I regret very much leaving the hot Tom and Jerry, but then I am also very enthusiastic about going along to help Dancing Dan play Santa Claus, while Good Time Charley is practically overjoyed, as it is the first time in his life Charley is ever mixed up in so much holiday spirit. In fact, nothing will do Charley but that we stop in a couple of spots and have a few drinks to Santa Claus's health, and these visits are a big success, although everybody is much surprised to see Charley and me with Santa Claus, especially Charley, although nobody recognizes Dancing Dan.

But of course there are no hot Tom and Jerrys in these spots we visit, and we have to drink whatever is on hand, and personally I will always believe that the noggin I have on me afterwards comes of mixing the drinks we get in these spots with my Tom and Jerry.

As we go up Broadway, headed for Forty-ninth Street, Charley and I see many citizens we know and give them a large hello, and wish them Merry Christmas, and some of these citizens shake hands with Santa Claus, not knowing he is nobody but Dancing Dan, although later I understand there is some gossip among these citizens because they claim a Santa Claus with such a breath on him as our Santa Claus has is a little out of line.

And once we are somewhat embarrassed when a lot of little kids going home with their parents from a late Christmas party somewhere gather about Santa Claus with shouts of childish glee, and some of them wish to climb up Santa Claus's legs. Naturally, Santa Claus gets a little peevish, and calls them a few names, and one of the parents comes up and wishes to know what is the idea of Santa Claus using such language, and Santa Claus takes a punch at the parent, all of which is no doubt most astonishing to the little kids who have an idea of Santa Claus as a very kindly old guy. But of course they do not know about Dancing Dan mixing the liquor we get in the spots we visit with his Tom and Jerry, or they will understand how even Santa Claus can lose his temper.

Well, finally we arrive in front of the place where Dancing Dan says Miss Muriel O'Neill and her grandmamma live, and it is nothing but a tenement house not far back of Madison Square Garden, and furthermore it is a walk-up, and at this time there are no lights burning in the joint except a gas jet in the main hall, and by the light of this jet we look at the names on the letter-boxes, such as you always find in the hall of these joints, and we see that Miss Muriel O'Neill and her grandmamma live on the fifth floor.

This is the top floor, and personally I do not like the idea of walking up five flights of stairs, and I am willing to let Dancing Dan and Good Time Charley go, but Dancing Dan insists we must all go, and finally I agree because Charley is commencing to argue that the right way for us to do is to get on the roof and let Santa Claus go down a chimney, and is making so much noise I am afraid he will wake somebody up.

So up the stairs we climb and finally we come to a door on the top floor that has a little card in a slot that says O'Neill, so we know we reach our destination. Dancing Dan first tries the knob, and right away the door opens, and we are in a little two- or three-room flat, with not much furniture in it, and what furniture there is is very poor. One single gas jet is burning near a bed in a room just off the one the door opens into, and by this light we see a very old doll is sleeping on the bed, so we judge this is nobody but Gammer O'Neill.

On her face is a large smile, as if she is dreaming of something very pleasant. On a chair at the head of the bed is hung a long black stocking, and it seems to be such a stocking as is often patched and mended, so I can see what Miss Muriel O'Neill tells Dancing Dan about her grandmamma hanging up her stocking is really true, although up to this time I have my doubts.

Well, I am willing to pack in after one gander at the old doll, especially as Good Time Charley is commencing to prowl around the flat to see if there is a chimney where Santa Claus can come down, and is knocking things over, but Dancing Dan stands looking down at Gammer O'Neill for a long time.

Finally he unslings the sack on his back, and takes out his package, and unties this package, and all of a sudden out pops a raft of big diamond bracelets, and diamond rings, and diamond brooches, and diamond necklaces, and I do not know what all else in the way of diamonds, and Dancing Dan and I begin stuffing these diamonds into the stocking and Good Time Charley pitches in and helps us.

There are enough diamonds to fill the stocking to the muzzle, and it is no small stocking, at that, and I judge that Gammer O'Neill has a pretty fair set of bunting sticks when she is young. In fact, there are so many diamonds that we have enough left over to make a nice little pile on the chair after we fill the stocking plumb up, leaving a nice diamond-studded vanity case sticking out the top where we figure it will hit Gammer O'Neill's eye when she wakes up.

And it is not until I get out in the fresh air again that all of a sudden I remember seeing large headlines in the afternoon papers about a five-hundred-G's stick-up in the afternoon of one of the biggest diamond merchants in Maiden Lane while he is sitting in his office, and I also recall once hearing rumours that Dancing Dan is one of the best lone-hand git-'em-up guys in the world.

Naturally I commence to wonder if I am in the proper company when I am with Dancing Dan, even if he is Santa Claus. So I leave him on the next corner arguing with Good Time Charley about whether they ought to go and find some more presents somewhere, and look for other stockings to stuff, and I hasten on home, and go to bed.

The next day I find I have such a noggin that I do not care to stir around, and in fact I do not stir around much for a couple of weeks.

Then one night I drop around to Good Time Charley's little speakeasy, and ask Charley what is doing. 'Well,' Charley says, 'many things are doing, and personally,' he says, 'I am greatly surprised I do not see you at Gammer O'Neill's wake. You know Gammer O'Neill leaves this wicked old world a couple of days after Christmas,' Good Time Charley says, 'and,' he says, 'Miss Muriel O'Neill states that Doc Moggs claims it is at least a day after she is entitled to go, but she is sustained,' Charley says, 'by great happiness on finding her stocking filled with beautiful gifts on Christmas morning.

'According to Miss Muriel O'Neill,' Charley says, 'Gammer O'Neill dies practically convinced that there is a Santa Claus, although of course,' he says, 'Miss Muriel O'Neill does not tell her the real owner of the gifts, an all-right guy by the name of Shapiro, leaves the gifts with her after Miss Muriel O'Neill notifies him of the finding of same.

'It seems,' Charley says, 'this Shapiro is a tender-hearted guy, who is willing to help keep Gammer O'Neill with us a little longer when Doc Moggs says leaving the gifts with her will do it.

'So,' Charley says, 'everything is quite all right, as the coppers cannot figure anything except that maybe the rascal who takes the gifts from Shapiro gets conscience stricken, and leaves them the first place he can, and Miss Muriel O'Neill receives a ten-G's reward for finding the gifts and returning them. And,' Charley says, 'I hear Dancing Dan is in San Francisco and is figuring on reforming and becoming a dancing teacher, so he can marry Miss Muriel O'Neill, and of course,' he says, 'we all hope and trust she never learns any details of Dancing Dan's career.'

Well, it is Christmas Eve a year later that I run into a guy by the name of Shotgun Sam, who is mobbed up with Heine Schmitz in Harlem, and who is a very, very obnoxious character indeed.

'Well, well, well,' Shotgun says, 'the last time I see you is another Christmas Eve like this, and you are coming out of Good Time Charley's joint, and,' he says, 'you certainly have your pots on.'

'Well, Shotgun,' I say, 'I am sorry you get such a wrong impression of me, but the truth is,' I say, 'on the occasion you speak of, I am suffering from a dizzy feeling in my head.'

'It is all right with me,' Shotgun says. 'I have a tip this guy Dancing Dan is in Good Time Charley's the night I see you, and Mockie Morgan and Gunner Jack and me are casing the joint, because,' he says, 'Heine Schmitz is all sored up at Dan over some doll, although of course,' Shotgun says, 'it is all right now, as Heine has another doll.

'Anyway,' he says, 'we never get to see Dancing Dan. We watch the joint from six-thirty in the evening until daylight Christmas morning, and nobody goes in all night but old Ooky the Santa Claus guy in his Santa Claus make-up, and,' Shotgun says, 'nobody comes out except you and Good Time Charley and Ooky.

'Well,' Shotgun says, 'it is a great break for Dancing Dan he never goes in or comes out of Good Time Charley's, at that, because,' he says, 'we are waiting for him on the second-floor front of the building across the way with some nice little sawed-offs, and are under orders from Heine not to miss.'

'Well, Shotgun,' I say, 'Merry Christmas.'

'Well, all right,' Shotgun says, 'Merry Christmas.'

Damon Runyon
Furthermore

Damon Runyon (1884–1946) saw service in the Spanish-American war of 1898. He then became a journalist for the *New York American*. During World War I he was a war correspondent for the Hearst newspaper group. His short stories were told in a unique style: humour, slang and the present tense were used to describe the adventures of gamblers, show girls, crooks, drunks and other shady characters from New York's underworld. His story collection *Guys and Dolls* became a very popular musical and also a film.

SANTA CLAUS IN THE BUSH

It chanced out back at the Christmas time,
When the wheat was ripe and tall,
A stranger rode to the farmer's gate—
A sturdy man and a small.

"Rin doon, rin doon, my little son Jack,
And bid the stranger stay;
And we'll hae a crack for Auld Lang Syne,
For the morn is Christmas Day."

"Nay noo, nay noo," said the dour guidwife,
"But ye should let him be;
He's maybe only a drover chap
Frae the land o' the Darling Pea.

"Wi' a drover's tales, and a drover's thirst
To swiggle the hail nicht through;
Or he's maybe a life assurance carle
To talk ye black and blue,"

"Guidwife, he's never a drover chap,
For their swags are neat and thin;
And he's never a life assurance carle,
Wi' the brick-dust burnt in his skin.

"Guidwife, guidwife, be nae sae dour,
For the wheat stands ripe and tall,
And we shore a seven-pound fleece this year,
Ewes and weaners and all.

"There is grass tae spare, and the stock are fat.
Where they whiles are gaunt and thin,
And we owe a tithe to the travelling poor,
So we maun ask him in.

"Ye can set him a chair tae the table side,
And gi' him a bite tae eat;
An omelette made of a new-laid egg,
Or a tasty bit of meat."

"But the native cats have taen the fowls,
They havena left a leg;
And he'll get nae omelette at a'
Till the emu lays an egg!"

"Rin doon, rin doon, my little son Jack,
To whaur the emus bide,
Ye shall find the auld hen on the nest,
While the auld cock sits beside.

"But speak them fair, and speak them saft,
Lest they kick ye a fearsome jolt.
Ye can gi' them a feed of thae half-inch nails
Or a rusty carriage bolt."

So little son Jack ran blithely down
With the rusty nails in hand,
Till he came where the emus fluffed and scratched
By their nest in the open sand.

And there he has gathered the new-laid egg—
'Twould feed three men or four—
And the emus came for the half-inch nails
Right up to the settler's door.

"A waste o' food," said the dour guidwife,
As she took the egg, with a frown,
"But he gets nae meat, unless ye rin
A paddy-melon* down."

"Gang oot, gang oot, my little son Jack,
Wi' your twa-three doggies sma';
Gin ye come nae back wi' a paddy-melon,
Then come nae back at a'."

So little son Jack he raced and he ran,
And he was bare o' the feet,
And soon he captured a paddy-melon,
Was gorged with the stolen wheat.

"Sit doon, sit doon, my bonny wee man,
To the best that the hoose can do—
An omelette made of the emu egg
And a paddy-melon stew."

"'Tis well, 'tis well," said the bonny wee man;
"I have eaten the wide world's meat,
And the food that is given with right good-will
Is the sweetest food to eat.

"But the night draws on to the Christmas Day
And I must rise and go,
For I have a mighty way to ride
To the land of the Esquimaux.

"And it's there I must load my sledges up,
With the reindeers four-in-hand,
That go to the North, South, East, and West,
To every Christian land."

"Tae the Esquimaux," said the dour guidwife,
"Ye suit my husband well!"
For when he gets up on his journey horse
He's a bit of a liar himsel'."

Then out with a laugh went the bonny wee man
To his old horse grazing nigh,
And away like a meteor flash they went
Far off to the Northern sky.

When the children woke on the Christmas morn
They chattered with might and main—
For a sword and gun had little son Jack,
And a braw new doll had Jane,
And a packet o' screws had the twa emus;
But the dour guidwife gat nane.

Andrew Barton 'Banjo' Paterson

Originally a solicitor, the Australian Andrew Barton 'Banjo' Paterson (1864–1941) switched to journalism in 1899, when he became a war correspondent in South Africa. As well as journalism, he wrote novels, but it is his poetry for which he is famous. His collection *The Man from Snowy River* was a best-seller. Often using a ballad form, Paterson also employed humour and slang to portray Australian life. He collected traditional material as well: his adaptation of one of these songs, 'Waltzing Matilda', became Australia's national song and is world-famous. *A paddy-melon is a very small kangaroo, considered a pest.

CHRISTMAS DINNER

The dinner was served up in the great hall, where the squire always held his Christmas banquet. A blazing crackling fire of logs had been heaped on to warm the spacious apartment, and the flame went sparkling and wreathing up the wide-mouthed chimney. The great picture of the crusader and his white horse had been profusely decorated with greens for the occasion, and holly and ivy had like-wise been wreathed round the helmet and weapons on the opposite wall, which I understood were the arms of the same warrior. … A sideboard was set out just under this chivalric trophy, on which was a display of plate that might have vied (at least in variety) with Belshazzar's parade of the vessels of the temple: "flagons, cans, cups, beakers, goblets, basins, and ewers," the gorgeous utensils of good companionship that had gradually accumulated through many generations of jovial housekeepers. Before these stood the two Yule candles, beaming like two stars of the first magnitude; other lights were distributed in branches, and the whole array glittered like a firmament of silver.

We were ushered into this banqueting scene with the sound of minstrelsy, the old harper being seated on a stool beside the fireplace and twanging, his instrument with a vast deal more power than melody. Never did Christmas board display a more goodly and gracious assemblage of countenances; those who were not handsome were at least happy, and happiness is a rare improver of your hard-favored visage. …

The parson said grace, which was not a short familiar one, such as is commonly addressed to the Deity in these unceremonious days, but a long, courtly, well-worded one of the ancient school. There was now a pause, as if something was expected, when suddenly the butler entered the hall with some degree of bustle: he was attended by a servant on each side with a large wax-light, and bore a silver dish on which was an enormous pig's head decorated with rosemary, with a lemon in its mouth, which was placed with great formality at the head of the table.

Though prepared to witness many of these little eccentricities, from being apprised of the peculiar hobby of mine host, yet I confess the parade with which so odd a dish was introduced somewhat perplexed me, until I gathered from the conversation of the squire and the parson that it was meant to represent the bringing in of the boar's head, a dish formerly served up with much ceremony and the sound of minstrelsy and song at great tables on Christmas Day. ...

The table was literally loaded with good cheer, and presented an epitome of country abundance in this season of overflowing larders. A distinguished post was allotted to "ancient sirloin," as mine host termed it, being, as he added, "the standard of old English hospitality, and a joint of goodly presence, and full of expectation." There were several dishes quaintly decorated, and which had evidently something traditional in their embellishments, but about which, as I did not like to appear overcurious, I asked no questions. ...

When the cloth was removed the butler brought in a huge silver vessel of rare and curious workmanship, which he placed before the squire. Its appearance was hailed with acclamation, being the Wassail Bowl, so renowned in Christmas festivity. The contents had been prepared by the squire himself; for it was a beverage in the skilful mixture of which he particularly prided himself, alleging that it was too abstruse and complex for the comprehension of an ordinary servant. It was a potation, indeed, that might well make the heart of a toper leap within him, being composed of the richest and raciest wines, highly spiced and sweetened, with roasted apples bobbing about the surface ....

The old gentleman's whole countenance beamed with a serene look of indwelling delight as he stirred this mighty bowl. Having raised it to his lips, with a hearty wish of a merry Christmas to all present, he sent it brimming round the board, for every one to follow his example, according to the primitive style, pronouncing it "the ancient fountain of good feeling, where all hearts met together."

Washington Irving
The Sketch-book of Geoffrey Crayon, Gent

Washington Irving (1783–1859) had established his reputation as a writer in his native America before he came to England to work in the family business. Making friends with authors such as Sir Walter Scott and Mary Shelley he became the first American to gain an international reputation when he published *The Sketch Book of Geoffrey Crayon, Gent*. This collection of stories and sketches includes some of his most famous work, including 'Rip van Winkle' and 'The Legend of Sleepy Hollow', as well as 'The Christmas Dinner', from which this extract has been taken.

MR PICKWICK GOES SKATING

'Now,' said Wardle, after a substantial lunch, with the agreeable items of strong beer and cherry-brandy, had been done ample justice to, 'what say you to an hour on the ice? We shall have plenty of time.'

'Capital!' said Mr. Benjamin Allen.

'Prime!' ejaculated Mr. Bob Sawyer.

'You skate, of course, Winkle?' said Wardle.

'Ye-yes; oh, yes,' replied Mr. Winkle. 'I—I—am rather out of practice.'

'Oh, do skate, Mr. Winkle,' said Arabella. 'I like to see it so much.'

'Oh, it is so graceful,' said another young lady.

A third young lady said it was elegant, and a fourth expressed her opinion that it was 'swan-like.'

'I should be very happy, I'm sure,' said Mr. Winkle, reddening; 'but I have no skates.'

This objection was at once overruled. Trundle had a couple of pair, and the fat boy announced that there were half a dozen more downstairs; whereat Mr. Winkle expressed exquisite delight, and looked exquisitely uncomfortable.

Old Wardle led the way to a pretty large sheet of ice; and the fat boy and Mr. Weller, having shovelled and swept away the snow which had fallen on it during the night, Mr. Bob Sawyer adjusted his skates with a dexterity which to Mr. Winkle was perfectly marvellous, and described circles with his left leg, and cut figures of eight, and inscribed upon the ice, without once stopping for breath, a great many other pleasant and astonishing devices, to the excessive satisfaction of Mr. Pickwick, Mr. Tupman, and the ladies; which reached a pitch of positive enthusiasm, when old Wardle and Benjamin Allen, assisted by the aforesaid Bob

Sawyer, performed some mystic evolutions, which they called a reel.

All this time, Mr. Winkle, with his face and hands blue with the cold, had been forcing a gimlet into the sole of his feet, and putting his skates on, with the points behind, and getting the straps into a very complicated and entangled state, with the assistance of Mr. Snodgrass, who knew rather less about skates than a Hindoo. At length, however, with the assistance of Mr. Weller, the unfortunate skates were firmly screwed and buckled on, and Mr. Winkle was raised to his feet.

'Now, then, Sir,' said Sam, in an encouraging tone; 'off vith you, and show 'em how to do it.'

'Stop, Sam, stop!' said Mr. Winkle, trembling violently, and clutching hold of Sam's arms with the grasp of a drowning man. 'How slippery it is, Sam!'

'Not an uncommon thing upon ice, Sir,' replied Mr. Weller. 'Hold up, Sir!'

This last observation of Mr. Weller's bore reference to a demonstration Mr. Winkle made at the instant, of a frantic desire to throw his feet in the air, and dash the back of his head on the ice.

'These—these—are very awkward skates; ain't they, Sam?' inquired Mr. Winkle, staggering.

'I'm afeerd there's a orkard gen'l'm'n in 'em, Sir,' replied Sam.

'Now, Winkle,' cried Mr. Pickwick, quite unconscious that there was anything the matter. 'Come; the ladies are all anxiety.'

'Yes, yes,' replied Mr. Winkle, with a ghastly smile. 'I'm coming.'

'Just a-goin' to begin,' said Sam, endeavouring to disengage himself. 'Now, Sir, start off!'

'Stop an instant, Sam,' gasped Mr. Winkle, clinging most affectionately to Mr. Weller. 'I find I've got a couple of coats at home that I don't want, Sam. You may have them, Sam.'

'Thank'ee, Sir,' replied Mr. Weller.

'Never mind touching your hat, Sam,' said Mr. Winkle hastily. 'You needn't take your hand away to do that. I meant to have given you five shillings this morning for a Christmas box, Sam. I'll give it you this afternoon, Sam.'

'You're wery good, sir,' replied Mr. Weller.

'Just hold me at first, Sam; will you?' said Mr. Winkle. 'There—that's right. I shall soon get in the way of it, Sam. Not too fast, Sam; not too fast.'

Mr. Winkle, stooping forward, with his body half doubled up, was being assisted over the ice by Mr. Weller, in a very singular and un-swan-like manner, when Mr. Pickwick most innocently shouted from the opposite bank—

'Sam!'

'Sir?'

'Here. I want you.'

'Let go, Sir,' said Sam. 'Don't you hear the governor a-callin'? Let go, sir.'

With a violent effort, Mr. Weller disengaged himself from the grasp of the agonised Pickwickian, and, in so doing, administered a considerable impetus to the unhappy Mr. Winkle. With an accuracy which no degree of dexterity or practice could have insured, that unfortunate gentleman bore swiftly down into the centre of the reel, at the very moment when Mr. Bob Sawyer was performing a flourish of unparalleled beauty. Mr. Winkle struck wildly against him, and with a loud crash they both fell heavily down. Mr. Pickwick ran to the spot. Bob Sawyer had risen to his feet, but Mr. Winkle was far too wise to do anything of the kind, in skates. He was seated on the ice, making spasmodic efforts to smile; but anguish was depicted on every lineament of his countenance.

'Are you hurt?' inquired Mr. Benjamin Allen, with great anxiety.

'Not much,' said Mr. Winkle, rubbing his back very hard.

'I wish you'd let me bleed you,' said Mr. Benjamin, with great eagerness.

'No, thank you,' replied Mr. Winkle hurriedly.

'I really think you had better,' said Allen.

'Thank you,' replied Mr. Winkle; 'I'd rather not.'

'What do you think, Mr. Pickwick?' inquired Bob Sawyer.

Mr. Pickwick was excited and indignant. He beckoned to Mr. Weller, and said in a stern voice, 'Take his skates off.'

'No; but really I had scarcely begun,' remonstrated Mr. Winkle.

'Take his skates off,' repeated Mr. Pickwick firmly.

The command was not to be resisted. Mr. Winkle allowed Sam to obey it, in silence.

'Lift him up,' said Mr. Pickwick. Sam assisted him to rise.

Mr. Pickwick retired a few paces apart from the bystanders; and, beckoning his friend to approach, fixed a searching look upon him, and uttered in a low, but distinct and emphatic tone, these remarkable words—

'You're a humbug, sir.'

A what?' said Mr. Winkle, starting.

'A humbug, Sir. I will speak plainer, if you wish it. An impostor, sir.'

With those words, Mr. Pickwick turned slowly on his heel, and rejoined his friends.

While Mr. Pickwick was delivering himself of the sentiment just recorded, Mr. Weller and the fat boy, having by their joint endeavours cut out a slide, were exercising themselves thereupon, in a very masterly and brilliant manner. Sam Weller, in particular, was displaying that beautiful feat of fancy-sliding which is currently denominated 'knocking at the cobbler's door,' and which is achieved by skimming over the ice on one foot, and occasionally giving a postman's knock upon it with the other. It was a good long slide, and there was something in the motion which Mr. Pickwick, who was very cold with standing still, could not help envying.

'It looks a nice warm exercise that, doesn't it?' he inquired of Wardle, when that gentleman was thoroughly out of breath, by reason of the indefatigable manner in which he had converted his legs into a pair of compasses, and drawn complicated problems on the ice.

'Ah, it does, indeed,' replied Wardle. 'Do you slide?'

'I used to do so, on the gutters, when I was a boy,' replied Mr. Pickwick.

'Try it now,' said Wardle.

'Oh, do, please, Mr. Pickwick!' cried all the ladies.

'I should be very happy to afford you any amusement,' replied Mr. Pickwick, 'but I haven't done such a thing these thirty years.'

'Pooh! pooh! Nonsense!' said Wardle, dragging off his skates with the impetuosity which characterised all his proceedings. 'Here; I'll keep you company; come along!' And away went the good-tempered old fellow down the slide, with a rapidity which came very close upon Mr. Weller, and beat the fat boy all to nothing.

Mr. Pickwick paused, considered, pulled off his gloves and put them in his hat; took two or three short runs, baulked himself as often, and at last took another run, and went slowly and gravely down the slide, with his feet about a yard and a quarter apart, amidst the gratified shouts of all the spectators.

'Keep the pot a-bilin', Sir!' said Sam; and down went Wardle again, and then Mr. Pickwick, and then Sam, and then Mr. Winkle, and then Mr. Bob Sawyer, and then the fat boy, and then Mr. Snodgrass, following closely upon each other's heels, and running after each other with as much eagerness as if their future prospects in life depended on their expedition.

It was the most intensely interesting thing, to observe the manner in which Mr. Pickwick performed his share in the ceremony; to watch the torture of anxiety with which he viewed the person behind, gaining upon him at the imminent hazard of tripping him up; to see him gradually expend the painful force he had put on at first, and turn slowly round on the slide, with his face towards the point from which he had started; to contemplate the playful smile which mantled on his face when he had accomplished the distance, and the eagerness with which he turned round when he had done so, and ran after his predecessor, his black gaiters tripping pleasantly through the snow, and his eyes beaming cheerfulness and gladness through his spectacles. And when he was knocked down (which happened upon the average every third round), it was the most invigorating sight that can possibly be imagined, to behold him gather up his hat, gloves, and handkerchief, with a glowing countenance, and resume his station in the rank, with an ardour and enthusiasm that nothing Could abate.

The sport was at its height, the sliding was at the quickest, the laughter was at the loudest, when a sharp smart crack was heard. There was a quick rush towards the bank, a wild scream from the ladies, and a shout from Mr. Tupman. A large mass of ice disappeared; the water bubbled up over it; Mr. Pickwick's hat, gloves, and handkerchief were floating on the surface; and this was all of Mr. Pickwick that anybody could see.

Dismay and anguish were depicted on every countenance; the males turned pale, and the females fainted; Mr. Snodgrass and Mr. Winkle grasped each other by the hand, and gazed at the spot where their leader had gone down, with frenzied eagerness; while Mr. Tupman, by way of rendering the promptest assistance, and at the same time conveying to any persons who might be within hearing, the clearest possible notion of the catastrophe, ran off across the country at his utmost speed, screaming 'Fire!' with all his might.

It was at this moment, when old Wardle and Sam Weller were approaching the hole with cautious steps, and Mr. Benjamin Allen was holding a hurried consultation with Mr. Bob Sawyer on the advisability of bleeding the company generally, as an improving little bit of professional practice—it was at this very moment, that a face, head, and shoulders, emerged from beneath the water, and disclosed the features and spectacles of Mr. Pickwick.

'Keep yourself up for an instant—for only one instant!' bawled Mr. Snodgrass.

'Yes, do; let me implore you—for my sake!' roared Mr. Winkle, deeply affected. The adjuration was rather unnecessary; the probability being, that if Mr. Pickwick had declined to keep himself up for anybody else's sake, it would have occurred to him that he might as well do so, for his own.

'Do you feel the bottom there, old fellow?' said Wardle.

'Yes, certainly,' replied Mr. Pickwick, wringing the water from his head and face, and gasping for breath. 'I fell upon my back. I couldn't get on my feet at first.'

The clay upon so much of Mr. Pickwick's coat as was yet visible, bore testimony to the accuracy of this statement; and as the fears of the spectators were still further relieved by the fat boy's suddenly recollecting that the water was nowhere more than five feet deep, prodigies of valour were performed to get him out. After a vast quantity of splashing, and cracking, and struggling, Mr. Pickwick was at length fairly extricated from his unpleasant position, and once more stood on dry land.

'Oh, he'll catch his death of cold,' said Emily.

'Dear old thing!' said Arabella. 'Let me wrap this shawl round you, Mr. Pickwick.'

'Ah, that's the best thing you can do,' said Wardle; 'and when you've got it on, run home as fast as your legs can carry you, and jump into bed directly.'

A dozen shawls were offered on the instant. Three or four of the thickest having been selected, Mr. Pickwick was wrapped up, and started off, under the guidance of Mr. Weller; presenting the singular phenomenon of an elderly gentleman, dripping wet, and without a hat, with his arms bound down to his sides, skimming over the ground, without any clearly-defined purpose, at the rate of six good English miles an hour.

But Mr. Pickwick cared not for appearances in such an extreme case, and urged on by Sam Weller, he kept at the very top of his speed until he reached the door of Manor Farm, where Mr. Tupman had arrived some five minutes before, and had frightened the old lady into palpitations of the heart by impressing her with the unalterable conviction that the kitchen chimney was on fire—a calamity which always presented itself in glowing colours to the old lady's mind, when anybody about her evinced the smallest agitation.

Mr. Pickwick paused not an instant until he was snug in bed. Sam Weller lighted a blazing fire in the room, and took up his dinner; a bowl of punch was carried up afterwards, and a grand carouse held in honour of his safety. Old Wardle would not hear of his rising, so they made the bed the chair, and Mr. Pickwick presided. A second and a third bowl were ordered in; and when Mr. Pickwick awoke next morning, there was not a symptom of rheumatism about him; which proves, as Mr. Bob Sawyer very justly observed, that there is nothing like hot punch in such cases; and that if ever hot punch did fail to act as a preventive, it was merely because the patient fell into the vulgar error of not taking enough of it.

Charles Dickens
The Pickwick Papers

At the age of twelve Charles Dickens (1812–1870) had to start work in a blacking factory, because his feckless father was in prison for debt: although he went to school before and after this experience, it left an indelible impression on him, which he used later to good effect. He became a journalist, and then started writing sketches for *The Monthly Magazine*, a journal edited by a friend. This was followed by similar work for other papers. In 1836 he started writing the stories which later became *The Pickwick Papers*. The comic adventures of the various colourful characters became immensely popular.

THE DOLPHIN

A.D. 1392: King Richard with Queen Anne his wife, foure bishops, as many Earles, the Duke of Yorke, many Lords, and fifteen Ladies held a royall Christmas at Langley neere to St. Albans. The same Christmas Day a Dolphin came foorth of the Sea and played himselfe in ye Thames at London to the bridge, foreshewing happily the tempests that were to follow within a week after, the which Dolphin being seene of the Citizens, and followed, was with much difficulty intercepted, and brought againe to London, shewing a spectacle to many, of the height of his body, for hee was ten foote in length. These Dolphins are fishes of the Sea that follow the voices of men, and rejoice in the playing of instruments & are wont to gather themselves at musicke. These when they play in rivers, with hasty springings or leapings doe signifie tempest to follow. The Seas containe nothing more swift nor nimble, for sometimes with their skips, they mount over the sailes of ships.

John Stow
Annales

John Stow (1525–1605) worked for many years as a tailor, but was also a self-taught historian and antiquary, building up an important collection of manuscripts. *The Chronicles of England*, published in 1580, came to be known as the *Annales of England*. His Survey of London and Westminster covers six centuries of history and customs: in the eighteenth century it was revised and enlarged by John Strype.

THE GREEN KNIGHT'S CHALLENGE

King Arthur lay at Camelot upon a Christmas-tide, with many a gallant lord and lovely lady, and all the noble brotherhood of the Round Table. There they held rich revels with gay talk and jest; one while they would ride forth to joust and tourney, and again back to the court to make carols; for there was the feast holden fifteen days with all the mirth that men could devise, song and glee, glorious to hear, in the daytime, and dancing at night. Halls and chambers were crowded with noble guests, the bravest of knights and the loveliest of ladies, and Arthur himself was the comeliest king that ever held a court. For all this fair folk were in their youth, the fairest and most fortunate under heaven, and the king himself of such fame that it were hard now to name so valiant a hero.

Now the New Year had but newly come in, and on that day a double portion was served on the high table to all the noble guests, and thither came the king with all his knights, when the service in the chapel had been sung to an end. And they greeted each other for the New Year, and gave rich gifts, the one to the other (and they that received them were not wroth, that may ye well believe!), and the maidens laughed and made mirth till it was time to get them to meat. Then they washed and sat them down to the feast in fitting rank and order, and Guinevere the queen, gaily clad, sat on the high daïs. Silken was her seat, with a fair canopy over her head, of rich tapestries of Tars, embroidered, and studded with costly gems; fair she was to look upon, with her shining grey eyes, a fairer woman might no man boast himself of having seen.

But Arthur would not eat till all were served, so full of joy and gladness was he, even as a child; he liked not either to lie long, or to sit long at meat, so worked upon him his young blood and his wild brain. And another custom he had also, that came of his nobility, that he would never eat upon an high day till he had been advised of some knightly deed, or some strange and marvellous tale, of his ancestors, or of arms, or of other ventures. Or till some stranger knight should seek of him leave to joust with one of the Round Table, that they might set their lives in jeopardy, one against another, as fortune might favour them. Such was the king's custom when he sat in hall at each high feast with his noble knights, therefore on that New Year tide, he abode, fair of face, on the throne, and made much mirth withal.

Thus the king sat before the high tables, and spake of many things; and there good Sir Gawain was seated by Guinevere the queen, and on her other side sat Agravain, à la dure main; both were the king's sister's sons and full gallant knights. And at the end of the table was Bishop Bawdewyn, and Ywain, King Urien's son, sat at the other side alone. These were worthily served on the daïs, and at the lower tables sat many valiant knights. Then they bare the first course with the blast of trumpets and waving of banners, with the sound of drums and pipes, of song and lute, that many a heart was uplifted at the melody. Many were the dainties, and rare the meats, so great was the plenty they might scarce find room on the board to set on the dishes. Each helped himself as he liked best, and to each two were twelve dishes, with great plenty of beer and wine.

Now I will say no more of the service, but that ye may know there was no lack, for there drew near a venture that the folk might well have left their labour to gaze upon. As the sound of the music ceased, and the first course had been fitly served, there came in at the hall door one terrible to behold, of stature greater than any on earth; from neck to loin so strong and thickly made, and with limbs so long and so great that he seemed even as a giant. And yet he was but a man, only the mightiest that might mount a steed; broad of chest and shoulders and slender of waist, and all his features of like fashion; but men marvelled much at his colour, for he rode even as a knight, yet was green all over.

For he was clad all in green, with a straight coat, and a mantle above; all decked and lined with fur was the cloth and the hood that was thrown back from his locks and lay on his shoulders. Hose had he of the same green, and spurs of bright gold with silken fastenings richly worked; and all his vesture was verily green. Around his waist and his saddle were bands with fair stones set upon silken work, ‹twere too long to tell of all the trifles that were embroidered thereon—birds and insects in gay gauds of green and gold. All the trappings of his steed were of metal of like enamel, even the stirrups that he stood in stained of the same, and stirrups and saddle-bow alike gleamed and shone with green stones. Even the steed on which he rode was of the same hue, a green horse, great and strong, and hard to hold, with broidered bridle, meet for the rider.

The knight was thus gaily dressed in green, his hair falling around his shoulders; on his breast hung a beard, as thick and green as a bush, and the beard and the hair of his head were clipped all round above his elbows. The lower part of his sleeves were fastened with clasps in the same wise as a king›s mantle. The horse›s mane was crisp and plaited with many a knot folded in with gold thread about the fair green, here a twist of the hair, here another of gold. The tail was twined in like manner, and both were bound about with a band of bright green set with many a precious stone; then they were tied aloft in a cunning knot, whereon rang many bells of burnished gold. Such a steed might no other ride, nor had such ever been looked upon in that hall ere that time; and all who saw that knight spake and said that a man might scarce abide his stroke.

The knight bore no helm nor hauberk, neither gorget nor breast-plate, neither shaft nor buckler to smite nor to shield, but in one hand he had a holly-bough, that is greenest when the groves are bare, and in his other an

axe, huge and uncomely, a cruel weapon in fashion, if one would picture it. The head was an ell-yard long, the metal all of green steel and gold, the blade burnished bright, with a broad edge, as well shapen to shear as a sharp razor. The steel was set into a strong staff, all bound round with iron, even to the end, and engraved with green in cunning work. A lace was twined about it, that looped at the head, and all adown the handle it was clasped with tassels on buttons of bright green richly broidered.

The knight rideth through the entrance of the hall, driving straight to the high daïs, and greeted no man, but looked ever upwards; and the first words he spake were, «Where is the ruler of this folk? I would gladly look upon that hero, and have speech with him." He cast his eyes on the knights, and mustered them up and down, striving ever to see who of them was of most renown.

Then was there great gazing to behold that chief, for each man marvelled what it might mean that a knight and his steed should have even such a hue as the green grass; and that seemed even greener than green enamel on bright gold. All looked on him as he stood, and drew near unto him wondering greatly what he might be; for many marvels had they seen, but none such as this, and phantasm and faërie did the folk deem it. Therefore were the gallant knights slow to answer, and gazed astounded, and sat stone still in a deep silence through that goodly hall, as if a slumber were fallen upon them. I deem it was not all for doubt, but some for courtesy that they might give ear unto his errand.

Then Arthur beheld this adventurer before his high daïs, and knightly he greeted him, for fearful was he never. «Sir,» he said, «thou art welcome to this place—lord of this hall am I, and men call me Arthur. Light thee down, and tarry awhile, and what thy will is, that shall we learn after.»

«Nay,» quoth the stranger, «so help me He that sitteth on high, ‹twas not mine errand to tarry any while in this dwelling; but the praise of this thy folk and thy city is lifted up on high, and thy warriors are holden for the best and the most valiant of those who ride mail-clad to the fight. The wisest and the worthiest of this world are they, and well proven in all knightly sports. And here, as I have heard tell, is fairest courtesy, therefore have I come hither as at this time. Ye may be sure by the branch that I bear here that I come in peace, seeking no strife. For had I willed to journey in warlike guise I have at home both hauberk and helm, shield and shining spear, and other weapons to mine hand, but since I seek no war my raiment is that of peace. But if thou be as bold as all men tell thou wilt freely grant me the boon I ask.»

And Arthur answered, «Sir Knight, if thou cravest battle here thou shalt not fail for lack of a foe.»

And the knight answered, «Nay, I ask no fight, in faith here on the benches are but beardless children, were I clad in armour on my steed there is no man here might match me. Therefore I ask in this court but a Christmas jest, for that it is Yule-tide, and New Year, and there are here many fain for sport. If any one in this hall holds himself so hardy, so bold both of blood and brain, as to dare strike me one stroke for another, I will give him as a gift this axe, which is heavy enough, in sooth, to handle as he may list, and I will abide the first blow, unarmed as I sit. If any knight be so bold as to prove my words let him come swiftly to me here, and take this weapon, I quit claim to it, he may keep it as his own, and I will abide his stroke, firm on the floor. Then shalt thou give me the right to deal him another, the respite of a year and a day shall he have. Now haste, and let see whether any here dare say aught.»

Now if the knights had been astounded at the first, yet stiller were they all, high and low, when they had heard his words. The knight on his steed straightened himself in the saddle, and rolled his eyes fiercely round the hall, red they gleamed under his green and bushy brows. He frowned and twisted his beard, waiting to see who should rise, and when none answered he cried aloud in mockery, «What, is this Arthur›s hall, and these the knights whose renown hath run through many realms? Where are now your pride and your conquests, your wrath, and anger, and mighty words? Now are the praise and the renown of the Round Table overthrown by one man›s speech, since all keep silence for dread ere ever they have seen a blow!»

With that he laughed so loudly that the blood rushed to the king›s fair face for very shame; he waxed wroth, as did all his knights, and sprang to his feet, and drew near to the stranger and said, «Now by heaven foolish is thy asking, and thy folly shall find its fitting answer. I know no man aghast at thy great words. Give me here thine axe and I shall grant thee the boon thou hast asked.» Lightly he sprang to him and caught at his hand, and the knight, fierce of aspect, lighted down from his charger.

Then Arthur took the axe and gripped the haft, and swung it round, ready to strike. And the knight stood before him, taller by the head than any in the hall; he stood, and stroked his beard, and drew down his coat, no more dismayed for the king›s threats than if one had brought him a drink of wine.

Then Gawain, who sat by the queen, leaned forward to the king and spake, «I beseech ye, my lord, let this venture be mine. Would ye but bid me rise from this seat, and stand by your side, so that my liege lady thought it not ill, then would I come to your counsel before this goodly court. For I think it not seemly when such challenges be made in your hall that ye yourself should undertake it, while there are many bold knights who sit beside ye, none are there, methinks, of readier will under heaven, or more valiant in open field. I am the weakest, I wot, and the feeblest of wit, and it will be the less loss of my life if ye seek sooth. For save that ye are mine uncle naught is there in me to praise, no virtue is there in my body save your blood, and since this challenge is such folly that it beseems ye not to take it, and I have asked it from ye first, let it fall to me, and if I bear myself ungallantly then let all this court blame me.»

Then they all spake with one voice that the king should leave this venture and grant it to Gawain.

Then Arthur commanded the knight to rise, and he rose up quickly and knelt down before the king, and caught hold of the weapon; and the king loosed his hold of it, and lifted up his hand, and gave him his blessing, and bade him be strong both of heart and hand. «Keep thee well, nephew,» quoth Arthur, «that thou give him but the one blow, and if thou redest him rightly I trow thou shalt well abide the stroke he may give thee after."

Gawain stepped to the stranger, axe in hand, and he, never fearing, awaited his coming. Then the Green Knight spake to Sir Gawain, «Make we our covenant ere we go further. First, I ask thee, knight, what is thy name? Tell me truly, that I may know thee.»

«In faith,» quoth the good knight, «Gawain am I, who give thee this buffet, let what may come of it; and at this time twelvemonth will I take another at thine hand with whatsoever weapon thou wilt, and none other.»

Then the other answered again, «Sir Gawain, so may I thrive as I am fain to take this buffet at thine hand,» and he quoth further, «Sir Gawain, it liketh me well that I shall take at thy fist that which I have asked here, and thou hast readily and truly rehearsed all the covenant that I asked of the king, save that thou shalt swear me, by thy troth, to seek me thyself wherever thou hopest that I may be found, and win thee such reward as thou dealest me to-day, before this folk.»   «Where shall I seek thee?» quoth Gawain. «Where is thy place? By Him that made me, I wot never where thou dwellest, nor know I thee, knight, thy court, nor thy name. But teach me truly all that pertaineth thereto, and tell me thy name, and I shall use all my wit to win my way thither, and that I swear thee for sooth, and by my sure troth.»

«That is enough in the New Year, it needs no more,» quoth the Green Knight to the gallant Gawain, «if I tell thee truly when I have taken the blow, and thou hast smitten me; then will I teach thee of my house and home, and mine own name, then mayest thou ask thy road and keep covenant. And if I waste no words then farest thou the better, for thou canst dwell in thy land, and seek no further. But take now thy toll, and let see how thy strikest.»

«Gladly will I,» quoth Gawain, handling his axe.

Then the Green Knight swiftly made him ready, he bowed down his head, and laid his long locks on the crown that his bare neck might be seen. Gawain gripped his axe and raised it on high, the left foot he set forward on the floor, and let the blow fall lightly on the bare neck. The sharp edge of the blade sundered the bones, smote through the neck, and clave it in two, so that the edge of the steel bit on the ground, and the fair head fell to the earth that many struck it with their feet as it rolled forth. The blood spurted forth, and glistened on the green raiment, but the knight neither

faltered nor fell; he started forward with out-stretched hand, and caught the head, and lifted it up; then he turned to his steed, and took hold of the bride, set his foot in the stirrup, and mounted. His head he held by the hair, in his hand. Then he seated himself in his saddle as if naught ailed him, and he were not headless. He turned his steed about, the grim corpse bleeding freely the while, and they who looked upon him doubted them much for the covenant.

For he held up the head in his hand, and turned the face towards them that sat on the high daïs, and it lifted up the eyelids and looked upon them and spake as ye shall hear. "Look, Gawain, that thou art ready to go as thou hast promised, and seek leally till thou find me, even as thou hast sworn in this hall in the hearing of these knights. Come thou, I charge thee, to the Green Chapel, such a stroke as thou hast dealt thou hast deserved, and it shall be promptly paid thee on New Year's morn. Many men know me as the knight of the Green Chapel, and if thou askest, thou shalt not fail to find me. Therefore it behoves thee to come, or to yield thee as recreant."

With that he turned his bridle, and galloped out at the hall door, his head in his hands, so that the sparks flew from beneath his horse›s hoofs. Whither he went none knew, no more than they wist whence he had come; and the king and Gawain they gazed and laughed, for in sooth this had proved a greater marvel than any they had known aforetime.

Though Arthur the king was astonished at his heart, yet he let no sign of it be seen, but spake in courteous wise to the fair queen: «Dear lady, be not dismayed, such craft is well suited to Christmas-tide when we seek jesting, laughter and song, and fair carols of knights and ladies. But now I may well get me to meat, for I have seen a marvel I may not forget.» Then he looked on Sir Gawain, and said gaily, «Now, fair nephew, hang up thine axe, since it has hewn enough,» and they hung it on the dossal above the daïs, where all men might look on it for a marvel, and by its true token tell of the wonder. Then the twain sat them down together, the king and the good knight, and men served them with a double portion, as was the share of the noblest, with all manner of meat and of minstrelsy. And they spent that day in gladness, but Sir Gawain must well bethink him of the heavy venture to which he had set his hand.

Anon.
Sir Gawain and the Green Knight, trans. Jesse Weston

Sir Gawain and the Green Knight, from which this extract comes, is a verse romance written in the late fourteenth century. From the vocabulary used, and other clues in the text, it appears to have been written by someone from the West Midlands, probably the same person who wrote three other poems, Pearl, Patience and Cleanliness, though these have religious themes and Sir Gawain and the Green Knight does not.

THE ADVENTURE OF THE BLUE CARBUNCLE

I HAD called upon my friend Sherlock Holmes upon the second morning after Christmas, with the intention of wishing him the compliments of the season. He was lounging upon the sofa in a purple dressing-gown, a pipe-rack within his reach upon the right, and a pile of crumpled morning papers, evidently newly studied, near at hand. Beside the couch was a wooden chair, and on the angle of the back hung a very seedy and disreputable hard felt hat, much the worse for wear, and cracked in several places. A lens and a forceps lying upon the seat of the chair suggested that the hat had been suspended in this manner for the purpose of examination.

"You are engaged," said I; "perhaps I interrupt you."

"Not at all. I am glad to have a friend with whom I can discuss my results. The matter is a perfectly trivial one"—he jerked his thumb in the direction of the old hat—"but there are points in connection with it which are not entirely devoid of interest and even of instruction."

I seated myself in his armchair and warmed my hands before his crackling fire, for a sharp frost had set in, and the windows were thick with the ice crystals. "I suppose," I remarked, "that, homely as it looks, this thing has some deadly story linked on to it—that it is the clue which will guide you in the solution of some mystery and the punishment of some crime."

"No, no. No crime," said Sherlock Holmes, laughing. "Only one of those whimsical little incidents which will happen when you have four million human beings all jostling each other within the space of a few square miles. Amid the action and reaction of so dense a swarm of humanity, every possible combination of events may be expected to take place, and many a little problem will be presented which may be striking and bizarre without being criminal. We have already had experience of such."

"So much so," I remarked, "that of the last six cases which I have added to my notes, three have been entirely free of any legal crime."

"Precisely. You allude to my attempt to recover the Irene Adler papers, to the singular case of Miss Mary Sutherland, and to the adventure of the man with the twisted lip. Well, I have no doubt that this small matter will fall into the same innocent category. You know Peterson, the commissionaire?"

"Yes."

"It is to him that this trophy belongs."

"It is his hat."

"No, no, he found it. Its owner is unknown. I beg that you will look upon it not as a battered billycock but as an intellectual problem. And, first, as to how it came here. It arrived upon Christmas morning, in company with a good fat goose, which is, I have no doubt, roasting at this moment in front of Peterson's fire. The facts are these: about four o'clock on Christmas morning, Peterson, who, as you know, is a very honest fellow, was returning from some small jollification and was making his way homeward down Tottenham Court Road. In front of him he saw, in the gaslight, a tallish man, walking with a slight stagger, and carrying a white goose slung over his shoulder. As he reached the corner of Goodge Street, a row broke out between this stranger and a little knot of roughs. One of the latter knocked off the man's hat, on which he raised his stick to defend himself and, swinging it over his head, smashed the shop window behind him. Peterson had rushed forward to protect the stranger from his assailants; but the man, shocked at having broken the window, and seeing an official-looking person in uniform rushing towards him, dropped his goose, took to his heels, and vanished amid the labyrinth of small streets which lie at the back of Tottenham Court Road. The roughs had also fled at the appearance of Peterson, so that he was left in possession of the field of battle, and also of the spoils of victory in the shape of this battered hat and a most unimpeachable Christmas goose."

"Which surely he restored to their owner?"

"My dear fellow, there lies the problem. It is true that 'For Mrs. Henry Baker' was printed upon a small card which was tied to the bird's left leg, and it is also true that the initials 'H. B.' are legible upon the lining of this hat, but as there are some thousands of Bakers, and some hundreds of Henry Bakers in this city of ours, it is not easy to restore lost property to any one of them."

"What, then, did Peterson do?"

"He brought round both hat and goose to me on Christmas morning, knowing that even the smallest problems are of interest to me. The goose we retained until this morning, when there were signs that, in spite of the slight frost, it would be well that it should be eaten without unnecessary delay. Its finder has carried it off, therefore, to fulfil the ultimate destiny of a goose, while I continue to retain the hat of the unknown gentleman who lost his Christmas dinner."

"Did he not advertise?"

"No."

"Then, what clue could you have as to his identity?"

"Only as much as we can deduce."

"From his hat?"

"Precisely."

"But you are joking. What can you gather from this old battered felt?"

"Here is my lens. You know my methods. What can you gather yourself as to the individuality of the man who has worn this article?"

I took the tattered object in my hands and turned it over rather ruefully. It was a very ordinary black hat of the usual round shape, hard and much the worse for wear. The lining had been of red silk, but was a good deal discoloured. There was no maker's name; but, as Holmes had remarked, the initials "H.B." were scrawled upon one side. It was pierced in the brim for a hat-securer, but the elastic was missing. For the rest, it was cracked, exceedingly dusty, and spotted in several places, although there seemed to have been some attempt to hide the discoloured patches by smearing them with ink.

"I can see nothing," said I, handing it back to my friend.

"On the contrary, Watson, you can see everything. You fail, however, to reason from what you see. You are too timid in drawing your inferences."

"Then, pray tell me what it is that you can infer from this hat?"

He picked it up and gazed at it in the peculiar introspective fashion which was characteristic of him. "It is perhaps less suggestive than it might have been," he remarked, "and yet there are a few inferences which are very distinct, and a few others which represent at least a strong balance of probability. That the man was highly intellectual is of course obvious upon the face of it, and also that he was fairly well-to-do within the last three years, although he has now fallen upon evil days. He had foresight, but has less now than formerly, pointing to a moral retrogression, which, when taken with the decline of his fortunes, seems to indicate some evil influence, probably drink, at work upon him. This may account also for the obvious fact that his wife has ceased to love him."

"My dear Holmes!"

"He has, however, retained some degree of self-respect," he continued, disregarding my remonstrance. "He is a man who leads a sedentary life, goes out little, is out of training entirely, is middle-aged, has grizzled hair which he has had cut within the last few days, and which he anoints with lime-cream. These are the more patent facts which are to be deduced from his hat. Also, by the way, that it is extremely improbable that he has gas laid on in his house."

"You are certainly joking, Holmes."

"Not in the least. Is it possible that even now, when I give you these results, you are unable to see how they are attained?"

"I have no doubt that I am very stupid, but I must confess that I am unable to follow you. For example, how did you deduce that this man was intellectual?"

For answer Holmes clapped the hat upon his head. It came right over the forehead and settled upon the bridge of his nose. "It is a question of cubic capacity," said he; "a man with so large a brain must have something in it."

"The decline of his fortunes, then?"

"This hat is three years old. These flat brims curled at the edge came in then. It is a hat of the very best quality. Look at the band of ribbed silk and the excellent lining. If this man could afford to buy so expensive a hat three years ago, and has had no hat since, then he has assuredly gone down in the world."

"Well, that is clear enough, certainly. But how about the foresight and the moral retrogression?"

Sherlock Holmes laughed. "Here is the foresight," said he putting his finger upon the little disc and loop of the hat-securer. "They are never sold upon hats. If this man ordered one, it is a sign of a certain amount of foresight, since he went out of his way to take this precaution against the wind. But since we see that he has broken the elastic and has not troubled to replace it, it is obvious that he has less foresight now than formerly, which is a distinct proof of a weakening nature. On the other hand, he has endeavoured to conceal some of these stains upon the felt by daubing them with ink, which is a sign that he has not entirely lost his self-respect."

"Your reasoning is certainly plausible."

"The further points, that he is middle-aged, that his hair is grizzled, that it has been recently cut, and that he uses limecream, are all to be gathered from a close examination of the lower part of the lining. The lens discloses a large number of hair-ends, clean cut by the scissors of the barber. They all appear to be adhesive, and there is a distinct odour of lime-cream. This dust, you will observe, is not the gritty, grey dust of the street but the fluffy brown dust of the house, showing that it has been hung up indoors most of the time, while the marks of moisture upon the inside are proof positive that the wearer perspired very freely, and could therefore, hardly be in the best of training."

"But his wife—you said that she had ceased to love him."

"This hat has not been brushed for weeks. When I see you, my dear Watson, with a week's accumulation of dust upon your hat, and when your wife allows you to go out in such a state, I shall fear that you also have been unfortunate enough to lose your wife's affection."

"But he might be a bachelor."

"Nay, he was bringing home the goose as a peace-offering to his wife. Remember the card upon the bird's leg."

"You have an answer to everything. But how on earth do you deduce that the gas is not laid on in his house?"

"One tallow stain, or even two, might come by chance; but when I see no less than five, I think that there can be little doubt that the individual must be brought into frequent contact with burning tallow—walks upstairs at night probably with his hat in one hand and a guttering candle in the other. Anyhow, he never got tallow-stains from a gas-jet. Are you satisfied?"

"Well, it is very ingenious," said I, laughing; "but since, as you said just now, there has been no crime committed, and no harm done save the loss of a goose, all this seems to be rather a waste of energy."

Sherlock Holmes had opened his mouth to reply, when the door flew open, and Peterson, the commissionaire, rushed into the apartment with flushed cheeks and the face of a man who is dazed with astonishment.

"The goose, Mr. Holmes! The goose, sir!" he gasped.

"Eh? What of it, then? Has it returned to life and flapped off through the kitchen window?" Holmes twisted himself round upon the sofa to get a fairer view of the man's excited face.

"See here, sir! See what my wife found in its crop!" He held out his hand and displayed upon the centre of the palm a brilliantly scintillating blue stone, rather smaller than a bean in size, but of such purity and radiance that it twinkled like an electric point in the dark hollow of his hand.

Sherlock Holmes sat up with a whistle. "By Jove, Peterson!" said he, "this is treasure trove indeed. I suppose you know what you have got?"

"A diamond, sir? A precious stone. It cuts into glass as though it were putty."

"It's more than a precious stone. It is the precious stone."

"Not the Countess of Morcar's blue carbuncle!" I ejaculated.

"Precisely so. I ought to know its size and shape, seeing that I have read the advertisement about it in The Times every day lately. It is absolutely unique, and its value can only be conjectured, but the reward offered of

£1,000 is certainly not within a twentieth part of the market price."

"A thousand pounds! Great Lord of mercy!" The commissionaire plumped down into a chair and stared from one to the other of us.

"That is the reward, and I have reason to know that there are sentimental considerations in the background which would induce the Countess to part with half her fortune if she could but recover the gem."

"It was lost, if I remember aright, at the Hotel Cosmopolitan," I remarked.

"Precisely so, on December 22d, just five days ago. John Horner, a plumber, was accused of having abstracted it from the lady's jewel-case. The evidence against him was so strong that the case has been referred to the Assizes. I have some account of the matter here, I believe." He rummaged amid his newspapers, glancing over the dates, until at last he smoothed one out, doubled it over, and read the following paragraph:

"Hotel Cosmopolitan Jewel Robbery. John Horner, 26, plumber, was brought up upon the charge of having upon the 22nd inst., abstracted from the jewel-case of the Countess of Morcar the valuable gem known as the blue carbuncle. James Ryder, upper-attendant at the hotel, gave his evidence to the effect that he had shown Horner up to the dressing-room of the Countess of Morcar upon the day of the robbery in order that he might solder the second bar of the grate, which was loose. He had remained with Horner some little time, but had finally been called away. On returning, he found that Horner had disappeared, that the bureau had been forced open, and that the small morocco casket in which, as it afterwards transpired, the Countess was accustomed to keep her jewel, was lying empty upon the dressing-table. Ryder instantly gave the alarm, and Horner was arrested the same evening; but the stone could not be found either upon his person or in his rooms. Catherine Cusack, maid to the Countess, deposed to having heard Ryder's cry of dismay on discovering the robbery, and to having rushed into the room, where she found matters as described by the last witness. Inspector Bradstreet, B division, gave evidence as to the arrest of Horner, who struggled frantically, and protested his innocence in the strongest terms. Evidence of a previous conviction for robbery having been given against the prisoner, the magistrate refused to deal summarily with the offence, but referred it to the Assizes. Horner, who had shown signs of intense emotion during the proceedings, fainted away at the conclusion and was carried out of court.

"Hum! So much for the police-court," said Holmes thoughtfully, tossing aside the paper. "The question for us now to solve is the sequence of events leading from a rifled jewel-case at one end to the crop of a goose in Tottenham Court Road at the other. You see, Watson, our little deductions have suddenly assumed a much more important and less innocent aspect. Here is the stone; the stone came from the goose, and the goose came from Mr. Henry Baker, the gentleman with the bad hat and all the other characteristics with which I have bored you. So now we must set ourselves very seriously to finding this gentleman and ascertaining what part he has played in this little mystery. To do this, we must try the simplest means first, and these lie undoubtedly in an advertisement in all the evening papers. If this fail, I shall have recourse to other methods."

"What will you say?"

"Give me a pencil and that slip of paper. Now, then:

'Found at the corner of Goodge Street, a goose and a black felt hat. Mr. Henry Baker can have the same by applying at 6:30 this evening at 221B, Baker Street.'

That is clear and concise."

"Very. But will he see it?"

"Well, he is sure to keep an eye on the papers, since, to a poor man, the loss was a heavy one. He was clearly so scared by his mischance in breaking the window and by the approach of Peterson that he thought of nothing but flight, but since then he must have bitterly regretted the impulse which caused him to drop his bird. Then, again, the introduction of his name will cause him to see it, for everyone who knows him will direct his attention to it. Here you are, Peterson, run down to the advertising agency and have this put in the evening papers."

"In which, sir?"

"Oh, in the Globe, Star, Pall Mall, St. James's, Evening News Standard, Echo, and any others that occur to you."

"Very well, sir. And this stone?"

"Ah, yes, I shall keep the stone. Thank you. And, I say, Peterson, just buy a goose on your way back and leave it here with me, for we must have one to give to this gentleman in place of the one which your family is now devouring."

When the commissionaire had gone, Holmes took up the stone and held it against the light. "It's a bonny thing," said he. "Just see how it glints and sparkles. Of course it is a nucleus and focus of crime. Every good stone is. They are the devil's pet baits. In the larger and older jewels every facet may stand for a bloody deed. This stone is not yet twenty years old.

It was found in the banks of the Amoy River in southern China and is remarkable in having every characteristic of the carbuncle, save that it is blue in shade instead of ruby red. In spite of its youth, it has already a sinister history. There have been two murders, a vitriol-throwing, a suicide, and several robberies brought about for the sake of this forty-grain weight of crystallised charcoal. Who would think that so pretty a toy would be a purveyor to the gallows and the prison? I'll lock it up in my strong box now and drop a line to the Countess to say that we have it."

"Do you think that this man Horner is innocent?"

"I cannot tell."

"Well, then, do you imagine that this other one, Henry Baker, had anything to do with the matter?"

"It is, I think, much more likely that Henry Baker is an absolutely innocent man, who had no idea that the bird which he was carrying was of considerably more value than if it were made of solid gold. That, however, I shall determine by a very simple test if we have an answer to our advertisement."

"And you can do nothing until then?"

"Nothing."

"In that case I shall continue my professional round. But I shall come back in the evening at the hour you have mentioned, for I should like to see the solution of so tangled a business."

"Very glad to see you. I dine at seven. There is a woodcock, I believe. By the way, in view of recent occurrences, perhaps I ought to ask Mrs. Hudson to examine its crop."

I had been delayed at a case, and it was a little after half-past six when I found myself in Baker Street once more. As I approached the house I saw a tall man in a Scotch bonnet with a coat which was buttoned up to his chin waiting outside in the bright semicircle which was thrown from the fanlight. Just as I arrived the door was opened, and we were shown up together to Holmes's room.

"Mr. Henry Baker, I believe," said he, rising from his armchair and greeting his visitor with the easy air of geniality which he could so readily assume. "Pray take this chair by the fire, Mr. Baker. It is a cold night, and I observe that your circulation is more adapted for summer than for winter. Ah, Watson, you have just come at the right time. Is that your hat, Mr. Baker?"

"Yes, sir, that is undoubtedly my hat."

He was a large man with rounded shoulders, a massive head, and a broad, intelligent face, sloping down to a pointed beard of grizzled brown. A touch of red in nose and cheeks, with a slight tremor of his extended hand, recalled Holmes's surmise as to his habits. His rusty black frock-coat was buttoned right up in front, with the collar turned up, and his lank wrists protruded from his sleeves without a sign of cuff or shirt. He spoke in a slow staccato fashion, choosing his words with care, and gave the impression generally of a man of learning and letters who had had ill-usage at the hands of fortune.

"We have retained these things for some days," said Holmes, "because we expected to see an advertisement from you giving your address. I am at a loss to know now why you did not advertise."

Our visitor gave a rather shamefaced laugh. "Shillings have not been so plentiful with me as they once were," he remarked. "I had no doubt that the gang of roughs who assaulted me had carried off both my hat and the bird. I did not care to spend more money in a hopeless attempt at recovering them."

"Very naturally. By the way, about the bird, we were compelled to eat it."

"To eat it!" Our visitor half rose from his chair in his excitement.

"Yes, it would have been of no use to anyone had we not done so. But I presume that this other goose upon the sideboard, which is about the same weight and perfectly fresh, will answer your purpose equally well?"

"Oh, certainly, certainly," answered Mr. Baker with a sigh of relief.

"Of course, we still have the feathers, legs, crop, and so on of your own bird, so if you wish——"

The man burst into a hearty laugh. "They might be useful to me as relics of my adventure," said he, "but beyond that I can hardly see what use the disjecta membra of my late acquaintance are going to be to me. No, sir, I think that, with your permission, I will confine my attentions to the excellent bird which I perceive upon the sideboard."

Sherlock Holmes glanced sharply across at me with a slight shrug of his shoulders.

"There is your hat, then, and there your bird," said he. "By the way, would it bore you to tell me where you got the other one from? I am somewhat of a fowl fancier, and I have seldom seen a better grown goose."

"Certainly, sir," said Baker, who had risen and tucked his newly gained property under his arm. "There are a few of us who frequent the Alpha Inn, near the Museum—we are to be found in the Museum itself during the day, you understand. This year our good host, Windigate by name, instituted a goose club, by which, on consideration of some few pence every week, we were each to receive a bird at Christmas. My pence were duly paid, and the rest is familiar to you. I am much indebted to you, sir, for a Scotch bonnet is fitted neither to my years nor my gravity." With a comical pomposity of manner he bowed solemnly to both of us and strode off upon his way.

"So much for Mr. Henry Baker," said Holmes when he had closed the door behind him. "It is quite certain that he knows nothing whatever about the matter. Are you hungry, Watson?"

"Not particularly."

"Then I suggest that we turn our dinner into a supper and follow up this clue while it is still hot."

"By all means."

It was a bitter night, so we drew on our ulsters and wrapped cravats about our throats. Outside, the stars were shining coldly in a cloudless sky, and the breath of the passers-by blew out into smoke like so many pistol shots. Our footfalls rang out crisply and loudly as we swung through the doctors' quarter, Wimpole Street, Harley Street, and so through Wigmore Street into Oxford Street. In a quarter of an hour we were in Bloomsbury at the Alpha Inn, which is a small public-house at the corner of one of the streets which runs down into Holborn. Holmes pushed open the door of the private bar and ordered two glasses of beer from the ruddy-faced, white-aproned landlord.

"Your beer should be excellent if it is as good as your geese," said he.

"My geese!" The man seemed surprised.

"Yes. I was speaking only half an hour ago to Mr. Henry Baker, who was a member of your goose club."

"Ah! yes, I see. But you see, sir, them's not our geese."

"Indeed! Whose, then?"

"Well, I got the two dozen from a salesman in Covent Garden."

"Indeed? I know some of them. Which was it?"

"Breckinridge is his name."

"Ah! I don't know him. Well, here's your good health landlord, and prosperity to your house. Good-night.

"Now for Mr. Breckinridge," he continued, buttoning up his coat as we came out into the frosty air. "Remember, Watson that though we have so homely a thing as a goose at one end of this chain, we have at the other a man who will certainly get seven years' penal servitude unless we can establish his innocence. It is possible that our inquiry may but confirm his guilt but, in any case, we have a line of investigation which has been missed by the police, and which a singular chance has placed in our hands. Let us follow it out to the bitter end. Faces to the south, then, and quick march!"

We passed across Holborn, down Endell Street, and so through a zigzag of slums to Covent Garden Market. One of the largest stalls bore the name of Breckinridge upon it, and the proprietor a horsy-looking man, with a sharp face and trim side-whiskers was helping a boy to put up the shutters.

"Good-evening. It's a cold night," said Holmes.

The salesman nodded and shot a questioning glance at my companion.

"Sold out of geese, I see," continued Holmes, pointing at the bare slabs of marble.

"Let you have five hundred to-morrow morning."

"That's no good."

"Well, there are some on the stall with the gas-flare."

"Ah, but I was recommended to you."

"Who by?"

"The landlord of the Alpha."

"Oh, yes; I sent him a couple of dozen."

"Fine birds they were, too. Now where did you get them from?"

To my surprise the question provoked a burst of anger from the salesman.

"Now, then, mister," said he, with his head cocked and his arms akimbo, "what are you driving at? Let's have it straight, now."

"It is straight enough. I should like to know who sold you the geese which you supplied to the Alpha."

"Well then, I shan't tell you. So now!"

"Oh, it is a matter of no importance; but I don't know why you should be so warm over such a trifle."

"Warm! You'd be as warm, maybe, if you were as pestered as I am. When I pay good money for a good article there should be an end of the business; but it's 'Where are the geese?' and 'Who did you sell the geese to?' and 'What will you take for the geese?' One would think they were the only geese in the world, to hear the fuss that is made over them."

"Well, I have no connection with any other people who have been making inquiries," said Holmes carelessly. "If you won't tell us the bet is off, that is all. But I'm always ready to back my opinion on a matter of fowls, and I have a fiver on it that the bird I ate is country bred."

"Well, then, you've lost your fiver, for it's town bred," snapped the salesman.

"It's nothing of the kind."

"I say it is."

"I don't believe it."

"D'you think you know more about fowls than I, who have handled them ever since I was a nipper? I tell you, all those birds that went to the Alpha were town bred."

"You'll never persuade me to believe that."

"Will you bet, then?"

"It's merely taking your money, for I know that I am right. But I'll have a sovereign on with you, just to teach you not to be obstinate."

The salesman chuckled grimly. "Bring me the books, Bill," said he.

The small boy brought round a small thin volume and a great greasy-backed one, laying them out together beneath the hanging lamp.

"Now then, Mr. Cocksure," said the salesman, "I thought that I was out of geese, but before I finish you'll find that there is still one left in my shop. You see this little book?"

"Well?"

"That's the list of the folk from whom I buy. D'you see? Well, then, here on this page are the country folk, and the numbers after their names are where their accounts are in the big ledger. Now, then! You see this other page in red ink? Well, that is a list of my town suppliers. Now, look at that third name. Just read it out to me."

"Mrs. Oakshott, 117, Brixton Road—249," read Holmes.

"Quite so. Now turn that up in the ledger."

Holmes turned to the page indicated. "Here you are, 'Mrs. Oakshott, 117, Brixton Road, egg and poultry supplier."

"Now, then, what's the last entry?"

"'December 22d. Twenty-four geese at 7s. 6d.'"

"Quite so. There you are. And underneath?"

"'Sold to Mr. Windigate of the Alpha, at 12s.'"

"What have you to say now?"

Sherlock Holmes looked deeply chagrined. He drew a sovereign from his pocket and threw it down upon the slab, turning away with the air of a man whose disgust is too deep for words. A few yards off he stopped under a lamp-post and laughed in the hearty, noiseless fashion which was peculiar to him.

"When you see a man with whiskers of that cut and the 'Pink 'un' protruding out of his pocket, you can always draw him by a bet," said he.

"I daresay that if I had put £100 down in front of him, that man would not have given me such complete information as was drawn from him by the idea that he was doing me on a wager. Well, Watson, we are, I fancy, nearing the end of our quest, and the only point which remains to be determined is whether we should go on to this Mrs. Oakshott to-night, or whether we should reserve it for to-morrow. It is clear from what that surly fellow said that there are others besides ourselves who are anxious about the matter, and I should—"

His remarks were suddenly cut short by a loud hubbub which broke out from the stall which we had just left. Turning round we saw a little rat-faced fellow standing in the centre of the circle of yellow light which was thrown by the swinging lamp, while Breckinridge, the salesman, framed in the door of his stall, was shaking his fists fiercely at the cringing figure.

"I've had enough of you and your geese," he shouted. "I wish you were all at the devil together. If you come pestering me any more with your silly talk I'll set the dog at you. You bring Mrs. Oakshott here and I'll answer her, but what have you to do with it? Did I buy the geese off you?"

"No; but one of them was mine all the same," whined the little man.

"Well, then, ask Mrs. Oakshott for it."

"She told me to ask you."

"Well, you can ask the King of Proosia, for all I care. I've had enough of it. Get out of this!" He rushed fiercely forward, and the inquirer flitted away into the darkness.

"Ha! this may save us a visit to Brixton Road," whispered Holmes. "Come with me, and we will see what is to be made of this fellow."

Striding through the scattered knots of people who lounged round the flaring stalls, my companion speedily overtook the little man and touched him upon the shoulder. He sprang round, and I could see in the gas-light that every vestige of colour had been driven from his face.

"Who are you, then? What do you want?" he asked in a quavering voice.

"You will excuse me," said Holmes blandly, "but I could not help overhearing the questions which you put to the salesman just now. I think that I could be of assistance to you."

"You? Who are you? How could you know anything of the matter?"

"My name is Sherlock Holmes. It is my business to know what other people don't know."

"But you can know nothing of this?"

"Excuse me, I know everything of it. You are endeavouring to trace some geese which were sold by Mrs. Oakshott, of Brixton Road, to a salesman named Breckinridge, by him in turn to Mr. Windigate, of the Alpha, and by him to his club, of which Mr. Henry Baker is a member."

"Oh, sir, you are the very man whom I have longed to meet," cried the little fellow with outstretched hands and quivering fingers. "I can hardly explain to you how interested I am in this matter."

Sherlock Holmes hailed a four-wheeler which was passing. "In that case we had better discuss it in a cosy room rather than in this wind-swept market-place," said he. "But pray tell me, before we go farther, who it is that I have the pleasure of assisting."

The man hesitated for an instant. "My name is John Robinson," he answered with a sidelong glance.

"No, no; the real name," said Holmes sweetly. "It is always awkward doing business with an alias."

A flush sprang to the white cheeks of the stranger. "Well then," said he, "my real name is James Ryder."

"Precisely so. Head attendant at the Hotel Cosmopolitan. Pray step into the cab, and I shall soon be able to tell you everything which you would wish to know."

The little man stood glancing from one to the other of us with half-frightened, half-hopeful eyes, as one who is not sure whether he is on the verge of a windfall or of a catastrophe. Then he stepped into the cab, and in half an hour we were back in the sitting-room at Baker Street. Nothing had been said during our drive, but the high, thin breathing of our new companion, and the claspings and unclaspings of his hands, spoke of the nervous tension within him.

"Here we are!" said Holmes cheerily as we filed into the room. "The fire looks very seasonable in this weather. You look cold, Mr. Ryder. Pray take the basket-chair. I will just put on my slippers before we settle this little matter of yours. Now, then! You want to know what became of those geese?"

"Yes, sir."

"Or rather, I fancy, of that goose. It was one bird, I imagine in which you were interested—white, with a black bar across the tail."

Ryder quivered with emotion. "Oh, sir," he cried, "can you tell me where it went to?"

"It came here."

"Here?"

"Yes, and a most remarkable bird it proved. I don't wonder that you should take an interest in it. It laid an egg after it was dead—the bonniest, brightest little blue egg that ever was seen. I have it here in my museum."

Our visitor staggered to his feet and clutched the mantelpiece with his right hand. Holmes unlocked his strong-box and held up the blue carbuncle, which shone out like a star, with a cold brilliant, many-pointed radiance. Ryder stood glaring with a drawn face, uncertain whether to claim or to disown it.

"The game's up, Ryder," said Holmes quietly. "Hold up, man, or you'll be into the fire! Give him an arm back into his chair, Watson. He's not got blood enough to go in for felony with impunity. Give him a dash of brandy. So! Now he looks a little more human. What a shrimp it is, to be sure!"

For a moment he had staggered and nearly fallen, but the brandy brought a tinge of colour into his cheeks, and he sat staring with frightened eyes at his accuser.

"I have almost every link in my hands, and all the proofs which I could possibly need, so there is little which you need tell me. Still, that little may as well be cleared up to make the case complete. You had heard, Ryder, of this blue stone of the Countess of Morcar's?"

"It was Catherine Cusack who told me of it," said he in a crackling voice.

"I see—her ladyship's waiting-maid. Well, the temptation of sudden wealth so easily acquired was too much for you, as it has been for better men before you; but you were not very scrupulous in the means you used. It seems to me, Ryder, that there is the making of a very pretty villain in you. You knew that this man Horner, the plumber, had been concerned in some such matter before, and that suspicion would rest the more readily upon him. What did you do, then? You made some small job in my lady's room—you and your confederate Cusack—and you managed that he should be the man sent for. Then, when he had left, you rifled the jewel-case, raised the alarm, and had this unfortunate man arrested. You then—"

Ryder threw himself down suddenly upon the rug and clutched at my companion's knees. "For God's sake, have mercy!" he shrieked. "Think of my father! of my mother! It would break their hearts. I never went wrong before! I never will again. I swear it. I'll swear it on a Bible. Oh, don't bring it into court! For Christ's sake, don't!"

"Get back into your chair!" said Holmes sternly. "It is very well to cringe and crawl now, but you thought little enough of this poor Horner in the dock for a crime of which he knew nothing."

"I will fly, Mr. Holmes. I will leave the country, sir. Then the charge against him will break down."

"Hum! We will talk about that. And now let us hear a true account of the next act. How came the stone into the goose, and how came the goose into the open market? Tell us the truth, for there lies your only hope of safety."

Ryder passed his tongue over his parched lips. "I will tell you it just as it happened, sir," said he. "When Horner had been arrested, it seemed to me that it would be best for me to get away with the stone at once, for I did not know at what moment the police might not take it into their heads to search me and my room. There was no place about the hotel where it would be safe. I went out, as if on some commission, and I made for my sister's house. She had married a man named Oakshott, and lived in Brixton Road, where she fattened fowls for the market. All the way there every man I met seemed to me to be a policeman or a detective; and, for all that it was a cold night, the sweat was pouring down my face before I came to the Brixton Road. My sister asked me what was the matter, and why I was so pale; but I told her that I had been upset by the jewel robbery at the hotel. Then I went into the back yard and smoked a pipe and wondered what it would be best to do.

"I had a friend once called Maudsley, who went to the bad, and has just been serving his time in Pentonville. One day he had met me, and fell into talk about the ways of thieves, and how they could get rid of what they stole. I knew that he would be true to me, for I knew one or two things about him; so I made up my mind to go right on to Kilburn, where he lived, and take him into my confidence. He would show me how to turn the stone into money. But how to get to him in safety? I thought of the agonies I had gone through in coming from the hotel. I might at any moment be seized and searched, and there would be the stone in my waistcoat pocket. I was leaning against the wall at the time and looking at the geese which were waddling about round my feet, and suddenly an idea came into my head which showed me how I could beat the best detective that ever lived.

"My sister had told me some weeks before that I might have the pick of her geese for a Christmas present, and I knew that she was always as good as her word. I would take my goose now, and in it I would carry my stone to Kilburn. There was a little shed in the yard, and behind this I drove one of the birds —a fine big one, white, with a barred tail. I caught it, and prying its bill open, I thrust the stone down its throat as far as my finger could reach. The bird gave a gulp, and I felt the stone pass along its gullet and down into its crop. But the creature flapped and struggled, and out came my sister to know what was the matter. As I turned to speak to her the brute broke loose and fluttered off among the others.

"Whatever were you doing with that bird, Jem?' says she.

"Well,' said I, 'you said you'd give me one for Christmas, and I was feeling which was the fattest.'

"Oh,' says she, 'we've set yours aside for you—Jem's bird, we call it. It's the big white one over yonder. There's twenty-six of them, which makes one for you, and one for us, and two dozen for the market.'

"Thank you, Maggie,' says I; 'but if it is all the same to you, I'd rather have that one I was handling just now.'

"The other is a good three pound heavier,' said she, 'and we fattened it expressly for you.'

"Never mind. I'll have the other, and I'll take it now,' said I.

"Oh, just as you like,' said she, a little huffed. 'Which is it you want, then?'

"That white one with the barred tail, right in the middle of the flock.'

"Oh, very well. Kill it and take it with you.'

"Well, I did what she said, Mr. Holmes, and I carried the bird all the way to Kilburn. I told my pal what I had done, for he was a man that it was easy to tell a thing like that to. He laughed until he choked, and we got a knife and opened the goose. My heart turned to water, for there was no sign of the stone, and I knew that some terrible mistake had occurred. I left the bird rushed back to my sister's, and hurried into the back yard. There was not a bird to be seen there.

"Where are they all, Maggie?' I cried.

"Gone to the dealer's, Jem.'

"Which dealer's?'

"Breckinridge, of Covent Garden.'

"But was there another with a barred tail?' I asked, 'the same as the one I chose?'

"Yes, Jem; there were two barred-tailed ones, and I could never tell them apart.'

"Well, then, of course I saw it all, and I ran off as hard as my feet would carry me to this man Breckinridge; but he had sold the lot at once, and not one word would he tell me as to where they had gone. You heard him yourselves to-night. Well, he has always answered me like that. My sister thinks that I am going mad. Sometimes I think that I am myself. And now —and now I am myself a branded thief, without ever having touched the wealth for which I sold my character. God help me! God help me!" He burst into convulsive sobbing, with his face buried in his hands.

There was a long silence, broken only by his heavy breathing and by the measured tapping of Sherlock Holmes's finger-tips upon the edge of the table. Then my friend rose and threw open the door.

"Get out!" said he.

"What, sir! Oh, Heaven bless you!"

"No more words. Get out!"

And no more words were needed. There was a rush, a clatter upon the stairs, the bang of a door, and the crisp rattle of running footfalls from the street.

"After all, Watson," said Holmes, reaching up his hand for his clay pipe, "I am not retained by the police to supply their deficiencies. If Horner were in danger it would be another thing; but this fellow will not appear against him, and the case must collapse. I suppose that I am commuting a felony, but it is just possible that I am saving a soul. This fellow will not go wrong again; he is too terribly frightened. Send him to jail now, and you make him a jail-bird for life. Besides, it is the season of forgiveness. Chance has put in our way a most singular and whimsical problem, and its solution is its own reward. If you will have the goodness to touch the bell, Doctor, we will begin another investigation, in which, also a bird will be the chief feature."

Sir Arthur Conan Doyle
The Adventures of Sherlock Holmes

Arthur Conan Doyle (1859–1930) trained as a doctor, but he was so poor he turned to writing to try and supplement his income. His first book, *A Study in Scarlet*, introduced the world to Sherlock Holmes and his method of solving a crime by observation and deduction. Short stories about Holmes appeared in the *Strand Magazine*, and made Doyle's name. Holmes was so popular Doyle could not get rid of him, though he tried. He also wrote historical novels (which he considered were better books) and science fiction.

YES, VIRGINIA, THERE IS A SANTA

VIRGINIA, your little friends are wrong. They have been affected by the skepticism of a skeptical age. They do not believe except they see. They think that nothing can be which is not comprehensible by their little minds. All minds, Virginia, whether they be men's or children's, are little. In this great universe of ours man is a mere insect, an ant, in his intellect, as compared with the boundless world about him, as measured by the intelligence capable of grasping the whole of truth and knowledge.

Yes, VIRGINIA, there is a Santa Claus. He exists as certainly as love and generosity and devotion exist, and you know that they abound and give to your life its highest beauty and joy. Alas! how dreary would be the world if there were no Santa Claus. It would be as dreary as if there were no VIRGINIAS. There would be no childlike faith then, no poetry, no romance to make tolerable this existence. We should have no enjoyment, except in sense and sight. The eternal light with which childhood fills the world would be extinguished.

Not believe in Santa Claus! You might as well not believe in fairies! You might get your papa to hire men to watch in all the chimneys on Christmas Eve to catch Santa Claus, but even if they did not see Santa Claus coming down, what would that prove? Nobody sees Santa Claus, but that is no sign that there is no Santa Claus. The most real things in

the world are those that neither children nor men can see. Did you ever see fairies dancing on the lawn? Of course not, but that's no proof that they are not there. Nobody can conceive or imagine all the wonders there are unseen and unseeable in the world.

You may tear apart the baby's rattle and see what makes the noise inside, but there is a veil covering the unseen world which not the strongest man, nor even the united strength of all the strongest men that ever lived, could tear apart. Only faith, fancy, poetry, love, romance, can push aside that curtain and view and picture the supernal beauty and glory beyond. Is it all real? Ah, VIRGINIA, in all this world there is nothing else real and abiding.

No Santa Claus! Thank God! he lives, and he lives forever. A thousand years from now, Virginia, nay, ten times ten thousand years from now, he will continue to make glad the heart of childhood.

Francis Pharcellus Church
Editorial, *The New York Sun*

Virginia O'Hanlon, aged eight, wrote to the *New York Sun* newspaper, asking if Santa existed. Some of her friends had told her there wasn't a Santa, and she was confused. Her father had told her that 'if you see it in the *Sun* it's so' and the little girl wanted an answer to this important question. When Francis Pharcellus Church (1839–1906), the editor, saw the child's letter, his reply became his most famous editorial.

ST NICHOLAS

DEAR GIRL AND BOY – No, there are more! Here they come! There they come! Near by, far off, everywhere, we can see them, – coming by dozens, hundreds, thousands, troops upon troops, and all pressing closer and closer.

Why, this is delightful. And how fresh, eager, and hearty you look! Glad to see us? Thank you. The same to you, and many happy returns. Well, well, we might have known it; we did know it, but we hardly thought it would be like this. Hurrah for dear St. Nicholas! He has made us friends in a moment.

And no wonder. Is he not the boys' and girls' own Saint, the especial friend of young Americans? That he is. And isn't he the acknowledged patron Saint of New York—one of America›s great cities—dear to old hearts as well as young? Didn't his image stand at the prow of the first emigrant ship that ever sailed into New York Bay, and wasn't the very first church the New Yorkers built named after him? Didn't he come over with the Dutch, ever so long ago, and take up his abode here? Certainly. And, what is more, isn't he the kindest, best, and jolliest old dear that ever was known? Certainly, again.

Another thing you know: He is fair and square. He comes when he says he will. At the very outset he decided to visit our boys and girls every Christmas; and doesn't he do it? Yes; and that makes it all the harder when trouble or poverty shuts him out at that time from any of the children.

Dear old St. Nicholas, with his pet names—Santa Claus, Kriss Kringle, St. Nick, and we don›t know how many others. What a host of wonderful stories are told about him—you may hear them all some day—and what loving, cheering thoughts follow in his train! He has attended so many heart-warmings in his long, long day that he glows without knowing it, and, coming as he does, at a holy time, casts a light upon the children's faces that lasts from year to year.

Never to dim this light, young friends, by word or token, to make it even brighter, when we can, in good, pleasant, helpful ways, and to clear away clouds that sometimes shut it out, is our aim and prayer.

Mary Mapes Dodge
Editor's letter, *St Nicholas Magazine*, Vol. 1 No. 1, November 1873

When her husband died, Mary Mapes Dodge (1831–1905) started to write to support herself and her children: one of her books, *Hans Brinker, or the Silver Skates*, is considered to be a classic. In 1873 she was invited to edit a new periodical for children, *St Nicholas*. From the first, Mrs Dodge was determined that it should be of the highest quality, with 'no sermonizing'. Many famous authors contributed; Frances Hodgson Burnett's Little Lord Fauntleroy first appeared within, and Rudyard Kipling's Jungle Book stories made their first appearance in America in *St Nicholas*. Mark Twain, Louisa Alcott, and R L Stevenson were among other notable contributors. This is the editor's letter for the first issue of the magazine. The orginal St Nicholas (270–343) was the Greek Bishop of Myra, now in Turkey.

GRANDMA'S STORY

"It is too bad to have our jolly vacation spoiled by this provoking storm. Didn't mind it yesterday, because we could eat all the time; but here we are cooped up for a week, perhaps, and I'd like to know what we are to do," growled Geoff, as he stood at the window looking gloomily at the bleak scene without. It certainly was discouraging; for the north wind howled, the air was dark with falling snow, and drifts were rising over fences, roads, and fields, as if to barricade the Christmas party in the great country house.

"We can bear it pleasantly, since it can't be helped," said gentle sister Mary, with a kind hand on his shoulder, and a face full of sympathy for his disappointment. "I'm sorry for the coasting, skating, and sleighing frolics we have lost; but if we must be shut up, I'm sure we couldn't have a pleasanter prison or a kinder jailer. Don't let grandma hear us complain, for she has made great exertions to have our visit a merry one, and it will trouble her if we are not gay and contented."

"That's easy for a parcel of girls, who only want to mull over the fire, and chatter, and drink tea; but it's rough on us fellows, who come for the outside fun. House is well enough; but when you've seen it once, there's an end. Eating is jolly, but you can't stuff forever. We might dig, or snowball, if it didn't blow a gale. Never saw such a beast of a storm!"—and Geoff flattened his nose against the window-pane and scowled at the elements.

A laugh made him turn around, and forget his woes to stare at the quaint little figure that stood curtseying in the door-way of the keeping-room, where a dozen young people were penned while the maids cleared up the remains of yesterday's feast in the kitchen, the mothers were busy with the babies upstairs, and the fathers read papers in the best parlor; for this was a family gathering under the roof of the old homestead.

A rosy, dark-eyed face looked out from the faded green calash, a gayly flowered gown was looped up over a blue quilted petticoat, and a red camlet cloak hung down behind. A big reticule and a funny umbrella were held in either hand, and red hose and very high-heeled, pointed shoes covered a trim pair of feet.

"God bless you, merry gentlemen!
May nothing you dismay;
Here's your ancient granny come
To call, this Christmas day,"

sang Minnie, the lively member of the flock, as she bobbed little curtseys and smiled so infectiously that even cross Geoff cheered up.

"Where did you get that rigging?" "Isn't it becoming?" "What queer stuff!" "Did grandma ever look so, I wonder?"

These and many other questions rained upon the wearer of the old costume, and she answered them as fast as she could.

"I went rummaging up garret for something to read, and found two chests of old duds. Thought I'd dress up and see how you liked me. Grandma said I might, and told me I looked like her when she was young. She was a beauty, you know; so I feel as proud as a peacock." And Min danced away to stand before the portrait of a blooming girl in a short-waisted, white-satin gown and a pearl necklace, which hung opposite the companion portrait of an officer in an old-fashioned uniform.

"So you do. Wonder if I should look like grandpa if I got into his old toggery!" said Geoff, looking up at the handsome man with the queue and the high coat-collar.

"Go and try; the uniform is in the chest, and not much moth-eaten. Let's have a jolly rummage, and see what we can find. We didn't eat ourselves sick, so we will amuse these lazy invalids;" and Min glanced pityingly at several cousins who lay about on sofas or in easy chairs, pretending to read, but evidently suffering from too great devotion to the bountiful dinner and evening feast of yesterday.

Away went Min and Lotty, Geoff and Walt, glad of anything to beguile the stormy afternoon. Grandma smiled as she heard the tramp of feet overhead, the peals of laughter, and the bang of chest-lids, well knowing that a scene of dire confusion awaited her when the noisy frolic was done, but thankful for the stores of ancient finery which would keep the restless children happy for a day.

It was truly a noble garret, for it extended the whole length of the great square house, with windows at either end, and divided in the middle by a solid chimney. All around stood rows of chests, dilapidated furniture, and wardrobes full of old relics, while the walls were hung with many things for which modern tongues can find no names. In one corner was a book-case full of musty books and papers; in another, kitchen utensils and rusty weapons; the third was devoted to quilts hung on lines, and in the fourth stood a loom with a spinning-wheel beside it, both seemingly well cared for, as the dust lay lightly on them, and flax was still upon the distaff.

A glorious rummage followed the irruption of the Goths and Vandals into this quiet spot, and soon Geoff quite forgot the storm as he pranced about in the buff-and-blue coat, with a cocked hat on his head, and grandfather's sword at his side. Lotty arrayed herself in a pumpkin hood and quilted cloak for warmth, while Walt, the book-worm, went straight to the ancient library, and became absorbed in faded souvenirs, yellow newspapers, and almanacs of a century ago.

Having displayed themselves below and romped all over the house, the masqueraders grew tired at last, and early twilight warned them to leave before ghostly shadows began to haunt the garret.

"I mean to take this down and ask grandma to show me how it's done. I've heard her tell about spinning and weaving when she was a girl, and I know I can learn," said Minnie, who had fallen in love with the little wheel, and vainly tried to twist the flax into as smooth a thread as the one hanging from the distaff, as if shadowy fingers had lately spun it.

"Queen Victoria set the fashion in England, and we might do it here. Wouldn't it be fun to have a wheel in the parlor at home, and really use it; not keep it tied up with blue ribbons, as the other girls do!" cried Lotty, charmed with the new idea.

"Come, Geoff, take it down for us. You ought to do it out of gratitude for my cheering you up so nicely," said Min, leading the way.

"So I will. Here, Walt, give it a hoist, and come behind to pick up the pieces, for the old machine must be about a hundred, I guess."

Shouldering the wheel, Geoff carried it down; but no bits fell by the way, for the stout little wheel was all in order, kept so by loving hands that for more than eighty years had been spinning the mingled thread of a long and useful life.

Glorious fires were roaring up the wide chimneys in parlor and keeping-room, and old and young were gathering around them, while the storm beat on the window-panes, and the wintry wind howled as if angry at being shut out.

"See what we've stolen, grandma," cried Min, as the procession came in, rosy, dusty, gay, and eager.

"Bless the child! What possessed you to lug that old thing down?" asked Madam Shirley, much amused as the prize was placed before her, where she sat in her high-backed chair,—a right splendid old lady in her stately cap, black silk gown, and muslin apron, with a bunch of keys at her side, like a model housekeeper, as she was.

"You don't mind our playing with it, do you? And will you teach me to spin? I think it's such a pretty little thing, and I want to be like you in all ways, grandma dear," answered Min, sitting on the arm of the great chair, with her fresh cheek close to the wrinkled one where winter roses still bloomed.

"You wheedling gypsy! I'll teach you with all my heart, for it is pretty work, and I often wonder ladies don't keep it up. I did till I was too busy, and now I often take a turn at it when I'm tired of knitting. The hum is very soothing, and the thread much stronger than any we get nowadays."

As she spoke, the old lady dusted the wheel, and gave it a skilful turn or two, till the soft whir made pleasant music in the room.

"Is it really a hundred years old?" asked Geoff, drawing nearer with the others to watch the new work.

"Just about. It was one of my mother's wedding presents, and she gave it to me when I was fifteen. Deary me, how well I remember that day!" and grandma seemed to fall a-dreaming as her eyes rested on the letters E. R. M. rudely cut in the wood, and below these were three others with something meant for a true lover's knot between.

"Whose initials are these?" asked Min, scenting a romance with girlish quickness, for grandma was smiling as if her eyes read the title to some little story in those worn letters.

"Elizabeth Rachel Morgan, and Joel Manlius Shirley. Your blessed grandfather cut our names there the day I was sixteen, and put the flourish between to show what he wanted," added the old lady, laughing as she made the wheel hum again.

"Tell about it, please do," begged Min, remembering that grandma had been a beauty and a belle.

"It's a long tale, my darling, and I couldn't tell it now. Sometime when I'm teaching you to spin I'll do it, maybe."

But the girl was determined to have her story; and after tea, when the little ones were in bed, the elders playing whist in the parlor, and the young folks deciding what game to begin, Minnie sat down and tried to spin, sure that the familiar sound would lure grandma to give the lesson and tell the tale.

She was right, for the wheel had not gone around many times, when the tap of the cane was heard, and the old lady came rustling in, quite ready for a chat, now that three cups of her own good tea and a nap in the chimney corner had refreshed her.

"No, dear, that's not the way; you need a dish of water to wet your fingers in, and you must draw the flax out slow and steady, else it runs to waste, and makes a poor thread. Fetch me that chair, and I'll show you how, since you are bent on learning."

Establishing herself in the straight-backed seat, a skilful tap of the foot set the wheel in swift and easy motion, and the gray thread twisted fine and evenly from the distaff.

"Isn't it a pretty picture?" said Min to Lotty, as they watched the old lady work.

"Not so pretty as the one I used to see when my dear mother sat here, and I, a little child, at her knee. Ah, my dears, she could have told you stories all night long, and well worth hearing. I was never tired of them."

"Please tell one now, grandma. We don't know what to play, and it would be so nice to sit around the fire and hear it this stormy night," suggested Min, artfully seizing the hint.

"Do! Do! We all love stories, and we'll be as still as mice," added Geoff, beckoning to the others as he took the big arm-chair, being the oldest grandson and leader of the flock.

Camping on the rug, or nestling in the sofa corner, the boys and girls all turned expectant faces toward grandma, who settled her cap-strings and smoothed her spotless apron, with an indulgent smile at her little audience.

"I don't know which one to tell first."

"The ghost story; that's a splendid one, and most of the children never heard it," said Walt.

"Have Indians and fighting in it. I like that kind," added Geoff.

"No; tell a love story. They are so interesting," said Lotty.

"I want the story about the initials first. I know it is very sentimental. So do begin with that, grandma," begged Min.

"Well, dears, perhaps I'd better choose that one, for it has the battle of New Orleans, and wolves, and spinning, and sweethearts in it; so it will suit you all, I hope."

"Oh, lovely! Do begin right away," cried Minnie, as the clapping of hands showed how satisfactory the prospect was.

Grandma gave a loud "hem!" and began at once, while the little wheel hummed a soft accompaniment to her words.

Grandma's Story

"When I was fifteen, my mother gave me this wheel, and said: 'Now, daughter Betsey, it is time for you to begin your wedding outfit, for I mistrust you'll marry young.' In those days girls spun and wove webs of fine linen and laid 'em up in chests, with lavender and rosemary, for sheets and table-linen after they married. So I spun away, making all manner of fine plans in my silly head, for I was a pretty piece, they all said, and young as I was, two or three fine lads used to come evenings and sit staring at me while I worked.

"Among these, was my neighbor Joel Manlius Shirley, and I was fond of him; but he hadn't much money, so I put on airs, and tried his patience very much. One day he came in and said: 'Betsey, I'm going a-soldiering; they need men, and I'm off. Will you think of poor Joe when I'm gone?'

"I don't know how I looked, but I felt as if I couldn't bear it. Only I was too proud to show my trouble; so I laughed, and gave my wheel a twist, and said I was glad of it, since anything was better than hanging round at home.

"That hurt him; but he was always gentle to saucy Betsey, and taking out his knife, he cut those letters under mine, saying, with a look I never could forget:—

"'That will remind you of me if you are likely to forget. Good-by; I'm going right away, and may never come back.'

"He kissed me, and was off before I could say a word, and then I cried till my flax was wet and my thread tangled, and my heart 'most broken. Deary me, how well I remember that heavy day!"

Grandma smiled, but something shone in her old eyes very like a tear, and sentimental Lotty felt deeply interested at this point.

"Where does the fighting come in?" asked Geoff, who was of a military turn, as became the descendant of a soldier.

"I didn't know or care much about the War of 1812, except as far as the safety of one man was concerned. Joe got on without any harm till the battle of New Orleans, when he was nearly killed behind the cotton-bale breastworks General Jackson built."

"Yes, I know all about it. Jackson fought against twelve thousand, and lost only seven men. That was the last battle of the war, January 8, 1815. Three cheers for grandpa!" shouted Geoff, waving a tidy, as no hat was at hand.

The others echoed the hurrah, and grandma beamed with pride as she went on: "We couldn't get news from the army very often in those troublous times, and Joe was gone two years before the war ended. After the great battle we had no news for a long spell, and we feared he was one of the seven men killed. Those were dreadful days for all of us. My honored mother was a pious soul, and so was Mrs. Shirley; and they kept up their hearts with hope and prayer; but I, poor thing, was young and weak, and I cried myself half blind, remembering how naughty I had been. I would spin no more, but set the wheel away, saying I should have no need of wedding gear, as I should never marry; and I wore black ribbon on my caps, and one of Joe's buttons strung about my neck, mourning dismally for my lost dear.

"So the winter ended, and the summer went, and no news came of Joe. All said he was dead, and we had prayers at church, and talked of setting up a stone in the grave-yard, and I thought my life was done; for I pined sadly, and felt as if I could never laugh again. But I did; for the Lord was very good to us, and out of danger and captivity delivered that dear boy."

Grandma spoke solemnly, and folded her hands in thanksgiving as she looked up at the picture of the handsome officer hanging on the wall before her. The elder children could just remember grandpa as a very old and feeble man, and it struck them as funny to speak of him as a "dear boy;" but they never smiled, and dutifully lifted their eyes to the queue and the high-collared coat, wondering if Joe was as rosy in real life as in the portrait.

"Well, that's the sentimental part; now comes the merry part, and that will suit the boys," said the old lady, briskly, as she spun away,—and went on in a lively tone:—

"One December day, as I sat by that very window, dreaming sorrowfully at my sewing work, while old Sally nodded over her knitting by the fire, I saw a man come creeping along by the fence and dodge behind the wood-pile. There were many bad folks 'round in those times; for war always leaves a sight of lazy rascals afloat, as well as poor fellows maimed and homeless.

"Mother had gone over to the sewing society at Mrs. Shirley's, and I was all alone; for Sally was so stiff with rheumatics she could scarce stir, and that was why I stayed to take care of her. The old musket always hung over the kitchen chimney-piece, loaded, and I knew how to fire it, for Joe had taught me. So away I went and got it down; for I saw the man popping up his head now and then to spy the land, and I felt sure he meant mischief. I knew Sally would only scream like a scared hen, so I let her sleep; and getting behind the shutter I pointed my gun, and waited to blaze away as soon as the enemy showed signs of attacking.

"Presently he came creeping up to the back door, and I heard him try the latch. All was fast, so I just slipped into the kitchen and stood behind the settle, for I was surer than ever he was a rascal since I'd seen him nearer. He was a tall man, dreadful shabby in an old coat and boots, a ragged hat over his eyes, and a great beard hiding the lower part of his face. He had a little bundle and a big stick in his hands, and limped as if foot-sore or lame.

"I was much afeard; but those were times that made heroes of men, and taught women to be brave for love of home and country. So I kept steady, with my eye on the window, and my finger on the trigger of the old gun, that hadn't been fired for years. Presently the man looked in, and I saw what a strange roll his great eyes had, for he was thin-faced and looked half-starved. If mother had been there, she'd have called him in and fed him well, but I dared not, and when he tried the window I aimed, but did not fire; for finding the button down he went away, and I dropped on the settle, shaking like a leaf. All was still, and in a minute I plucked up courage to go to look out a bit; but just as I reached the middle of the kitchen, the buttery door opened, and there stood the robber, with a carving knife in one hand and my best loaf of spice bread in the other. He said something, and made a rush at me; but I pulled the trigger, saw a flash, felt a blow, and fell somewhere, thinking, 'Now I'm dead!'"

Here grandma paused for breath, having spoken rapidly and acted out the scene dramatically, to the intense delight of the children, who sat like images of interest, staring at her with round eyes.

"But you weren't dead? What next?" cried Walt, eagerly.

"Bless you, no! I only fell into Joe's arms, and when I came to, there the dear fellow was, crying over me like a baby, while old Sally danced round us like a bedlamite, in spite of her rheumatics, shouting: 'Hosanna! Thanks and praise! He's come, he's come!'"

"Was he shot?" asked Geoff, anxious for a little bloodshed.

"No, dear; the old gun burst and hurt my hands, but not a mite of harm was done to Joe. I don't think I could tell all that happened for a spell, being quite dazed with joy and surprise; but by the time mother came home I was as peart as a wren, and Joe was at the table eating and drinking every mortal thing I could find in the house.

"He'd been kept a prisoner till exchanged, and had had a hard time getting home, with little money and a bad wound in the leg, besides being feeble with jail fever. But we didn't fret over past troubles, being so glad to get him back. How my blessed mother did laugh, when we told her the reception I gave the poor lad! But I said it served him right, since he came sneaking home like a thief, instead of marching in like a hero. Then he owned that he came there to get something to eat, being ashamed to go in upon his mother with all her company about her. So we fed and comforted him; and when we'd got our wits about us, I whipped away to Mrs. Shirley's and told my news, and every one of those twenty-five women went straight over to our house and burst in upon poor Joe, as he lay resting on the settle. That was my revenge for the scare he gave me, and a fine one it was; for the women chattered over him like a flock of magpies, and I sat in the corner and laughed at him. Ah, I was a sad puss in those days!"

The old lady's black eyes twinkled with fun, and the children laughed with her, till Walt caused a lull by asking:—

"Where do the wolves come in, grandma?"

"Right along, dear; I'm not likely to forget 'em, for they 'most cost me my life, to say nothing of my new slippers. There was great rejoicing over Joe, and every one wanted to do something to honor our hero; for he had done well, we found out, when the General heard his story. We had a great dinner, and Judge Mullikin gave a supper; but Major Belknap was bound to outshine the rest, so he invited all the young folks over to his house, nigh ten miles away, to a ball, and we all went. I made myself fine, you may believe, and wore a pair of blue kid slippers, with mother's best buckles to set 'em off. Joe had a new uniform, and was an elegant figure of a man, I do assure you. He couldn't dance, poor dear, being still very lame: but I was a proud girl when I marched into that ball-room, on the arm of my limping beau. The men cheered, and the ladies stood up in chairs to see him, and he was as red as my ribbons, and I could hardly keep from crying, as I held him up,—the floor being slippery as glass with the extra waxing it had got.

"I declared I wouldn't dance, because Joe couldn't; but he made me, saying he could see me better; so I footed it till two o'clock, soon forgetting all my sorrow and my good resolutions as well. I wanted to show Joe that I was as much a favorite as ever, though I'd lived like a widow for a year. Young folks will be giddy, and I hope these girls will take warning by me and behave better when their time comes. There mayn't be any wolves to sober 'em, but trouble of some sort always follows foolish actions; so be careful, my dears, and behave with propriety when you 'come out,' as you call it nowadays."

Grandma held up a warning forefinger at the girls, and shook her head impressively, feeling that the moral of her tale must be made clear before she went on. But the lassies blushed a little, and the lads looked all impatience, so the dear old lady introduced the wolves as quickly as she could.

"About half-past two, Joe and I drove off home with four fine hams in the bottom of the sleigh, sent by the Major to our mothers. It was a bitter-cold February night, with just light enough to see the road, and splendid sleighing; so we went along at a good pace, till we came to the great woods. They are all gone now, and the woollen mills stand there, but then they were a thick forest of pines, and for more than three miles the road led through them. In former days Indians had lurked there; bears and foxes were still shot, and occasionally wolves were seen, when cold weather drove them to seek food near the sheep-folds and barn-yards.

"Well, we were skimming along pleasantly enough, I rather sleepy, and Joe very careful of me, when, just as I was beginning to doze a bit with my head on his arm I felt him start. Old Buck, the horse, gave a jump that woke me up, and in a minute I knew what the trouble was, for from behind us came the howl of a wolf.

"'Just the night to bring 'em out,' muttered Joe, using the whip till Buck went at his quickest trot, with his ears down and every sign of hurry and worry about him.

"'Are you afraid of them?' I asked, for I'd never had a scare of this sort, though I'd heard other people tell of the fierceness of the brutes when hunger made them bold.

"'Not a bit, only I wish I had my gun along,' said Joe, looking over his shoulder anxiously.

"'Pity I hadn't brought mine—I do so well with it,' I said, and I laughed as I remembered how I aimed at Joe and hurt myself.

"'Are they chasing us?' I asked, standing up to look back along the white road, for we were just on the edge of the woods now.

"'Shouldn't wonder. If I had a better horse it would be a lively race; but Buck can't keep this pace long, and if he founders we are in a fix, for I can't run, and you can't fight. Betsey, there's more than one; hold tight and try to count 'em.'

"Something in Joe's voice told me plainer than words that we were in danger, and I wished we'd waited till the rest of our party came; but I was tired, and so we had started alone.

"Straining my eyes, I could see three black spots on the snow, and hear three howls as the wolves came galloping after us. I was a brave girl, but I'd never tried this kind of thing before, and in a minute all the wolf stories I'd ever heard came flying through my mind. I was mortally afeard, but I wouldn't show it, and turned to Joe, trying to laugh as I said: 'Only three as yet. Tell me just what to do, and I'll do it.'

"'Brave lass! I must see to Buck or he'll be down, for he's badly scared. You wait till the rascals are pretty close, then heave over one of these confounded hams to amuse 'em, while we make the most of their halt. They smell this meat, and that's what they are after,' said Joe, driving his best, for the poor old horse began to pant, and limp on his stiff legs.

"'Lucky for us we've got 'em,' says I, bound to be cool and gay; 'if we hadn't, they'd get fresh meat instead of smoked.'

"Joe laughed, but a long howl close by made me dive for a ham; for in the darkness of the woods the beasts had got closer, and now all I could see were several balls of fire not many yards away. Out went the ham, and a snarling sound showed that the wolves were busy eating it.

"'All right!' said Joe. 'Rest a bit, and have another ready. They'll soon finish that and want more. We must go easy, for Buck is nearly blown.'

"I prepared my ammunition, and, in what seemed five minutes, I heard the patter of feet behind us, and the fiery eyes were close by. Over went the second mouthful, and then the third, and the fourth; but they seemed more ravenous than ever, and each time were back sooner in greater numbers.

"We were nearly out of the woods when the last was gone, and if Buck had only had strength we should have been safe. But it was plain to see that he couldn't keep up much longer, for he was very old, though he'd been a fine horse in his prime.

"'This looks bad, little Betsey. Cover up in the robes, and hold fast to me. The beasts will begin to snatch presently, and I'll have to fight 'em off. Thank the powers, I've my arms left.'

"As he spoke, Joe pulled me close, and wrapped me up, then took the whip, ready to rap the first wolf that dared come near enough to be hit. We didn't wait long; up they raced, and began to leap and snarl in a way that made my heart stand still, at first. Then my temper rose, and catching up the hot brick I had for my feet, I fired it with such good aim that one sharp, black nose disappeared with a yelp of pain.

"'Hit 'em again, Betsey! Take the demijohn and bang 'em well. We are nearing Beaman's, and the brutes will soon drop off.'

"It was a lively scrimmage for a few minutes, as we both warmed to our work, Joe thrashing away with his whip on one side, and I on the other flourishing the demijohn in which we had carried some cider for the supper.

"But it was soon over, for in the fury of the fight Joe forgot the horse; poor Buck made a sudden bolt, upset the sleigh down a bank, and, breaking loose, tore back along the road with the wolves after him.

"Run, Betsey! run for your life, and send Beaman's folks back! I'm done for—my leg's broken. Never mind. I'll crawl under the sleigh, and be all right till you come. The wolves will take a good while to pick poor Buck's bones.'

"Just waiting to see Joe safe, I ran as I never ran before,—and I was always light of foot. How I did it I don't know, for I'd forgot to put on my moccasins (we didn't have snow-boots, you know, in my young days), and there I was, tearing along that snowy road in my blue kid slippers like a crazy thing. It was nigh a mile, and my heart was 'most broke before I got there; but I kept my eye on the light in Hetty's winder and tugged along, blessing her for the guide and comfort that candle was. The last bit was down hill, or I couldn't have done it; for when I fell on the doorstep my voice was clean gone, and I could only lie and rap, rap, rap! till they came flying. I just got breath enough to gasp out and point:—

"Joe—wolves—the big woods—go!' when my senses failed me, and I was carried in."

Here Madam Shirley leaned back in her chair quite used up, for she had been acting the scene to a breathless audience, and laying about her with her handkerchief so vigorously that her eyes snapped, her cheeks were red, and her dear old cap all awry.

"But Joe—did they eat him?" cried the boys in great excitement, while the girls held to one another, and the poor little wheel lay flat, upset by the blows of the imaginary demijohn, dealt to an equally imaginary wolf.

"Hardly,—since he lived to be your grandfather," laughed the old lady, in high feather at the success of her story.

"No, no,—we mean the horse;" shouted Geoff, while the others roared at the mistake.

"Yes, they did. Poor old Buck saved us, at the cost of his own life. His troubles were over, but mine were not; for when I came to, I saw Mr. Beaman, and my first thought and word was 'Joe?'"

"'Too late—they'd got him, so we turned back to tell you,' said that stupid man.

"I gave one cry and was going off again, when his wife shook me, and says, laughing: 'You little goose! He means the folks from the Major's. A lot came along and found Joe, and took him home, and soon's ever you're fit we'll send you along, too.'

"'I'm ready now,' says I, jumping up in a hurry. But I had to sit down again, for my feet were all cut and bleeding, and my slippers just rags. They fixed me up and off I went, to find mother in a sad taking. But Joe was all right; he hadn't broken his leg, but only sprained it badly, and being the wounded one he was laid up longer than I. We both got well, however, and the first time Joe went out he hobbled over to our house. I was spinning again then, and thought I might need my wedding outfit, after all—On the whole, I guess we'll end the story here; young folks wouldn't care for that part."

As grandma paused, the girls cried out with one voice: "Yes, we do! we like it best. You said you would. Tell about the wedding and all."

"Well, well, it isn't much. Joe came and sat by me, and, as we talked over our adventure, he cut that true lover's knot between the letters. I didn't seem to mind, and spun away till he pointed to it, saying, with the look that always made me meek as a lamb, 'May it stand so, my little Betsey?'

"I said 'Yes, Joe,' and then—well, never mind that bit;—we were married in June, and I spun and wove my wedding things afterward. Dreadful slack, my mother thought, but I didn't care. My wedding gown was white lutestring, full trimmed with old lace. Hair over a cushion with white roses, and the pearl necklace, just as you see up there. Joe wore his uniform, and I tied up his hair with a white satin ribbon. He looked beautiful,—and so did I."

At this artless bit of vanity, the girls smiled, but all agreed that grandma was right, as they looked at the portraits with fresh interest.

"I call that a pretty good story," said Walt, with the air of an accomplished critic.

"'Specially the wolf part. I wanted that longer," added Geoff.

"It was quite long enough for me, my dear, and I didn't hear the last of it for years. Why, one of my wedding presents was four hams done up elegantly in white paper, with posies on 'em, from the Major. He loved a joke, and never forgot how well we fought with the pigs' legs that night. Joe gave me a new sleigh, the next Christmas, with two wolf-skin robes for it,—shot the beasts himself, and I kept those rugs till the moths ate the last bit. He kept the leavings of my slippers, and I have them still. Fetch 'em, Minnie—you know where they are."

Grandma pointed to the tall secretary that stood in a corner, and Minnie quickly took a box from one of the many drawers. All the heads clustered around grandma, and the faded, ragged shoes went from hand to hand, while questions rained upon the story-teller till she bade them go to bed.

Nothing but the promise of more tales would appease them; then, with thanks and kisses, the young folks trooped away, leaving the old lady to put the little wheel to rights, and sit thinking over her girlhood, in the fire-light.

Louisa Alcott
Spinning-Wheel Stories

Bronson Alcott, father of Louisa Alcott (1832–1888) was a philosopher and educationist who failed to make a living to support his family. As soon as she was old enough to work Louisa contributed to the household income, eventually trying to repay her parents' debts. At the same time as teaching, sewing, nursing during the American Civil War and other jobs, Louisa Alcott wrote, sometimes under pseudonyms, in a variety of genres from short stories and serious novels to lurid stories for dime-novel publishers. A Boston publisher asked her for a book for girls: this did not appeal but drawing on her own experiences she produced *Little Women* – the first American classic for children.

THE WREN, THE WREN

The Wren, the Wren the king of all birds,
St. Stephenses day, he was caught in the furze.
Although he is little, his honor is great,
Rise up, kind sir, and give us a trate.

We followed this Wren ten miles or more
Through hedges and ditches and heaps of snow,
We up with our wattles and gave him a fall
And brought him here to show you all.

For we are the boys that came your way
To bury the Wren on Saint Stephenses Day,
So up with the kettle and down with the pan!
Give us some help for to bury the Wren!

Trad.

Boxing Day – 26 December – is also St Stephen's Day. St Stephen, the first Christian martyr, was stoned to death and in some places it was the custom for people to hunt down a wren and stone it to death to commemorate the saint. More recently an imitation wren has been put on the top of a pole, and paraded around to the music of a band. Money is collected to fund celebrations.

JOURNEY OF THE MAGI

A cold coming they had of it, at this time of the yeare; just the worst time of the yeare, to take a journey, and specially a long journey, in. The waies deep, the weather sharp, the daies short, the sun farthest off in solstitio brumali, the very dead of winter. Venimus, wee are come, if that be one; Venimus, Wee are (now) come, come at this time, that (sure) is another.

Lancelot Andrewes
Epiphany Sermon, XCVI Sermons

A scholar, linguist (he spoke fifteen languages) and theologian, Lancelot Andrewes (1555–1626) was one of the most important of the team of translators chosen by James I in 1604 to work on what became the Authorised Version of the Bible. Later he became bishop of Chichester and then Bishop of Winchester. This extract – some of which was used later by T S Eliot in his poem 'The Coming of the Magi' – was the beginning of a sermon preached for Epiphany 1622. *Right*: Dürer woodcut, 'Adoration of the Magi' (*c.* 1501).

TWELFTH NIGHT: OR, KING AND QUEEN

NOW, now the mirth comes
    With the cake full of plums,
Where bean's the king of the sport here ;
    Beside we must know,
    The pea also
Must revel, as queen, in the court here.

Begin then to choose,
    This night as ye use,
Who shall for the present delight here,
    Be a king by the lot,
    And who shall not
Be Twelfth-day queen for the night here.

Which known, let us make
    Joy-sops with the cake ;
And let not a man then be seen here,
    Who unurg›d will not drink
    To the base from the brink
A health to the king and queen here.

Next crown a bowl full
    With gentle lamb›s wool :
Add sugar, nutmeg, and ginger,
    With store of ale too ;
    And thus ye must do
To make the wassail a swinger.

Give then to the king
    And queen wassailing :
And though with ale ye be whet here,
    Yet part from hence
    As free from offence
As when ye innocent met here.

Robert Herrick

TWELFTH NIGHT IN LONDON

During the entire twelve months there is no such illumination of pastry-cooks' shops, as on Twelfth-night. Each sends forth a blaze of light; and is filled with glorious cakes, "decorated," to use the words of Mr. Hone, "with all imaginable images of thing animate and inanimate. Stars, castles, kings, cottages, dragons, trees, fish, palaces, cats, dogs, churches, lions, milkmaids, knights, serpents, and innumerable other forms, in snow-white confectionery, painted with variegated colors." "This 'paradise of dainty devices,'" he continues, "is crowded by successive, and successful, desirers of the seasonable delicacies; while alternate tappings of hammers and peals of laughter, from the throng surrounding the house, excite smiles from the inmates." This last observation requires explanation, for our country readers.

Let all idle gazers, then, in the streets of London beware of Twelfth-night! There is then that spirit of mischievous fun abroad, which, carried on without the superintending power of a Lord of Misrule, exhibits itself in transfixing the coat-skirts of the unconscious stranger to the frame of the door or window, at which he may have paused to stare and wonder. Once fairly caught, lucky is the wight who can disengage himself, without finding that, in the interim, his other skirt has been pinned to the pelisse or gown of some alarmed damsel, whose dress is perhaps dragged, at the same moment, in opposite directions, so that he can neither stand still nor move, without aiding the work of destruction. These practical faceti are the performances of that class of nondescript lads, "perplexers of Lord Mayors and irritators of the police," whose character Mr. Leigh Hunt has as truly drawn as our artist has depicted their persons: "those equivocal animal-spirits of the streets, who come whistling along, you know not whether thief or errand-boy, sometimes with a bundle and sometimes not, in corduroys, a jacket, and a cap or bit of hat, with hair sticking through a hole in it. His vivacity gets him into scrapes in the street; and he is not ultra-studious of civility in his answers. If the man he runs against is not very big, he gives him abuse for abuse, at once; if otherwise, he gets at a convenient distance, and then halloos out, 'Eh, stupid!' or 'Can't you see before you?' or 'Go and get your face washed!' This last is a favorite saying of his, out of an instinct referable to his own visage. He sings 'Hokee-Pokee,' and 'A shiny Night,' varied, occasionally, with an uproarious 'Rise, gentle Moon,' or 'Coming through the Rye.'

On winter evenings, you may hear him indulging himself, as he goes along, in a singular undulation of yowl, a sort of gargle, as if a wolf was practising the rudiments of a shake. This he delights to do, more particularly in a crowded thoroughfare, as though determined that his noise should triumph over every other and show how jolly he is, and how independent of the ties to good behavior. If the street is a quiet one, and he has a stick in his hand (perhaps a hoop-stick), he accompanies the howl with a run upon the gamut of the iron rails. He is the nightingale of mud and cold. If he gets on in life, he will be a pot-boy. At present, as we said before, we hardly know what he is; but his mother thinks herself lucky if he is not transported."

Thomas K. Hervey
A Book of Christmas

THE NEW YEAR

THE WIND STORM

1 Jan. 1778 – This morning very early about 1. o'clock a most dreadful Storm of Wind with Hail & Snow happened here and the Wind did not quite abait till the Evening. – A little before 2. o'clock I got up, my bedstead rocking under me, and never in my Life that I know of , did I remember the Wind so high or of so long continuance – I expected every Moment that some Part or other of my House must have been blown down, but blessed be God the whole stood, only a few Tiles displaced... My Chancel received great Damage as did my Barn – the Leads from my Chancel were almost all blown up with some Parts of the Roof – the North West Window blown in & smashed all to pieces.

James Woodforde
Diary of a Country Parson

James Woodforde (1740–1803) was a country clergyman. He kept a diary for forty-five years, starting when he was an undergraduate at Oxford. His diary is full of the minute details of country life – public events are occasionally mentioned, but not discussed. It provides a unique account of ordinary, uneventful rural life in the last half of the eighteenth century.

HOW ARTHUR WAS CHOSEN KING

THEN stood the realm in great jeopardy long while, for every lord that was mighty of men made him strong, and many weened to have been king. Then Merlin went to the Archbishop of Canterbury, and counselled him for to send for all the lords of the realm, and all the gentlemen of arms, that they should to London come by Christmas, upon pain of cursing; and for this cause, that Jesus, that was born on that night, that he would of his great mercy show some miracle, as he was come to be king of mankind, for to show some miracle who should be rightwise king of this realm. So the Archbishop, by the advice of Merlin, sent for all the lords and gentlemen of arms that they should come by Christmas even unto London. And many of them made them clean of their life, that their prayer might be the more acceptable unto God. So in the greatest church of London, whether it were Paul's or not the French book maketh no mention, all the estates were long or day in the church for to pray. And when matins and the first mass was done, there was seen in the churchyard, against the high altar, a great stone four square, like unto a marble stone; and in midst thereof was like an anvil of steel a foot on high, and therein stuck a fair sword naked by the point, and letters there were written in gold about the sword that said thus:—Whoso pulleth out this sword of this stone and anvil, is rightwise king born of all England. Then the people marvelled, and told it to the Archbishop. I command, said the Archbishop, that ye keep you within your church and pray unto God still, that no man touch the sword till the high mass be all done. So when all masses were done all the lords went to behold the stone and the sword. And when they saw the scripture some assayed, such as would have been king. But none might stir the sword nor move it. He is not here, said the Archbishop, that shall achieve the sword, but doubt not God will make him known. But this is my counsel, said the Archbishop, that we let purvey ten knights, men of good fame, and they to keep this sword. So it was ordained, and then there was made a cry, that every man should assay that would, for to win the sword. And upon New Year's Day the barons let make a jousts and a tournament, that all knights that would joust or tourney there might play, and all this was ordained for to keep the lords together and the commons, for the Archbishop trusted that God would make him known that should win the sword.

So upon New Year's Day, when the service was done, the barons rode unto the field, some to joust and some to tourney, and so it happened that Sir Ector, that had great livelihood about London, rode unto the jousts, and with him rode Sir Kay his son, and young Arthur that was his nourished brother; and Sir Kay was made knight at All Hallowmass afore. So as they rode to the jousts-ward, Sir Kay lost his sword, for he had left it at his father's lodging, and so he prayed young Arthur for to ride for his sword. I will well, said Arthur, and rode fast after the sword, and when he came home, the lady and all were out to see the jousting. Then was Arthur wroth, and said to himself, I will ride to the churchyard, and take the sword with me that sticketh in the stone, for my brother Sir Kay shall not be without a sword this day. So when he came to the churchyard, Sir Arthur alighted and tied his horse to the stile, and so he went to the tent, and found no knights there, for they were at the jousting. And so he handled the sword by the handles, and lightly and fiercely pulled it out of the stone, and took his horse and rode his way until he came to his brother Sir Kay, and delivered him the sword. And as soon as Sir Kay saw the sword, he wist well

it was the sword of the stone, and so he rode to his father Sir Ector, and said: Sir, lo here is the sword of the stone, wherefore I must be king of this land. When Sir Ector beheld the sword, he returned again and came to the church, and there they alighted all three, and went into the church. And anon he made Sir Kay swear upon a book how he came to that sword. Sir, said Sir Kay, by my brother Arthur, for he brought it to me. How gat ye this sword? said Sir Ector to Arthur. Sir, I will tell you. When I came home for my brother's sword, I found nobody at home to deliver me his sword; and so I thought my brother Sir Kay should not be swordless, and so I came hither eagerly and pulled it out of the stone without any pain. Found ye any knights about this sword? said Sir Ector. Nay, said Arthur. Now, said Sir Ector to Arthur, I understand ye must be king of this land. Wherefore I, said Arthur, and for what cause? Sir, said Ector, for God will have it so; for there should never man have drawn out this sword, but he that shall be rightwise king of this land. Now let me see whether ye can put the sword there as it was, and pull it out again. That is no mastery, said Arthur, and so he put it in the stone; wherewithal Sir Ector assayed to pull out the sword and failed.

Now assay, said Sir Ector unto Sir Kay. And anon he pulled at the sword with all his might; but it would not be. Now shall ye assay, said Sir Ector to Arthur. I will well, said Arthur, and pulled it out easily. And therewithal Sir Ector knelt down to the earth, and Sir Kay. Alas, said Arthur, my own dear father and brother, why kneel ye to me? Nay, nay, my lord Arthur, it is not so; I was never your father nor of your blood, but I wot well ye are of an higher blood than I weened ye were. And then Sir Ector told him all, how he was betaken him for to nourish him, and by whose commandment, and by Merlin's deliverance.

Then Arthur made great dole when he understood that Sir Ector was not his father. Sir, said Ector unto Arthur, will ye be my good and gracious lord when ye are king? Else were I to blame, said Arthur, for ye are the man in the world that I am most beholden to, and my good lady and mother your wife, that as well as her own hath fostered me and kept. And if ever it be God's will that I be king as ye say, ye shall desire of me what I may do, and I shall not fail you; God forbid I should fail you Sir, said Sir Ector, I will ask no more of you, but that ye will make my son, your foster brother, Sir Kay, seneschal of all your lands. That shall be done, said Arthur, and more, by the faith of my body, that never man shall have that office but he, while he and I live Therewithal they went unto the Archbishop, and told him how the sword was achieved, and by whom; and on Twelfth-day all the barons came thither, and to assay to take the sword, who that would assay. But there afore them all, there might none take it out but Arthur; wherefore there were many lords wroth, and said it was great shame unto them all and the realm, to be overgoverned with a boy of no high blood born. And so they fell out at that time that it was put off till Candlemas and then all the barons should meet there again; but always the ten knights were ordained to watch the sword day and night, and so they set a pavilion over the stone and the sword, and five always watched. So at Candlemas many more great lords came thither for to have won the sword, but there might none prevail. And right as Arthur did at Christmas, he did at Candlemas, and pulled out the sword easily, whereof the barons were sore aggrieved and put it off in delay till the high feast of Easter. And as Arthur sped before, so did he at Easter; yet there were some of the great lords had indignation that Arthur should be king, and put it off in a delay till the feast of Pentecost.

Then the Archbishop of Canterbury by Merlin's providence let purvey then of the best knights that they might get, and such knights as Uther Pendragon loved best and most trusted in his days. And such knights were put about Arthur as Sir Baudwin of Britain, Sir Kay, Sir Ulfius, Sir Brastias. All these, with many other, were always about Arthur, day and night, till the feast of Pentecost.

Sir Thomas Malory
Le Morte d'Arthur

Quite who Sir Thomas Malory (d. ?1471) was is uncertain. Caxton's edition of his book tells readers he was a knight, and that *Le Morte d'Arthur* was wholly or largely written while he was in Newgate prison. One possibility is Sir Thomas Malory of Newbold Revel in Warwickshire, who was imprisoned by Edward IV after quarrelling with a neighbour and also because he was a Lancastrian.

GREEN GROWETH THE HOLLY

Green groweth the holly,
So doth the ivy.
Though winter blasts blow never so high,
Green groweth the holly.

As the holly groweth green
And never changeth hue,
So I am, ever hath been,
Unto my lady true.

As the holly groweth green
With ivy all alone
When flowers cannot be seen
And greenwood leaves be gone,

Now unto my lady
Promise to her I make,
From all other only
To her I me betake.

Adieu, mine own lady,
Adieu, my special
Who hath my heart truly
Be sure, and ever shall.

Green groweth the holly,
So doth the ivy.
Though winter blasts blow never so high,
Green groweth the holly

Henry VIII

Henry VIII (1491–1547) was musical. He was taught music from childhood, and it was an important feature at his court, where the best musicians were welcomed and encouraged. At one point he could count on the services of some hundred musicians and composers. Henry could sing and play several musical instruments well, and also wrote and composed, though much of his music has been lost. Today, thirty-three of his pieces – twenty songs and thirteen instrumental compositions - are known. Henry VIII's Songbook, a collection of over one hundred pieces including Henry's own, is in the British Library. This poem is a love-song, but is sometimes sung as a carol.

REJOICINGS UPON THE NEW YEAR'S COMING OF AGE

The Old Year being dead, and the New Year coming of age, which he does, by Calendar Law, as soon as the breath is out of the old gentleman's body, nothing would serve the young spark but he must give a dinner upon the occasion, to which all the Days in the year were invited. The Festivals, whom he deputed as his stewards, were mightily taken with the notion. They had been engaged time out of mind, they said, in providing mirth and good cheer for mortals below; and it was time they should have a taste of their own bounty. It was stiffly debated among them, whether the Fasts should be admitted. Some said, the appearance of such lean, starved guests, with their mortified faces, would pervert the ends of the meeting. But the objection was over-ruled by Christmas Day, who had a design upon Ash Wednesday (as you shall hear), and a mighty desire to see how the old Domine would behave himself in his cups. Only the Vigils were requested to come with their lanterns, to light the gentlefolks home at night.

All the Days came to their day. Covers were provided for three hundred and sixty-five guests at the principal table: with an occasional knife and fork at the side-board for the Twenty–Ninth of February.

I should have told you, that cards of invitation had been issued. The carriers were the Hours; twelve little, merry, whirligig foot-pages, as you should desire to see, that went all round, and found out the persons invited well enough, with the exception of Easter Day, Shrove Tuesday, and a few such Moveables, who had lately shifted their quarters.

Well, they all met at last, foul Days, fine Days, all sorts of Days, and a rare din they made of it. There was nothing but, Hail! fellow Day — well met — brother Day— sister Day — only Lady Day kept a little on the aloof, and seemed somewhat scornful. Yet some said, Twelfth Day cut her out and out, for she came in a tiffany suit, white and gold, like a queen ona frost-cake, all royal, glittering, and Epiphanous. The rest came, some in green, some in white — but old Lent and his family were not yet out of mourning. Rainy Days came in, dripping; and sun-shiny Days helped them to change their stockings. Wedding Day was there in his marriage finery, a little the worse for wear. Pay Day came late, as he always does; and Doomsday sent word — he might be expected.

April Fool (as my young lord's jester) took upon himself to marshal the guests, and wild work he made with it. It would have posed old Erra

Pater to have found out any given Day in the year, to erect a scheme upon — good Days, bad Days, were so shuffled together, to the confounding of all sober horoscopy.

He had stuck the Twenty First of June next to the Twenty Second of December, and the former looked like a Maypole siding a marrow-bone. Ash Wednesday got wedged in (as was concerted) betwixt Christmas and Lord Mayor's Days. Lord! how he laid about him! Nothing but barons of beef and turkeys would go down with him — to the great greasing and detriment of his new sackcloth bib and tucker. And still Christmas Day was at his elbow, plying him the wassail-bowl, till he roared, and hiccup'd, and protested there was no faith in dried ling, but commended it to the devil for a sour, windy, acrimonious, censorious, hy-po-crit-crit-cri-tical mess, and no dish for a gentleman. Then he dipt his fist into the middle of the great custard that stood before his left-hand neighbour, and daubed his hungry beard all over with it, till you would have taken him for the Last Day in December, it so hung in icicles.

At another part of the table, Shrove Tuesday was helping the Second of September to some cock broth — which courtesy the latter returned with the delicate thigh of a hen pheasant — so there was no love lost for that matter. The Last of Lent was spunging upon Shrovetide's pancakes; which April Fool perceiving, told him he did well, for pancakes were proper to a good fry-day.

In another part, a hubbub arose about the Thirtieth of January, who, it seems, being a sour puritanic character, that thought nobody's meat good or sanctified enough for him, had smuggled into the room a calf's head, which he had had cooked at home for that purpose, thinking to feast thereon incontinently; but as it lay in the dish, March manyweathers, who is a very fine lady, and subject to the megrims, screamed out there was a "human head in the platter," and raved about Herodias' daughter to that degree, that the obnoxious viand was obliged to be removed; nor did she recover her stomach till she had gulped down a Restorative, confected of Oak Apple, which the merry Twenty Ninth of May always carries about with him for that purpose.

The King's health21 being called for after this, a notable dispute arose between the Twelfth of August (a zealous old Whig gentlewoman,) and the Twenty Third of April (a new-fangled lady of the Tory stamp,) as to which of them should have the honour to propose it. August grew hot upon the matter, affirming time out of mind the prescriptive right to have lain with her, till her rival had basely supplanted her; whom she represented as little better than a kept mistress, who went about in fine clothes, while she (the legitimate BIRTHDAY) had scarcely a rag, &c.

April fool, being made mediator, confirmed the right in the strongest form of words to the appellant, but decided for peace' sake that the exercise of it should remain with the present possessor. At the same time, he slily rounded the first lady in the ear, that an action might lie against the Crown for bi-geny.

It beginning to grow a little duskish, Candlemas lustily bawled out for lights, which was opposed by all the Days, who protested against burning daylight. Then fair water was handed round in silver ewers, and the same lady was observed to take an unusual time in Washing herself.

May Day, with that sweetness which is peculiar to her, in a neat speech proposing the health of the founder, crowned her goblet (and by her example the rest of the company) with garlands. This being done, the lordly New Year from the upper end of the table, in a cordial but somewhat lofty tone, returned thanks. He felt proud on an occasion of meeting so many of his worthy father's late tenants, promised to improve their farms, and at the same time to abate (if any thing was found unreasonable) in their rents.

At the mention of this, the four Quarter Days involuntarily looked at each other, and smiled; April Fool whistled to an old tune of "New Brooms;" and a surly old rebel at the farther end of the table (who was discovered to be no other than the Fifth of November,) muttered out, distinctly enough to be heard by the whole company, words to this effect, that, "when the old one is gone, he is a fool that looks for a better." Which rudeness of his, the guests resenting, unanimously voted his expulsion; and the male-content was thrust out neck and heels into the cellar, as the properest place for such a boutefeu and firebrand as he had shown himself to be.

Order being restored — the young lord (who to say truth, had been a little ruffled, and put beside his oratory) in as few, and yet as obliging words as possible, assured them of entire welcome; and, with a graceful turn, singling out poor Twenty Ninth of February, that had sate all this while mumchance at the side-board, begged to couple his health with that of the good company before him — which he drank accordingly; observing, that he had not seen his honest face any time these four years, with a number of endearing expressions besides. At the same time, removing the solitary Day from the forlorn seat which had been assigned him, he stationed him at his own board, somewhere between the Greek Calends and Latter Lammas. Ash Wednesday, being now called upon for a song, with his eyes fast stuck in his head, and as well as the Canary he had swallowed would give him leave, struck up a Carol, which Christmas Day had taught him for the nonce; and was followed by the latter, who gave "Miserere" in fine style, hitting off the mumping notes and lengthened drawl of Old Mortification.

Charles Lamb
The Last Essays of Elia

Charles Lamb (1775–1824) worked for the East India Company as a clerk. With his sister Mary he published *Tales from Shakespeare* for young readers: this was a success and the brother and sister wrote more for children. Lamb also wrote essays published in different periodicals, and was invited to join the staff of *The London Magazine*. The essays he contributed to this periodical under his penname 'Elia' are his best known.

ST DISTAFF'S DAY

Thus, on the day which followed Twelfth-night, the implements of labor were prepared and the team was even yoked for a space; but the business of turning the soil was not required to be laboriously engaged in until the Monday which followed, and which therefore bore (and bears) the title of Plough Monday. After a few hours of morning labor, a sort of half-holiday was the concluding privilege of this privileged season; and the husbandman laid aside his plough, and the maiden her distaff, to engage in certain revels which were peculiar to the day and to the country districts. From the partial resumption of the spinning labors of the women on this morning, the festival in question takes its name; and it is (or was) sometimes called also "Rockday," in honor of the rock, which is another name for the distaff. It is described as being "a distaff held in the hand, from whence wool is spun by twirling a ball below."

Thomas K. Hervey
A Book of Christmas

PLOUGH MONDAY

The first Monday after Twelfth-day is called Plough Monday, and appears to have received that name because it was the first day after Christmas that husbandmen resumed the plough. In some parts of the country, and especially in the north, they draw the plough in procession to the doors of the villagers and townspeople. Long ropes are attached to it, and thirty or forty men, stripped to their clean white shirts, but protected from the weather by waistecoats beneath, drag it along. Their arms and shoulders are decorated with gay-coloured ribbons, tied in large knots and bows, and their hats are smartened in the same way. They are usually accompanied by an old woman, or a boy dressed up to represent one; she is gaily bedizened, and called the Bessy. Sometimes the sport is assisted by a humorous countryman to represent a fool. He is covered with ribbons, and attired in skins, with a depending tail, and carries a box to collect money from the spectators. They are attended by music, and Morris-dancers when they can be got; but there is always a sportive dance with a few lasses in all their finery, and a superabundance or ribbons. When this merriment is well managed, it is very pleasing. The money collected is spent at night in conviviality. It must not be supposed, however, that in these times, the twelve days of Christmas are devoted to pastime, although the custom remains. Formerly, indeed, little was done in the field at this season, and according to "Tusser Redivivus," during the Christmas holidays, gentlemen feasted the farmers, and every farmer feasted his servants and taskmen. Then Plough Monday reminded them of their business, and on the morning of that day, the men and maids strove who should show their readiness to commence the labours of the years, by rising the earliest. If the plough-man could get his whip, his plough-staff, hatched, or any field implement, by the fireside, before the maid could get her kettle on, she lost her Shrove-tide cock to the men. Thus did our forefathers strive to allure youth to their duty, and provided them innocent mirth as well as labour. On Plough Monday night the farmer gave them a good supper and strong ale. In some places, where the ploughman went to work on Plough Monday, if, on his return at night, he came with his whip to the kitchen-hatch, and cried "Cock on the dunghill," he gained a cock for Shrove Tuesday.

William Hone
The Every-day Book

William Hone (1780–1842) spent much of his life as a radical journalist and political satirist, which brought him into conflict with the law. He was tried on three separate charges in 1817, but was acquitted. This struck a useful blow for press freedom. Various businesses, such as bookselling and running a coffee house, failed. In the course of research for his defence, he collected miscellaneous information about old customs and antiquities. Some of this he published in *The Every-day Book*.

THE GREAT WINTER

Before Sir Ensor Doone was buried, the greatest frost of the century had set in, with its iron hand, and step of stone, on everything. How it came is not my business, nor can I explain it; because I never have watched the skies; as people now begin to do, when the ground is not to their liking. Though of all this I know nothing, and less than nothing I may say (because I ought to know something); I can hear what people tell me; and I can see before my eyes.

The strong men broke three good pickaxes, ere they got through the hard brown sod, streaked with little maps of gray where old Sir Ensor was to lie, upon his back, awaiting the darkness of the Judgment-day. It was in the little chapel-yard; I will not tell the name of it; because we are now such Protestants, that I might do it an evil turn; only it was the little place where Lorna's Aunt Sabina lay. ...

After all was over, I strode across the moors very sadly; trying to keep the cold away by virtue of quick movement. Not a flake of snow had fallen yet; all the earth was caked and hard, with a dry brown crust upon it; all the sky was banked with darkness, hard, austere, and frowning. The fog of the last three weeks was gone, neither did any rime remain; but all things had a look of sameness, and a kind of furzy colour. It was freezing hard and sharp, with a piercing wind to back it; and I had observed that the holy water froze upon Sir Ensor's coffin.

One thing struck me with some surprise, as I made off for our fireside (with a strong determination to heave an ash-tree up the chimney-place), and that was how the birds were going, rather than flying as they used to fly. All the birds were set in one direction, steadily journeying westward, not with any heat of speed, neither flying far at once; but all (as if on business bound), partly running, partly flying, partly fluttering along; silently, and without a voice, neither pricking head nor tail. This movement of the birds went on, even for a week or more; every kind of thrushes passed us, every kind of wild fowl, even plovers went away, and crows, and snipes and wood-cocks. And before half the frost was over, all we had in the snowy ditches were hares so tame that we could pat them; partridges that came to hand, with a dry noise in their crops; heath-poults, making cups of snow; and a few poor hopping redwings, flipping in and out the hedge, having lost the power to fly. And all the time their great black eyes, set with gold around them, seemed to look at any man, for mercy and for comfort.

Annie took a many of them, all that she could find herself, and all the boys would bring her; and she made a great hutch near the fire, in the back-kitchen chimney-place. Here, in spite of our old Betty (who sadly wanted to roast them), Annie kept some fifty birds, with bread and milk, and raw chopped meat, and all the seed she could think of, and lumps of rotten apples, placed to tempt them, in the corners. Some got on, and some died off; and Annie cried for all that died, and buried them under the woodrick; but, I do assure you, it was a pretty thing to see, when she went to them in the morning. There was not a bird but knew her well, after one day of comforting; and some would come to her hand, and sit, and shut one eye, and look at her. Then she used to stroke their heads, and feel their breasts, and talk to them; and not a bird of them all was there but liked to have it done to him. And I do believe they would eat from her hand things unnatural to them, lest she should be grieved and hurt by not knowing what to do for them. One of them was a noble bird, such as I never had seen before, of very fine bright plumage, and larger than a missel-thrush. He was the hardest of all to please: and yet he tried to do his best. I have heard since then, from a man who knows all about birds, and beasts, and fishes, that he must have been a Norwegian bird, called in this country a Roller, who never comes to England but in the most tremendous winters. …

But lo, in the very night which followed old Sir Ensor's funeral, such a storm of snow began as never have I heard nor read of, neither could have dreamed it. At what time of night it first began is more than I can say, at least from my own knowledge, for we all went to bed soon after supper, being cold and not inclined to talk. At that time the wind was moaning sadly, and the sky as dark as a wood, and the straw in the yard swirling round and round, and the cows huddling into the great cowhouse, with their chins upon one another. But we, being blinder than they, I suppose, and not having had a great snow for years, made no preparation against the storm, except that the lambing ewes were in shelter.

It struck me, as I lay in bed, that we were acting foolishly; for an ancient shepherd had dropped in and taken supper with us, and foretold a heavy fall and great disaster to live stock. He said that he had known a frost beginning, just as this had done, with a black east wind, after days of raw cold fog, and then on the third night of the frost, at this very time of year (to wit on the 15th of December) such a snow set in as killed half of the sheep and many even of the red deer and the forest ponies. It was three-score years agone, he said; and cause he had to remember it, inasmuch as two of his toes had been lost by frost-nip, while he dug out his sheep on the other side of the Dunkery. Hereupon mother nodded at him, having heard from her father about it, and how three men had been frozen to death, and how badly their stockings came off from them.

Remembering how the old man looked, and his manner of listening to the wind and shaking his head very ominously (when Annie gave him a glass of schnapps), I grew quite uneasy in my bed, as the room got colder and colder; and I made up my mind, if it only pleased God not to send the snow till the morning, that every sheep, and horse, and cow, ay, and even the poultry, should be brought in snug, and with plenty to eat, and fodder enough to roast them.

Alas what use of man's resolves, when they come a day too late; even if they may avail a little, when they are most punctual!

In the bitter morning I arose, to follow out my purpose, knowing the time from the force of habit, although the room was so dark and gray. An odd white light was on the rafters, such as I never had seen before; while all the length of the room was grisly, like the heart of a mouldy oat-rick. I went to the window at once, of course; and at first I could not understand what was doing outside of it. It faced due east (as I may have said), with the walnut-tree partly sheltering it; and generally I could see the yard, and the woodrick, and even the church beyond.

But now, half the lattice was quite blocked up, as if plastered with gray lime; and little fringes, like ferns, came through, where the joining of the lead was; and in the only undarkened part, countless dots came swarming, clustering, beating with a soft, low sound, then gliding down in a slippery manner, not as drops of rain do, but each distinct from his neighbour. Inside the iron frame (which fitted, not to say too comfortably, and went along the stonework), at least a peck of snow had entered, following its own bend and fancy; light as any cobweb.

With some trouble, and great care, lest the ancient frame should yield, I spread the lattice open; and saw at once that not a moment must be lost, to save our stock. All the earth was flat with snow, all the air was thick with snow; more than this no man could see, for all the world was snowing.

I shut the window and dressed in haste; and when I entered the kitchen, not even Betty, the earliest of all early birds, was there. I raked the ashes together a little, just to see a spark of warmth; and then set forth to find John Fry, Jem Slocombe, and Bill Dadds. But this was easier thought than done; for when I opened the courtyard door, I was taken up to my knees at once, and the power of the drifting cloud prevented sight of anything. However, I found my way to the woodrick, and there got hold of a fine ash-stake, cut by myself not long ago. With this I ploughed along pretty well, and thundered so hard at John Fry's door, that he thought it was the Doones at least, and cocked his blunderbuss out of the window.

John was very loth to come down, when he saw the meaning of it; for he valued his life more than anything else; though he tried to make out that his wife was to blame. But I settled his doubts by telling him, that I would have him on my shoulder naked, unless he came in five minutes; not that he could do much good, but because the other men would be

sure to skulk, if he set them the example. With spades, and shovels, and pitch-forks, and a round of roping, we four set forth to dig out the sheep; and the poor things knew that it was high time.

It must have snowed most wonderfully to have made that depth of covering in about eight hours. For one of Master Stickles' men, who had been out all the night, said that no snow began to fall until nearly midnight. And here it was, blocking up the doors, stopping the ways, and the water courses, and making it very much worse to walk than in a saw-pit newly used. However, we trudged along in a line; I first, and the other men after me; trying to keep my track, but finding legs and strength not up to it. Most of all, John Fry was groaning; certain that his time was come, and sending messages to his wife, and blessings to his children. For all this time it was snowing harder than it ever had snowed before, so far as a man might guess at it; and the leaden depth of the sky came down, like a mine turned upside down on us. Not that the flakes were so very large; for I have seen much larger flakes in a shower of March, while sowing peas; but that there was no room between them, neither any relaxing, nor any change of direction.

Watch, like a good and faithful dog, followed us very cheerfully, leaping out of the depth, which took him over his back and ears already, even in the level places; while in the drifts he might have sunk to any distance out of sight, and never found his way up again. However, we helped him now and then, especially through the gaps and gateways; and so after a deal of floundering, some laughter, and a little swearing, we came all safe to the lower meadow, where most of our flock was hurdled.

But behold, there was no flock at all! None, I mean, to be seen anywhere; only at one corner of the field, by the eastern end, where the snow drove in, a great white billow, as high as a barn, and as broad as a house. This great drift was rolling and curling beneath the violent blast, tufting and combing with rustling swirls, and carved (as in patterns of cornice) where the grooving chisel of the wind swept round. Ever and again the tempest snatched little whiffs from the channelled edges, twirled them round and made them dance over the chime of the monster pile, then let them lie like herring-bones, or the seams of sand where the tide has been. And all the while from the smothering sky, more and more fiercely at every blast, came the pelting, pitiless arrows, winged with murky white, and pointed with the barbs of frost.

But although for people who had no sheep, the sight was a very fine one (so far at least as the weather permitted any sight at all); yet for us, with our flock beneath it, this great mount had but little charm. Watch began to scratch at once, and to howl along the sides of it; he knew that his charge was buried there, and his business taken from him. But we four men set to in earnest, digging with all our might and main, shovelling away at the great white pile, and fetching it into the meadow. Each man made for himself a cave, scooping at the soft, cold flux, which slid upon him at every stroke, and throwing it out behind him, in piles of castled fancy. At last we drove our tunnels in (for we worked indeed for the lives of us), and all converging towards the middle, held our tools and listened.

The other men heard nothing at all; or declared that they heard nothing, being anxious now to abandon the matter, because of the chill in their feet and knees. But I said, "Go, if you choose all of you. I will work it out by myself, you pie-crusts," and upon that they gripped their shovels, being more or less of Englishmen; and the least drop of English blood is worth the best of any other when it comes to lasting out.

But before we began again, I laid my head well into the chamber; and there I hears a faint "ma-a-ah," coming through some ells of snow, like a plaintive, buried hope, or a last appeal. I shouted aloud to cheer him up, for I knew what sheep it was, to wit, the most valiant of all the wethers, who had met me when I came home from London, and been so glad to see me. And then we all fell to again; and very soon we hauled him out. Watch took charge of him at once, with an air of the noblest patronage, lying on his frozen fleece, and licking all his face and feet, to restore his warmth to him. Then fighting Tom jumped up at once, and made a little butt at Watch, as if nothing had ever ailed him, and then set off to a shallow place, and looked for something to nibble at.

Further in, and close under the bank, where they had huddled themselves for warmth, we found all the rest of the poor sheep packed, as closely as if they were in a great pie. It was strange to observe how their vapour and breath, and the moisture exuding from their wool had scooped, as it were, a coved room for them, lined with a ribbing of deep yellow snow. Also the churned snow beneath their feet was as yellow as gamboge. Two or three of the weaklier hoggets were dead, from want of air, and from pressure; but more than three-score were as lively as ever; though cramped and stiff for a little while.

"However shall us get 'em home?" John Fry asked in great dismay, when we had cleared about a dozen of them; which we were forced to do very carefully, so as not to fetch the roof down. "No manner of maning to draive 'un, drough all they girt driftnesses."

"You see to this place, John," I replied, as we leaned on our shovels a moment, and the sheep came rubbing round us; "let no more of them out for the present; they are better where they be. Watch, here boy, keep them!"

Watch came, with his little scut of a tail cocked as sharp as duty, and I set him at the narrow mouth of the great snow antre. All the sheep sidled away, and got closer, that the other sheep might be bitten first, as the foolish things imagine; whereas no good sheep-dog even so much as lips a sheep to turn it.

Then of the outer sheep (all now snowed and frizzled like a lawyer's wig) I took the two finest and heaviest, and with one beneath my right arm, and the other beneath my left, I went straight home to the upper sheppey, and set them inside and fastened them. Sixty and six I took home in that way, two at a time on each journey; and the work grew harder and harder each time, as the drifts of the snow were deepening. No other man should meddle with them; I was resolved to try my strength against the strength of the elements; and try it I did, ay, and proved it. A certain fierce delight burned in me, as the struggle grew harder; but rather would I die than yield; and at last I finished it. People talk of it to this day; but none can tell what the labour was, who have not felt that snow and wind.

Of the sheep upon the mountain, and the sheep upon the western farm, and the cattle on the upper barrows, scarcely one in ten was saved; do what we would for them, and this was not through any neglect (now that our wits were sharpened), but from the pure impossibility of finding them at all. That great snow never ceased a moment for three days and nights; and then when all the earth was filled, and the topmost hedges were unseen, and the trees broke down with weight (wherever the wind had not lightened them), a brilliant sun broke forth and showed the loss of all our customs.

All our house was quite snowed up, except where we had purged a way, by dint of constant shovellings. The kitchen was as dark and darker than the cider-cellar, and long lines of furrowed scollops ran even up to the chimney-stacks. Several windows fell right inwards, through the weight of the snow against them; and the few that stood, bulged in, and bent like an old bruised lanthorn. We were obliged to cook by candle-light; we were forced to read by candle-light; as for baking, we could not do it, because the oven was too chill; and a load of faggots only brought a little wet down the sides of it.

For when the sun burst forth at last upon that world of white, what he brought was neither warmth, nor cheer, nor hope of softening; only a clearer shaft of cold, from the violet depths of sky. Long-drawn alleys of white haze seemed to lead towards him, yet such as he could not come down, with any warmth remaining. Broad white curtains of the frost-fog looped around the lower sky, on the verge of hill and valley, and above the laden trees. Only round the sun himself, and the spot of heaven he claimed, clustered a bright purple-blue, clear, and calm, and deep.

That night such a frost ensued as we had never dreamed of, neither read in ancient books, or histories of Frobisher. The kettle by the fire froze, and the crock upon the hearth-cheeks; many men were killed, and cattle rigid in their head-ropes. Then I heard that fearful sound, which never I had heard before, neither since have heard (except during that same winter), the sharp yet solemn sound of trees burst open by the frost-blow. Our great walnut lost three branches, and has been dying ever since; though growing meanwhile, as the soul does. And the ancient oak at the cross was rent, and many score of ash trees. But why should I tell all this? the people who have not seen it (as I have) will only make faces, and disbelieve; till such another frost comes; which perhaps may never be.

This terrible weather kept Tom Faggus from coming near our house for weeks; at which indeed I was not vexed a quarter so much as Annie was; for I had never half approved of him, as a husband for my sister; in spite of his purchase from Squire Bassett, and the grant of the Royal pardon. It may be, however, that Annie took the same view of my love for Lorna, and could not augur well of it; but if so, she held her peace, though I was not so sparing. For many things contributed to make me less good-humoured now than my real nature was; and the very least of all these things would have been enough to make some people cross, and rude, and fractious. I mean the red and painful chapping of my face and hands, from working in the snow all day, and lying in the frost all night. For being of a fair complexion, and a ruddy nature, and pretty plump withal, and fed on plenty of hot victuals, and always forced by my mother to sit nearer the fire than I wished, it was wonderful to see how the cold ran revel on my cheeks and knuckles. And I feared that Lorna (if it should ever please God to stop the snowing) might take this for a proof of low and rustic blood and breeding.

And this I say was the smallest thing; for it was far more serious that we were losing half our stock, do all we would to shelter them. Even the horses in the stables (mustered all together for the sake of breath and steaming) had long icicles from their muzzles, almost every morning. But of all things the very gravest, to my apprehension, was the impossibility of hearing, or having any token of or from my loved one. Not that those three days alone of snow (tremendous as it was) could have blocked the country so; but that the sky had never ceased, for more than two days at a time, for full three weeks thereafter, to pour fresh piles of fleecy mantle; neither had the wind relaxed a single day from shaking them. As a rule, it snowed all day, cleared up at night, and froze intensely, with the stars as bright as jewels, earth spread out in lustrous twilight, and the sounds in the air as sharp and crackling as artillery; then in the morning, snow again; before the sun could come to help.

It mattered not what way the wind was. Often and often the vanes went round, and we hoped for change of weather; the only change was that it seemed (if possible) to grow colder. Indeed, after a week or so, the wind would regularly box the compass (as the sailors call it) in the course of every day, following where the sun should be, as if to make a mock of him. And this of course immensely added to the peril of the drifts; because they shifted every day; and no skill or care might learn them.

I believe it was on Epiphany morning, or somewhere about that period, when Lizzie ran into the kitchen to me, where I was thawing my goose-grease, with the dogs among the ashes—the live dogs, I mean, not the iron ones, for them we had given up long ago,—and having caught me, by way of wonder (for generally I was out shoveling long before my "young lady" had her nightcap off), she positively kissed me, for the sake of warming her lips perhaps, or because she had something proud to say.

"You great fool, John," said my lady, as Annie and I used to call her, on account of her airs and graces; "what a pity you never read, John!"

"Much use, I should think, in reading!" I answered, though pleased with her condescension; "read, I suppose, with roof coming in, and only this chimney left sticking out of the snow!"

"The very time to read, John," said Lizzie, looking grander; "our worst troubles are the need, whence knowledge can deliver us."

"Amen," I cried out; "are you parson or clerk? Whichever you are, good-morning."

Thereupon I was bent on my usual round (a very small one nowadays), but Eliza took me with both hands, and I stopped of course; for I could not bear to shake the child, even in play, for a moment, because her back was tender. Then she looked up at me with her beautiful eyes, so large, unhealthy and delicate, and strangely shadowing outward, as if to spread their meaning; and she said,—

"Now, John, this is no time to joke. I was almost frozen in bed last night; and Annie like an icicle. Feel how cold my hands are. Now, will you listen to what I have read about climates ten times worse than this; and where none but clever men can live?" ...

She told me that in the Arctic Regions, as they call some places, a long way north, where the Great Bear lies all across the heavens, and no sun is up, for whole months at a time, and yet where people will go exploring, out of pure contradiction, and for the sake of novelty, and love of being frozen—that here they always had such winters as we were having now. It never ceased to freeze, she said; and it never ceased to snow; except when it was too cold; and then all the air was choked with glittering spikes; and a man's skin might come off of him, before he could ask the reason. Nevertheless the people there (although the snow was fifty feet deep, and all their breath fell behind them frozen, like a log of wood dropped from their shoulders), yet they managed to get along, and make the time of the year to each other, by a little cleverness. For seeing how the snow was spread, lightly over everything, covering up the hills and valleys, and the foreskin of the sea, they contrived a way to crown it, and to glide like a flake along. Through the sparkle of the whiteness, and the wreaths of windy tossings, and the ups and downs of cold, any man might get along with a boat on either foot, to prevent his sinking.

She told me how these boats were made; very strong and very light, of ribs with skin across them; five feet long, and one foot wide; and turned up at each end, even as a canoe is. But she did not tell me, nor did I give it a moment's thought myself, how hard it was to walk upon them without early practice. Then she told me another thing equally useful to me; although I would not let her see how much I thought about it. And this concerned the use of sledges, and their power of gliding, and the lightness of their following; all of which I could see at once, through knowledge of our own farm-sleds; which we employ in lieu of wheels, used in flatter districts. When I had heard all this from her, a mere chit of a girl as she was, unfit to make a snowball even, or to fry snow pancakes, I looked down on her with amazement, and began to wish a little that I had given more time to books. ...

Therefore, I fell to at once, upon that hint from Lizzie, and being used to thatching-work, and the making of traps, and so on, before very long I built myself a pair of strong and light snow-shoes, framed with ash and ribbed of withy, with half-tanned calf-skin stretched across, and an inner sole to support my feet. At first I could not walk at all, but floundered about most piteously, catching one shoe in the other, and both of them in the snow-drifts, to the great amusement of the girls, who were come to look at me. But after a while I grew more expert, discovering what my errors were, and altering the inclination of the shoes themselves, according to a print which Lizzie found in a book of adventures. And this made such a difference, that I crossed the farmyard and came back again (though turning was the worst thing of all) without so much as falling once, or getting my staff entangled.

But oh, the aching of my ankles, when I went to bed that night; I was forced to help myself upstairs with a couple of mopsticks! and I rubbed the joints with neatsfoot oil, which comforted them greatly. And likely enough I would have abandoned any further trial, but for Lizzie's ridicule, and pretended sympathy; asking if the strong John Ridd would have old Betty to lean upon. Therefore I set to again, with a fixed resolve not to notice pain or stiffness, but to warm them out of me. And sure enough, before dark that day, I could get along pretty freely; especially improving every time, after leaving off and resting. The astonishment of poor John Fry, Bill Dadds, and Jem Slocombe, when they saw me coming down the hill upon them, in the twilight, where they were clearing the furze rick and trussing it for cattle, was more than I can tell you; because they did not let me see it, but ran away with one accord, and floundered into a snowdrift. They believed, and so did every one else (especially when I grew able to glide along pretty rapidly), that I had stolen Mother Melldrum's sieves, on which she was said to fly over the foreland at midnight every Saturday.

R. D. Blackmore
Lorna Doone

Richard Doddridge Blackmore (1825–1900) spent his childhood in Devon. At Oxford he studied law, but did not practice, preferring market gardening and writing. Several of his fifteen novels are set in Devon: the historical novel *Lorna Doone* brought him fame and success.

SHEEP IN WINTER

The sheep get up and make their many tracks
And bear a load of snow upon their backs
And gnaw the frozen turnip to the ground
With sharp quick bite and then go noising round
The boy that pecks the turnips all the day
And knocks his hands to keep the cold away
And laps his legs in straw to keep them warm
And hides behind the hedges from the storm
The sheep as tame as dogs go where he goes
And try to shake their fleeces from the snows
Then leave their frozen meal and wander round
The stubble stack that stands beside the ground
And lye all night and face the drizzling storm
And shun the hovel where they might be warm.

John Clare
Oxford 263: 1–14

FAMINE

793. This year dire forwarnings came over the land of the North-humbrians, and miserably terrified the people; these were excessive whirlwinds, and lightnings; and fiery dragons were seen flying in the air. A great famine soon followed these tokens; and a little after that, in the same year, on the 6th before the Ides of January, the ravaging of heathen men lamentably destroyed God's church at Lindisfarne through rapine and slaughter.

The Anglo-Saxon Chronicle

King Alfred the Great arranged for a record of annual events to be kept – written in Old English, the Chronicles were compiled in places where literate scribes could be found, usually monasteries. Several copies survive, giving detailed information about what occurred each year. *The Peterborough Chronicle*, which started off as a copy of the one compiled in Canterbury, was kept until 1155, and contains information up to and including the reign of King Stephen.

TRYING TO CATCH A GOOSE

It happened that in January some winters ago, there was a very great fall of snow in England, especially in the south and west. The snow fell without intermission all day and all night, and on the following morning Wells appeared half buried in it. He was then living with a daughter who kept house for him in a cottage standing in its own grounds on the outskirts of the town. On attempting to leave the house he found they were shut in by the snow, which had banked itself against the walls to the height of the eaves. Half an hour's vigorous spade work enabled him to get out from the kitchen door into the open, and the sun in a blue sky shining on a dazzling white and silent world. But no milkman was going his rounds, and there would be no baker nor butcher nor any other tradesman to call for orders. And there were no provisions in the house! But the milk for breakfast was the first thing needed, and so with a jug in his hand he went bravely out to try and make his way to the milk shop which was not far off.

A wall and hedge bounded his front garden on one side, and this was now entirely covered by an immense snowdrift, sloping up to a height of about seven feet. It was only when he paused to look at this vast snow heap in his garden that he caught sight of a goose, a very big snow-white bird without a grey spot in its plumage, standing within a few yards of him, about four feet from the ground. Its entire snowy whiteness with snow for a background had prevented him from seeing it until he looked directly at it. He stood still gazing in astonishment and admiration at this noble bird, standing so motionless with its head raised high that it was like the figure of a goose carved out of some crystalline white stone and set up at that spot on the glittering snowdrift. But it was no statue; it had living eyes which without the least turning of the head watched him and every motion he made. Then all at once the thought came into his head that here was something, very good succulent food in fact, sent, he almost thought providentially, to provision his house; for how easy it would be for him as he passed the bird to throw himself suddenly upon and capture it! It had belonged to some one, no doubt, but that great snowstorm and the furious north-east wind had blown it far far from its native place and it was lost to its owner for ever. Practically it was now a wild bird free for him to take without any qualms and to nourish himself on its flesh while the snow siege lasted. Standing there, jug in hand, he thought it out, and then took a few steps towards the bird in order to see if there was any sign of suspicion in it; but there was none, only he could see that the goose without turning its head was all the time regarding him out of the corner of one eye. Finally he came to the conclusion that his best plan was to go for the milk and on his return to set the jug down by the gate when coming in, then to walk in a careless, unconcerned manner towards the door, taking no notice of the goose until he got abreast of it, and then turn suddenly and hurl himself upon it. Nothing could be easier; so away he went and in about twenty minutes was back again with the milk, to find the bird in the same place standing as before motionless in the same attitude. It was not disturbed at his coming in at the gate, nor did it show the slightest disposition to move when he walked towards it in his studied careless manner. Then, when within three yards of it, came the supreme moment, and wheeling suddenly round he hurled himself with violence upon his victim, throwing out his arms to capture it, and so great was the impulse he had given himself that he was buried to the ankles in the drift. But before going into it, in that brief moment, the fraction of a second, he saw what happened; just as his hands were about to touch it the wings opened and the bird was lifted from its stand and out of his reach as if by a miracle. In the drift he was like a drowning man, swallowing snow into his lungs for water. For a few dreadful moments he thought it was all

over with him; then he succeeded in struggling out and stood trembling and gasping and choking, blinded with snow. By-and-bye he recovered and had a look round, and lo! there stood his goose on the summit of the snow bank about three yards from the spot where it had been! It was standing as before, perfectly motionless, its long neck and head raised, and was still in appearance the snow-white figure of a carved bird, only it was more conspicuous and impressive now, being outlined against the blue sky, and as before it was regarding him out of the corner of one eye. He had never, he said, felt so ashamed of himself in his life! If the bird had screamed and fled from him it would not have been so bad, but there it had chosen to remain, as if despising his attempt at harming it too much even to feel resentment. A most uncanny bird! it seemed to him that it had divined his intention from the first and had been prepared for his every movement; and now it appeared to him to be saying mentally: "Have you got no more plans to capture me in your clever brain, or have you quite given it up?"

Yes, he had quite, quite given it up!

And then the goose, seeing there were no more plans, quietly unfolded its wings and rose from the snowdrift and flew away over the town and the cathedral away on the further side, and towards the snow-covered Mendips; he standing there watching it until it was lost to sight in the pale sky.

W. H. Hudson
Birds in Town and Village

THE SEVEREST WINTER KNOWN

7th March, 1658. To London, to hear Dr. Taylor in a private house on Luke xiii. 23, 24. After the sermon, followed the blessed Communion, of which I participated. In the afternoon, Dr. Gunning, at Exeter House, expounding part of the Creed.

This had been the severest winter that any man alive had known in England. The crows' feet were frozen to their prey. Islands of ice inclosed both fish and fowl frozen, and some persons in their boats.

John Evelyn
Diary

cheerio my deario

well boss i met
mehitabel the cat
trying to dig a
frozen lamb chop
out of a snow
drift the other day
a heluva comedown
that is for me archy
she says a few
brief centuries
ago one of old
king
tut
ank
hamens favorite
queens and today
the village scavenger
butwotthehell
archy wotthehell
its cheerio
my deario that
pulls a lady through
see here mehitabel
i said i thought
you told me that
it was cleopatra
you used to be
before you
transmigrated into
the carcase of a cat
where do you get
this tut
ank
hamen stuff
uestion mark
i was several
ladies my little
insect says she
being cleopatra was

only an incident
in my career
and i was always getting
the rough end of it
always being
misunderstood by some
strait laced
prune faced bunch
of prissy mouthed
sisters of uncharity
the things that
have been said
about me archy
exclamation point
and all simply
because i was a
live dame
the palaces i have
been kicked out of
in my time
exclamation point
but wotthehell
little archy wot
thehell
its cheerio
my deario
that pulls a
lady through
exclamation point
framed archy always
framed that is the
story of all my lives
no chance for a dame
with the anvil chorus
if she shows a little
motion it seems to
me only yesterday
that the luxor local
number one of
the ladies axe
association got me in
dutch with king tut and

he slipped me the
sarcophagus always my
luck yesterday an empress
and today too
emaciated to interest
a vivisectionist but
toujours gai archy
toujours gai and always
a lady in spite of hell
and transmigration
once a queen
always a queen
archy
period
one of her
feet was frozen
but on the other three
she began to caper and
dance singing its
cheerio my deario
that pulls a lady
through her morals may
have been mislaid somewhere
in the centuries boss but
i admire her spirit.....................

archy

Don Marquis
archie and mehitabel

Don Marquis (1878–1937) was a journalist and humorist. While working
for the *New York Sun*, he introduced his readers to archie the cockroach,
once a free verse poet, who uses Marquis's typewriter at night by climbing
up the frame then hurling himself at the key he wants. He can't reach the
shift key, so the poems don't use capital letters. archie's friend mehitabel,
who features some of archie's poems, is an alley cat. The cockroach's
comments make a very interesting social commentary on American life at
the time of Prohibition and Depression.

PEPYS AND A WINTER WIND

24th. By agreement my Lord Bruncker called me up, and though it was a very foule, windy, and rainy morning, yet down to the waterside we went, but no boat could go, the storme continued so. So my Lord to stay till fairer weather carried me into the Tower to Mr. Hore's and there we staid talking an houre, but at last we found no boats yet could go, so we to the office, where we met upon an occasion extraordinary of examining abuses of our clerkes in taking money for examining of tickets, but nothing done in it. ... My Lord and I, the wind being again very furious, so as we durst not go by water, walked to London quite round the bridge, no boat being able to stirre; and, Lord! what a dirty walk we had, and so strong the wind, that in the fields we many times could not carry our bodies against it, but were driven backwards. We went through Horsydowne, where I never was since a little boy, that I went to enquire after my father, whom we did give over for lost coming from Holland. It was dangerous to walk the streets, the bricks and tiles falling from the houses that the whole streets were covered with them; and whole chimneys, nay, whole houses in two or three places, blowed down. But, above all, the pales on London-bridge on both sides were blown away, so that we were fain to stoop very low for fear of blowing off of the bridge. We could see no boats in the Thames afloat, but what were broke loose, and carried through the bridge, it being ebbing water. And the greatest sight of all was, among other parcels of ships driven here and there in clusters together, one was quite overset and lay with her masts all along in the water, and keel above water. So walked home, my Lord away to his house and I to dinner, Mr. Creed being come to towne and to dine with me, though now it was three o'clock. After dinner he and I to our accounts and very troublesome he is.

Samuel Pepys
Diary entry for 26 January 1666

Samuel Pepys (1633–1703) worked for the navy, eventually becoming secretary to the Admiralty and instigating a number of useful reforms. He also belonged to the Royal Society, like his friend John Evelyn, becoming President in 1684. At the Revolution of 1688 he lost his

position. During the years 1660–1669 Pepys kept a diary – in code – which recorded his life, both public and private, in extraordinary detail. Public events, such as the Plague and the Fire of London are included, as well as private adventures and thoughts – being attacked by a dog, or thinking that *A Midsummer Night's Dream* was 'the most insipid ridiculous play that ever I saw in my life'. First decoded at the beginning of the nineteenth century, Pepys's Diary gives a wonderfully colourful record of a very lively decade.

FARMING IN JANUARY

In January, husbandes that powcheth the grotes :
will breake vp their lay, or be sowing of otes.
Sow Jauiuer Otes, and lay them by thy wheate ;
in May, bye thy hay for thy cattel to eate.

In Feuerell, rest not for taking thine ease :
get into the grounde with thy beanes, and thy pease.
Sow peason betimes, and betimes they will come :
the sooner, the better they fill vp a rome,

In euery grene, where the fence is not thine :
the thornes stub out cleane, that the grasse may be fine.
Thy neighbours wil borow, els hack them beliue :
so neither thy grasse, nor the bushes shall thriue.

Thy seruant, in walking thy pastures aboute :
for yokes, forkes and rakes, let him loke to finde oute.
And after at leyser let this be his hier :
to trimme them and make them at home by the fier.

When frostes will not suffer to ditche nor to hedge :
then get the an heate, with thy betill and wedge.
A blocke at the harthe, cowched close for thy life :
shall helpe to saue fier bote, and please well thy wife.

Then lop for thy fewel, the powlinges well growen :
that hindreth the corne, or the grasse to be mowen.

In lopping, and cropping, saue Edder and stake
thyne hedges, where nede is to mende or to make.

No stick, nor no stone, leaue vnpicked vp clene :
for hurting thy sieth, or for harming thy grene.
For sauing of al thing, get home with the rest,
the snow frozen hardest, thy cart may goe best.

Thomas Tusser
Five Hundred Points of Good Husbandry

THAT SPOT

I don't think much of Stephen Mackaye any more, though I used to swear by him. I know that in those days I loved him more than my own brother. If ever I meet Stephen Mackaye again, I shall not be responsible for my actions. It passes beyond me that a man with whom I shared food and blanket, and with whom I mushed over the Chilcoot Trail, should turn out the way he did. I always sized Steve up as a square man, a kindly comrade, without an iota of anything vindictive or malicious in his nature. I shall never trust my judgment in men again. Why, I nursed that man through typhoid fever; we starved together on the headwaters of the Stewart; and he saved my life on the Little Salmon. And now, after the years we were together, all I can say of Stephen Mackaye is that he is the meanest man I ever knew.

We started for the Klondike in the fall rush of 1897, and we started too late to get over Chilcoot Pass before the freeze-up. We packed our outfit on our backs part way over, when the snow began to fly, and then we had to buy dogs in order to sled it the rest of the way. That was how we came to get that Spot. Dogs were high, and we paid one hundred and ten dollars for him. He looked worth it. I say looked, because he was one of the finest appearing dogs I ever saw. He weighed sixty pounds, and he had all the lines of a good sled animal. We never could make out his breed. He wasn't husky, nor Malemute, nor Hudson Bay; he looked like all of them and he didn't look like any of them; and on top of it all he had some of the white man's dog in him, for on one side, in the thick of the mixed yellow-brown-red-and-dirty-white that was his prevailing color, there was a spot of coal-black as big as a water-bucket. That was why we called him Spot.

He was a good looker all right. When he was in condition his muscles stood out in bunches all over him. And he was the strongest looking brute I ever saw in Alaska, also the most intelligent looking. To run your eyes over him, you'd think he could outpull three dogs of his own weight. Maybe he could, but I never saw it. His intelligence didn't run that way. He could steal and forage to perfection; he had an instinct that was positively grewsome for divining when work was to be done and for making a sneak accordingly; and for getting lost and not staying lost he was nothing short of inspired. But when it came to work, the way that intelligence dribbled out of him and left him a mere clot of wobbling, stupid jelly would make your heart bleed.

There are times when I think it wasn't stupidity. Maybe, like some men I know, he was too wise to work. I shouldn't wonder if he put it all over us with that intelligence of his. Maybe he figured it all out and decided that a licking now and again and no work was a whole lot better than work all the time and no licking. He was intelligent enough for such a computation. I tell you, I've sat and looked into that dog's eyes till the shivers ran up and down my spine and the marrow crawled like yeast, what of the intelligence I saw shining out. I can't express myself about that intelligence. It is beyond mere words. I saw it, that's all. At times it was like gazing into a human soul, to look into his eyes; and what I saw there frightened me and started all sorts of ideas in my own mind of reincarnation and all the rest. I tell you I sensed something big in that brute's eyes; there was a message there, but I wasn't big enough myself to catch it. Whatever it was (I know I'm making a fool of myself)— whatever it was, it baffled me. I can't give an inkling of what I saw in that brute's eyes; it wasn't light, it wasn't color; it was something that moved, away back, when the eyes themselves weren't moving. And I guess I didn't see it move, either; I only sensed that it moved. It was an expression,— that's what it was,—and I got an impression of it. No; it was different from a mere expression; it was more than that. I don't know what it was, but it gave me a feeling of kinship just the same. Oh, no, not sentimental kinship. It was, rather, a kinship of equality. Those eyes never pleaded like a deer's eyes. They challenged. No, it wasn't defiance. It was just a calm assumption of equality. And I don't think it was deliberate. My belief is that it was unconscious on his part. It was there because it was there, and it couldn't help shining out. No, I don't mean shine. It didn't shine; it moved. I know I'm talking rot, but if you'd looked into that animal's eyes the way I have, you'd understand. Steve was affected the same way I was. Why, I tried to kill that Spot once—he was no good for anything; and I fell down on it. I led him out into the brush, and he came along slow and unwilling. He knew what was going on. I stopped in a likely place, put my foot on the rope, and pulled my big Colt's. And that dog sat down and looked at me. I tell you he didn't plead. He just looked. And I saw all kinds of incomprehensible things moving, yes, moving, in those eyes of his. I didn't really see them move; I thought I saw them, for, as I said before, I guess I only sensed them. And I want to tell you right now that it got beyond me. It was like killing a man, a conscious, brave man who looked calmly into your gun as much as to say, "Who's afraid?" Then, too, the message seemed so near that, instead of pulling the trigger quick, I stopped to see if I could catch the message. There it was, right before me, glimmering all around in those eyes of his. And then it was too late. I got scared. I was trembly all over, and my stomach generated a nervous palpitation that made me seasick. I just sat down and looked at that dog, and he looked at me, till I thought I was going crazy. Do you want to know what I did? I threw down the gun and ran back to camp with the fear of God in my heart. Steve laughed at me. But I notice that Steve led Spot into the woods, a week later, for the same purpose, and that Steve came back alone, and a little later Spot drifted back, too.

At any rate, Spot wouldn't work. We paid a hundred and ten dollars for him from the bottom of our sack, and he wouldn't work. He wouldn't even tighten the traces. Steve spoke to him the first time we put him in harness, and he sort of shivered, that was all. Not an ounce on the traces. He just stood still and wobbled, like so much jelly. Steve touched him with the whip. He yelped, but not an ounce. Steve touched him again, a bit harder, and he howled—the regular long wolf howl. Then Steve got mad and gave him half a dozen, and I came on the run from the tent. I told Steve he was brutal with the animal, and we had some words—the first we'd ever had. He threw the whip down in the snow, and walked away mad. I picked it up and went to it. That Spot trembled and wobbled and cowered before ever I swung the lash, and with the first bite of it he howled like a lost soul. Next he lay down in the snow. I started the rest of the dogs, and they dragged him along while I threw the whip into him. He rolled over on his back and bumped along, his four legs waving in the air, himself howling as though he was going through a sausage machine. Steve came back and laughed at me, and I apologized for what I'd said.

There was no getting any work out of that Spot; and to make up for it, he was the biggest pig-glutton of a dog I ever saw. On top of that, he was the cleverest thief. There was no circumventing him. Many a breakfast we went without our bacon because Spot had been there first. And it was because of him that we nearly starved to death up the Stewart. He figured out the way to break into our meat-cache, and what he didn't eat, the rest of the team did. But he was impartial. He stole from every body. He was a restless dog always very busy snooping around or going somewhere. And there was never a camp within five miles that he didn't raid. The worst of it was that they always came back on us to pay his board bill, which was just, being the law of the land; but it was mighty hard on us, especially that first winter on the Chilcoot, when we were busted, paying for whole hams and sides of bacon that we never ate. He could fight, too, that Spot. He could do anything but work. He never pulled a pound, but he was the boss of the whole team. The way he made those dogs stand around was an education. He bullied them, and there was always one or more of them fresh-marked with his fangs. But he was more than a bully. He wasn't afraid of anything that walked on four legs; and I've seen him march, single-handed, into a strange team, without any provocation whatever, and put the kibosh on the whole outfit. Did I say he could eat? I caught him eating the whip once. That's straight. He started in at the lash, and when I caught him he

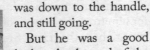

was down to the handle, and still going.

But he was a good looker. At the end of the first week we sold him for seventy-five dollars to the Mounted Police. They had experienced dog-drivers, and we knew that by the time he'd covered the six hundred miles to Dawson he'd be a good sled-dog. I say we knew, for we were just getting acquainted with that Spot. A little later we were not brash enough to know anything where he was concerned. A week later we woke up in the morning to the dangdest dog-fight we'd ever heard. It was that Spot came back and knocking the team into shape. We ate a pretty depressing breakfast, I can tell you; but cheered up two hours afterward when we sold him to an official courier, bound in to Dawson with government despatches. That Spot was only three days in coming back, and, as usual, celebrated his arrival with a rough-house.

We spent the winter and spring, after our own outfit was across the pass, freighting other people's outfits; and we made a fat stake. Also, we made money out of Spot. If we sold him once, we sold him twenty times. He always came back, and no one asked for their money. We didn't want the money. We'd have paid handsomely for any one to take him off our hands for keeps. We had to get rid of him, and we couldn't give him away, for that would have been suspicious. But he was such a fine looker that we never had any difficulty in selling him. "Unbroke," we'd say, and they'd pay any old price for him. We sold him as low as twenty-five dollars, and once we got a hundred and fifty for him. That particular party returned him in person, refused to take his money back, and the way he abused us was something awful. He said it was cheap at the price to tell us what he thought of us; and we felt he was so justified that we never talked back. But to this day I've never quite regained all the old self-respect that was mine before that man talked to me.

When the ice cleared out of the lakes and river, we put our outfit in a Lake Bennett boat and started for Dawson. We had a good team of dogs, and of course we piled them on top the outfit. That Spot was along—there was no losing him; and a dozen times, the first day, he knocked one or another of the dogs overboard in the course of fighting with them. It was close quarters, and he didn't like being crowded.

"What that dog needs is space," Steve said the second day. "Let's maroon him."

We did, running the boat in at Caribou Crossing for him to jump ashore. Two of the other dogs, good dogs, followed him; and we lost two whole days trying to find them. We never saw those two dogs again; but the quietness and relief we enjoyed made us decide, like the man who refused his hundred and fifty, that it was cheap at the price. For the first time in months Steve and I laughed and whistled and sang. We were as happy as clams. The dark days were over. The nightmare had been lifted. That Spot was gone.

Three weeks later, one morning, Steve and I were standing on the river-bank at Dawson. A small boat was just arriving from Lake Bennett. I saw Steve give a start, and heard him say something that was not nice and that was not under his breath. Then I looked; and there, in the bow of the boat, with ears pricked up, sat Spot. Steve and I sneaked immediately, like beaten curs, like cowards, like absconders from justice. It was this last that the lieutenant of police thought when he saw us sneaking. He surmised that there was law-officers in the boat who were after us. He didn't wait to find out, but kept us in sight, and in the M. & M. saloon got us in a corner. We had a merry time explaining, for we refused to go back to the boat and meet Spot; and finally he held us under guard of another policeman while he went to the boat. After we got clear of him, we started for the cabin, and when we arrived, there was that Spot sitting on the stoop waiting for us. Now how did he know we lived there? There were forty thousand people in Dawson that summer, and how did he savve our cabin out of all the cabins? How did he know we were in Dawson, anyway? I leave it to you. But don't forget what I have said about his intelligence and that immortal something I have seen glimmering in his eyes.

There was no getting rid of him any more. There were too many people in Dawson who had bought him up on Chilcoot, and the story got around. Half a dozen times we put him on board steamboats going down the Yukon; but he merely went ashore at the first landing and trotted back up the bank. We couldn't sell him, we couldn't kill him (both Steve and I had tried), and nobody else was able to kill him. He bore a charmed life. I've seen him go down in a dog-fight on the main street with fifty dogs on top of him, and when they were separated, he'd appear on all his four legs, unharmed, while two of the dogs that had been on top of him would be lying dead.

I saw him steal a chunk of moose meat from Major Dinwiddie's cache so heavy that he could just keep one jump ahead of Mrs. Dinwiddie's squaw cook, who was after him with an axe. As he went up the hill, after the squaw gave up, Major Dinwiddie himself came out and pumped his Winchester into the landscape. He emptied his magazine twice, and never touched that Spot. Then a policeman came along and arrested him for discharging firearms inside the city limits. Major Dinwiddie paid his fine, and Steve and I paid him for the moose meat at the rate of a dollar a pound, bones and all. That was what he paid for it. Meat was high that year.

I am only telling what I saw with my own eyes. And now I'll tell you something also. I saw that Spot fall through a water-hole. The ice was three and a half feet thick, and the current sucked him under like a straw. Three hundred yards below was the big water-hole used by the hospital. Spot crawled out of the hospital water-hole, licked off the water, bit out the ice that had formed between his toes, trotted up the bank, and whipped a big Newfoundland belonging to the Gold Commissioner.

In the fall of 1898, Steve and I poled up the Yukon on the last water, bound for Stewart River. We took the dogs along, all except Spot. We figured we'd been feeding him long enough. He'd cost us more time and trouble and money and grub than we'd got by selling him on the Chilcoot—especially grub. So Steve and I tied him down in the cabin and pulled our freight. We camped that night at the mouth of Indian River, and Steve and I were pretty facetious over having shaken him. Steve was a funny fellow, and I was just sitting up in the blankets and laughing when a tornado hit camp. The way that Spot walked into those dogs and gave them what-for was hair-raising. Now how did he get loose? It's up to you. I haven't any theory. And how did he get across the Klondike River? That's another facer. And anyway, how did he know we had gone up the Yukon? You see, we went by water, and he couldn't smell our tracks. Steve and I began to get superstitious about that dog. He got on our nerves, too; and, between you and me, we were just a mite afraid of him.

The freeze-up came on when we were at the mouth of Henderson Creek, and we traded him off for two sacks of flour to an outfit that was bound up White River after copper. Now that whole outfit was lost. Never trace nor hide nor hair of men, dogs, sleds, or anything was ever found. They dropped clean out of sight. It became one of the mysteries of the country. Steve and I plugged away up the Stewart, and six weeks afterward that Spot crawled into camp. He was a perambulating skeleton, and could just drag along; but he got there. And what I want to know is who told him we were up the Stewart? We could have gone a thousand other places. How did he know? You tell me, and I'll tell you.

No losing him. At the Mayo he started a row with an Indian dog. The buck who owned the dog took a swing at Spot with an axe, missed him, and killed his own dog. Talk about magic and turning bullets aside—I, for one, consider it a blamed sight harder to turn an axe aside with a big buck at the other end of it. And I saw him do it with my own eyes. That buck didn't want to kill his own dog. You've got to show me.

I told you about Spot breaking into our meat-cache. It was nearly the death of us. There wasn't any more meat to be killed and meat was all we had to live on. The moose had gone back several hundred miles and the Indians with them. There we were. Spring was on and we had to wait for the river to break. We got pretty thin before we decided to eat the dogs, and we decided to eat Spot first. Do you know what that dog did? He sneaked. Now how did he know our minds were made up to eat him? We sat up nights laying for him, but he never came back, and we ate the other dogs. We ate the whole team.

And now for the sequel. You know what it is when a big river breaks up and a few billion tons of ice go out, jamming and milling and grinding. Just in the thick of it, when the Stewart went out, rumbling and roaring, we sighted Spot out in the middle. He'd got caught as he was trying to cross up above somewhere. Steve and I yelled and shouted and ran up and down the bank, tossing our hats in the air. Sometimes we'd stop and hug each other, we were that boisterous, for we saw Spot's finish. He didn't have a chance in a million. He didn't have any chance at all. After the ice-run, we got into a canoe and paddled down to the Yukon, and down the Yukon to Dawson, stopping to feed up for a week at the cabins at the mouth of Henderson Creek. And as we came in to the bank at Dawson, there sat that Spot, waiting for us, his ears pricked up, his tail wagging, his mouth smiling, extending a hearty welcome to us. Now how did he get out of that ice? How did he know we were coming to Dawson, to the very hour and minute, to be out there on the bank waiting for us?

The more I think of that Spot, the more I am convinced that there are things in this world that go beyond science. On no scientific grounds can that Spot be explained. It's psychic phenomena, or mysticism, or something of that sort, I guess, with a lot of Theosophy thrown in. The Klondike is a good country. I might have been there yet, and become a millionaire, if it hadn't been for Spot. He got on my nerves. I stood him for two years all together, and then I guess my stamina broke. It was the summer of 1899 when I pulled out. I didn't say anything to Steve. I just sneaked. But I fixed it up all right. I wrote Steve a note, and enclosed a package of "rough-on-rats," telling him what to do with it. I was worn down to skin and bone by that Spot, and I was that nervous that I'd jump and look around when there wasn't anybody within hailing distance. But it was astonishing the way I recuperated when I got quit of him. I got back twenty pounds before I arrived in San Francisco, and by the time I'd crossed the ferry to Oakland I was my old self again, so that even my wife looked in vain for any change in me.

Steve wrote to me once, and his letter seemed irritated. He took it kind of hard because I'd left him with Spot. Also, he said he'd used the "rough-on-rats," per directions, and that there was nothing doing. A year went by. I was back in the office and prospering in all ways—even getting a bit fat. And then Steve arrived. He didn't look me up. I read his name in the steamer list, and wondered why. But I didn't wonder long. I got up one morning and found that Spot chained to the gatepost and holding up the milkman. Steve went north to Seattle, I learned, that very morning. I didn't put on any more weight. My wife made me buy him a collar and tag, and within an hour he showed his gratitude by killing her pet Persian cat. There is no getting rid of that Spot. He will be with me until I die, for he'll never die. My appetite is not so good since he arrived, and my wife says I am looking peaked. Last night that Spot got into Mr. Harvey's hen-house (Harvey is my next door neighbor) and killed nineteen of his fancy-bred chickens. I shall have to pay for them. My neighbors on the other side quarreled with my wife and then moved out. Spot was the cause of it. And that is why I am disappointed in Stephen Mackaye. I had no idea he was so mean a man.

Jack London
Brown Wolf and Other Jack London Stories

Jack London (John Griffith Chaney, 1876–1916) was born in San Francisco, where he was deserted by his father. He went to sea aged seventeen, travelling to the Arctic and Japan. Returning home, he could find no work, and he joined a march to Washington to petition for help for the poor. In 1897 he went to the Klondike in the hope of making his fortune. Back in California, he started to write, using his experiences as the basis for novels and short stories, some with a socialist theme. His novels *The Call of the Wild* and *White Fang* are considered classics. The wolf on page 266 is in Jack London Square, Oakland.

TO A SNOWFLAKE

What heart could have thought you? –
 Past our devisal (O filigree petal!)
 Fashioned so purely,
 Fragilely, surely, From what Paradisal
 Imagineless metal,
 Too costly for cost?
Who hammered you, wrought you,
 From argentine vapor? --
"God was my shaper.
Passing surmisal,
 He hammered, He wrought me,
 From curled silver vapor,
To lust of His mind --
Thou could'st not have thought me!
So purely, so palely,
Tinily, surely,
Mightily, frailly,
 Insculped and embossed,
With His hammer of wind,
And His graver of frost."

Francis Thompson

Francis Thompson (1859–1907) gave up studying for the Catholic priesthood, and also failed to complete his studies to become a doctor. He was discovered in London, addicted to opium and destitute, by the poet Alice Meynell and her husband. They rescued him, finding him a place to live, and encouraging him to write and publish his poetry. Much of this has a religious theme.

A BAD WINTER

Therefore the winds, piping to us in vain,
As in revenge, have suck'd up from the sea
Contagious fogs; which falling in the land
Have every pelting river made so proud
That they have overborne their continents:
The ox hath therefore stretch'd his yoke in vain,
The ploughman lost his sweat, and the green corn
Hath rotted ere his youth attain'd a beard;
The fold stands empty in the drowned field,
And crows are fatted with the murrion flock;
The nine men's morris is fill'd up with mud,
And the quaint mazes in the wanton green
For lack of tread are undistinguishable:
The human mortals want their winter here;
No night is now with hymn or carol blest:
Therefore the moon, the governess of floods,
Pale in her anger, washes all the air,
That rheumatic diseases do abound:
And thorough this distemperature we see
The seasons alter: hoary-headed frosts
Far in the fresh lap of the crimson rose,
And on old Hiems' thin and icy crown
An odorous chaplet of sweet summer buds
Is, as in mockery, set.

William Shakespeare
A Midsummer Night's Dream, Act 2, Scene 1

THE STRAITS OF MOYLE

And they came on the morrow to speak with their father and with their foster-father, and they bade them farewell, and Fionnuala made this complaint: -

"Farewell to you, Bodb Dearg, the man with whom all knowledge is in pledge. And farewell to our father along with you, Lir of the Hill of the White Field.

"The time is come, as I think, for us to part from you, O pleasant company; my grief it is not on a visit we are going to you.

"From this day out, O friends of our heart, our comrades, it is on the tormented course of the Maoil we will be, without the voice of any person near us.

"Three hundred years there, and three hundred years in the bay of the men of Domnann, it is a pity for the four comely children of Lir, the salt waves of the sea to be their covering by night.

"O three brothers, with the ruddy faces gone from you, let them all leave the lake now, the great troop that loved us, it is sorrowful our parting is." After that complaint they took to flight, lightly, airily, till they came to Sruth na Maoile between Ireland and Alban. And that was a grief to the men of Ireland, and they gave out an order no swan was to be killed from that out, whatever chance might be of killing one, all through Ireland.

It was a bad dwelling-place for the children of Lir they to be on Sruth na Maoile. When they saw the wide coast about them, they were filled with cold and with sorrow, and they thought nothing of all they had gone through before, in comparison to what they were going through on that sea.

Now one night while they were there a great storm came on them, and it is what Fionnuala said: "My dear brothers," she said, "it is a pity for us not to be making ready for this night, for it is certain the storm will separate us from one another. And let us," she said, "settle on some place where we can meet afterwards, if we are driven from one another in the night."

"Let us settle," said the others, "we meet one another at Carraig na Ron, the Rock of the Seals, for we all have knowledge of it"

And when midnight came, the wind came on them with it, and the noise of the waves increased, and the lightning was flashing, and a rough storm came sweeping down, the way the children of Lir were scattered over the great sea, and the wideness of it set them astray, so that no one of them could know what way the others went But after that storm a great quiet came on the sea, and Fionnuala was alone on Sruth na Maoile; and when she took notice that her brothers were wanting she was lamenting after them greatly, and she made this complaint: --

"It is a pity for me to be alive in the state I am; it is frozen to my sides my wings are; it is little that the wind has not broken my heart in my body, with the loss of Aodh.

"To be three hundred years on Loch Dairbhreach without going into my own shape, it is worse to me the time I am on Sruth na Maoile.

"The three I loved, Och! the three I loved, that slept under the shelter of my feathers; till the dead come back to the living I will see them no more for ever.

"It is a pity I to stay after Fiachra, and after Aodh, and after comely Conn, and with no account of them; my grief I to be here to face every hardship this night"

She stopped all night there upon the Rock of the Seals until the rising of the sun, looking out over the sea on every side till at last she saw Conn coming to her, his feathers wet through and his head hanging, and her heart gave him a great welcome; and then Fiachra came wet and perished and worn out, and he could not say a word they could understand with the dint of the cold and the hardship he had gone through. And Fionnuala put him under her wings, and she said: "We would be well off now if Aodh would but come to us."

It was not long after that, they saw Aodh coming, his head dry and his feathers beautiful, and Fionnuala gave him a great welcome, and she put him in under the feathers of her breast, and Fiachra under her right wing and Conn under her left wing, the way she could put her feathers over them all. "And Och! my brothers," she said, "this was a bad night to us, and it is many of its like are before us from this out."

They stayed there a long time after that, suffering cold and misery on the Maoil, till at last a night came on them they had never known the like of before, for frost and snow and wind and cold. And they were crying and lamenting the hardship of their life, and the cold of the night and the greatness of the snow and the hardness of the wind. And after they had suffered cold to the end of a year, a worse night again came on them, in the middle of winter. And they were on Carraig na Ron, and the water froze about them, and as they rested on the rock, their feet and their wings and their feathers froze to the rock, the way they were not able to move from it. And they made such a hard struggle to get away, that they left the skin of their feet and their feathers and the tops of their wings on the rock after them.

"My grief, children of Lir," said Fionnuala, "it is bad our state is now, for we cannot bear the salt water to touch us, and there are bonds on us not to leave it; and if the salt water goes into our sores," she said, "we will get our death." And she made this complaint: --

"It is keening we are to-night; without feathers to cover our bodies; it is cold the rough, uneven rocks are under our bare feet.

"It is bad our stepmother was to us the time she played enchantments on us, sending us out like swans upon the sea.

"Our washing place is on the ridge of the bay, in the foam of flying manes of the sea; our share of the ale feast is the salt water of the blue tide.

"One daughter and three sons; it is in the clefts of the rocks we are; it is on the hard rocks we are, it is a pity the way we are."

However, they came on to the course of the Maoil again, and the salt water was sharp and rough and bitter to them, but if it was itself, they were not able to avoid it or to get shelter from it. And they were there by the shore under that hardship till such time as their feathers grew again, and their wings, and till their sores were entirely healed. And then they used to go every day to the shore of Ireland or of Alban, but they had to come back to Sruth na Maoile every night.

The Fate of the Children of Lir, trans. Lady Gregory
(*Gods and Fighting Men*)

The Fate of the Children of Lir is an Old Irish romance, one of the tales known as the *Three Sorrows of Storytelling*. A jealous stepmother turns her husband's four children into swans, condemning them to spending three hundred years on a lough near their home, three hundred years in the Straits of Moyle between Ireland and Scotland, and three hundred years in the Atlantic off the west coast of Ireland. Only then, and when certain other conditions have been met, can they return to their human form. The swan children, of the magical race of the Tuatha De Danaaan, retain their voices, and can sing beautifully. They endure their long enchantment, but when it is lifted they are over nine hundred years old, and die almost at once.

A BAD WINTER AFTER CANDLEMAS

1046 And in this same year, after Candlemas, came the severe winter, with frost and with snow, and with all kinds of tempestuous weather, so that there was no man then alive who could remember so severe a winter as this was, as well through mortality of men as murrain of cattle; even birds and fishes perished through the great cold and famine.

The Anglo-Saxon Chronicle

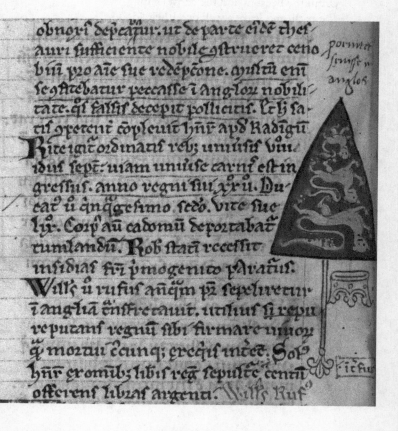

SNOW STORM

What a night! The wind howls, hisses, and but stops
To howl more loud, while the snow volley keeps
Incessant batter at the window pane,
Making our comfort feel as sweet again;
And in the morning, when the tempest drops,
At every cottage door mountainous heaps
Of snow lie drifted, that all entrance stops
Untill the beesom and the shovel gain
The path, and leave a wall on either side.
The shepherd rambling valleys white and wide
With new sensations his old memory fills,
When hedges left at night, no more descried,
Are turned to one white sweep of curving hills,
And trees turned bushes half their bodies hide.

The boy that goes to fodder with surprise
Walks oer the gate he opened yesternight.
The hedges all have vanished from his eyes;
Een some tree tops the sheep could reach to bite.
The novel scene emboldens new delight,
And, though with cautious steps his sports begin,
He bolder shuffles the huge hills of snow,
Till down he drops and plunges to the chin,
And struggles much and oft escape to win--
Then turns and laughs but dare not further go;
For deep the grass and bushes lie below,
Where little birds that soon at eve went in
With heads tucked in their wings now pine for day
And little feel boys oer their heads can stray.

John Clare

THE LANDSLIP

The months of January and February, in the year 1774, were remarkable for great melting snows and vast gluts of rain, so that by the end of the latter month the land-springs, or lavants, began to prevail, and to be near as high as in the memorable winter of 1764. The beginning of March also went on in the same tenor; when, in the night between the 8th and 9th of that month, a considerable part of the great woody hanger at Hawkley was torn from its place, and fell down, leaving a high freestone cliff naked and bare, and resembling the steep side of a chalk-pit. It appears that this huge fragment, being perhaps sapped and undermined by waters, foundered, and was engulfed, going down in a perpendicular direction; for a gate which stood in the field, on the top of the hill, after sinking with its posts for thirty or forty feet, remained in so true and upright a position as to open and shut with great exactness, just as in its first situation. Several oaks also are still standing, and in a state of vegetation, after taking the same desperate leap. That great part of this prodigious mass was absorbed in some gulf below, is plain also from the inclining ground at the bottom of the hill, which is free and unincumbered; but would have been buried in heaps of rubbish, had the fragment parted and fallen forward. About an hundred yards from the foot of this hanging coppice stood a cottage by the side of a lane; and two hundred yards lower, on the other side of the lane, was a farm- house, in which lived a labourer and his family; and, just by, a stout new barn. The cottage was inhabited by an old woman and her son and his wife. These people in the evening, which was very dark and tempestuous, observed that the brick floors of their kitchens began to heave and part; and that the walls seemed to open, and the roofs to crack: but they all agree that no tremor of the ground, indicating an earthquake, was ever felt; only that the wind continued to make a most tremendous roaring in the woods and hangers. The miserable inhabitants, not daring to go to bed, remained in the utmost solicitude and confusion, expecting every moment to be buried under the ruins of their shattered edifices. When day-light came they were at leisure to contemplate the devastations of the night: they then found that a deep rift, or chasm, had opened under their houses, and torn them, as it were, in two; and that one end of the barn had suffered in a similar manner; that a pond near the cottage had undergone a strange reverse, becoming deep at the shallow end, and so vice versa; that many large oaks were removed out of their perpendicular, some thrown down, and some fallen into the heads of neighbouring trees; and that a gate was thrust forward, with its hedge, full six feet, so as to require a new track to be made to it. From the foot of the cliff the general course of the ground, which is pasture, inclines in a moderate descent for half a mile, and is interspersed with some hillocks, which were rifted, in every direction, as well towards the great woody hanger, as from it. In the first pasture the deep clefts began: and running across the lane, and under the buildings, made such vast shelves that the road was impassable for some time; and so over to an arable field on the other side, which was strangely torn and disordered. The second pasture field, being more soft and springy, was protruded forward without many fissures in the turf, which was raised in long ridges resembling graves, lying at right angles to the motion. At the bottom of this enclosure the soil and turf rose many feet against the bodies of some oaks that obstructed their farther course and terminated this awful commotion.

The perpendicular height of the precipice, in general, is twenty-three yards; the length of the lapse, or slip, as seen from the fields below, one hundred and eighty-one; and a partial fall, concealed in the coppice, extends seventy yards more: so that the total length of this fragment that fell was two hundred and fifty-one yards. About fifty acres of land suffered from this violent convulsion; two houses were entirely destroyed; one end of a new barn was left in ruins, the walls being cracked through the very stones that composed them; a hanging coppice was changed to a naked rock; and some grass grounds and an arable field so broken and rifted by the chasms as to be rendered, for a time, neither fit for the plough or safe for pasturage, till considerable labour and expense had been bestowed in levelling the surface and filling in the gaping fissures.

Gilbert White
The Natural History of Selborne, Letter XLV to Daines Barrington

LOSS OF THE HALSEWELL EAST-INDIAMAN

Wrecked off Seacombe, in the Isle of Purbeck, on the Coast of Dorsetshire, January 6th, 1786.

The Haisewell East-Indiaman, of 758 tons burthen, Richard Pierce, Esq. commander, having been taken up by the Directors to make her third voyage to Coast and Bay, fell down to Gravesend the 16th of November, 1785, and there completed her lading. Having taken the ladies and other passengers on board at the Hope, she sailed through the Downs on Sunday, January the 1st, 1786, and the next morning, being abreast of Dunnose, it fell calm.

The ship was one of the finest in the service, and supposed to be in the most perfect condition for her voyage ; and the commander a man of distinguished ability and exemplary character. His officers possessed unquestioned knowledge in their profession ; the crew, composed of the best seamen that could be collected, was as numerous as the establishment admits. The vessel likewise contained a considerable body of soldiers, destined to recruit the forces of the Company in Asia.

The passengers were Miss Eliza Pierce, and Miss Mary-Anne Pierce, daughters of the commander ; Miss Amy Paul, and Miss Mary Paul, daughters of Mr. Paul, of Somersetshire, and relations of Captain Pierce; Miss Elizabeth Blackburne. daughter of Captain B. likewise in the service of the East-India Company ; Miss Mary Haggard, sister to an officer on the Madras establishment; Miss Ann Mansell, a native of Madras, but of European parents, who had received her education in England; and John-George Schutz, Esq. returning to Asia, where he had long resided, to collect a part of his fortune which he had left behind.

On Monday, the 2d of January, at three P. M. a breeze springing up from the south, they ran in shore to land the pilot. The weather coming on very thick in the evening, and the wind baffling, at nine they were obliged to anchor in eighteen fathom water. They furled their top sails, but were unable to furl (heir courses, the snow falling thick and freezing as it fell.

Tuesday, the 3d. at 4 A. M. a violent gale came on from E. N. E. and the ship driving, they were obliged to cut their cables and run out to sea. At noon they spoke with a brig to Dublin, and having put their pilot on board of her, bore down channel immediately. At eight in the evening the wind freshening, and coming to the southward, they reefed such sails as were judged necessary. At ten it blew a violent gale at south, and they were obliged to carry a press of sail to keep the ship off the shore. In this situation, the hawse-plugs, which, according to a recent improvement, were put Inside, were washed in, and the hawse-bags washed sway, in consequence of which they shipped a great quantity of water on the gun-deck.

Upon sounding the well they found that the vessel had sprung a leak, and had five feet of water m her hold ; they clued up the main top-sail, hauled up the main-sail, and immediately attempted to furl both, but failed in the attempt. All the pumps were set to work on the discovery of the leak.

Wednesday the 4th, at two A. M. they endeavored to wear the ship, but without success. The mizen-mast was instantly cut away, and a second attempt made to wear, which succeeded no better than the former. The ship having now seven feet water in her hold, and the leak gaining fast on the pumps, it was thought expedient for the preservation of the ship, which appeared to be in immediate danger of foundering, to cut away the main mast. In its fall Jonathan Moreton, coxswain, and four men, were carried overboard by the wreck and drowned. By eight o'clock the wreck was cleared, and the ship got before the wind. In this position she was kept about two hours, during which the pumps reduced the water in the hold two feet.

At ten in the morning the wind abated considerably, and the ship laboring extremely, rolled the fore top-mast over on the larboard side, which, in the fall, tore the foresail to pieces. At eleven the wind came to the westward, and the weather clearing up, the Berry-Head was distinguished, at the distance of four or five leagues. Having erected a jury main mast, and set a top-gallant sail, for a main sail, they bore up for Portsmouth, and employed the remainder of the day in getting up a jury mizen-mast.

On Thursday the 5th, at two in the morning the wind came to the southward, blew fresh, and the weather was very thick. At noon Portland was seen, bearing north by east, distant about two or three leagues. At eight at night it blew a strong gale at south ; the Portland lights were seen bearing northwest, distant four or five leagues, when they wore ship and got her head to the westward. Finding they lost ground on that tack, they wore her again, and kept stretching to the eastward, in the hope of weathering Peverel- Point, in which case they intended to have anchored in Studland Bay. At eleven they saw St. Alban's Head, a mile and a half to the leeward, upon which they took in sail immediately, and let go the small bower anchor, which brought up the ship at a whole cable, and she rode for about an hour, and then drove. They now let go the sheet anchor, and wore away a whole cable ; the ship rode about two hours longer when she drove again.

In this situation the captain sent for Mr. Henry Meriton, the chief officer, and asked his opinion concerning the probability of saving their lives. He replied with equal candor and calmness, that he apprehended there was very little hopes, as they were then driving fast on shore, and might expect every moment to strike. It was agreed that the boats could not then be of any use, but it was proposed that the officers should be confidentially requested, in case an opportunity presented itself, of making it serviceable, to reserve the long boat for the ladies and themselves, and this precaution was accordingly taken.

About two in the morning of Friday, the 6th, the ship still driving, and approaching the shore very fast, the same officer again went into the cuddy where the captain then was. Captain Pierce expressed extreme anxiety for the preservation of his beloved daughters, and earnestly asked Mr. Meriton, if he could devise any means of saving them. The latter expressed his fears that it would be impossible, adding, that their only chance would be to wait for the morning, upon which the captain lifted up his hands in silent distress.

At this moment the ship struck with such violence as to dash the heads of those who were standing in the cuddy against the deck above them, and the fatal blow was accompanied by a shriek of horror, which burst at the same instant from every quarter of the ship.

The seamen, many of whom had been remarkably inattentive and remiss in their duty during great part of the storm, and had actually skulked in their hammocks, leaving the exertions of the pump, and the other labors required by their situation, to the officers, roused to a sense of their danger, now poured upon the deck, to which the utmost endeavors of their officers could not keep them while their assistance might have been useful. But it was now too late ; the ship continued to beat upon the rocks, and soon bulged, falling with her broadside towards the shore. When the ship struck, several of the men caught hold of the ensign- staff, under the apprehension of her going to pieces immediately.

At this critical juncture Mr.Meriton offered his unhappy companions the best advice that possibly could be given, lie recommended that they should all repair to that side of the ship which lay lowest on the rocks, and take the opportunities that might then present themselves of escaping singly to the shore. He then returned to the round-house, where all the passengers and most of the officers were assembled. The latter were employed in affording consolation to the unfortunate ladies, and with unparalleled magnanimity, suffering their compassion for the amiable companions of their own danger, and the dread of almost inevitable destruction. At this moment what must have been the feelings of a father — of such a father as Captain Pierce ?

The ship had struck on the rocks near Seacombe, on the island of Purbeck, between Peverel-point and St. Alban's-Head. On this part of the shore the cliff is of immense height, and rises almost perpendicularly. In this particular spot the cliff is excavated at the base, presenting a cavern ten or twelve yards in depth, and equal in breadth to the length of a large ship. The sides of the cavern are so nearly upright as to be extremely difficult of access, and the bottom of it is strewed with sharp and uneven rocks which appear to have been rent from above by some convulsion of nature. It was at the mouth of this cavern that the unfortunate vessel lay stretched almost from side to side, and presented her broadside to the horrid chasm. But, at the time the ship struck it was too dark to -discover the extent of their danger, and the extreme horror of their situation.

The number in the round-house was now increased to nearly fifty, by the admission of three black women and two soldiers' wives, with the husband of one of the latter, though the sailors, who had demanded entrance to get a light, had been opposed and kept out by the officers. Captain Pierce was seated on a chair, or some other moveable, between his two daughters, whom he pressed alternately to his affectionate bosom. The rest of the melancholy assembly were seated on the deck, which was strewed with musical instruments, and the wreck of furniture, boxes, and packages.

Here Mr. Meriton, after having lighted several wax candles, and all the glass lanthorns he could find, likewise took his seat, intending to wait till day-light, in the hope that would afford him an opportunity of effecting his own escape, and also rendering assistance to the partners of his danger. But, observing that the ladies appeared parched and exhausted, he fetched a basket of oranges from some part of the round-house, with which he prevailed on some of them to refresh themselves.

On his return he perceived a considerable alteration in the appearance of the ship. The sides were visibly giving way, the deck seemed to heave, and he discovered other evident symptoms that she could not hold together much longer. Attempting to go forward to look out, he instantly perceived that the ship had separated in the middle and that the fore-part had changed its position, and lay rather farther out towards the sea.

In this emergency he determined to seize the present moment, as the next might have been charged with his fate, and to follow the example of the crew and the soldiers, who were leaving the ship in numbers, and making their way to a shore, with the horrors of which they were yet unacquainted.

To favor their escape an attempt had been made to lay the ensign-staff from the ship's side to the rocks, but without success, for it snapped to pieces before it reached them. By the light of a lanthorn, however, Mr. Meriton, discovered a spar, which appeared to be laid from the ship's side to the rocks, and upon which he determined to attempt his escape. He accordingly lay down upon it, and thrust himself forward, but soon found that the spar had no communication with the rock. He reached the end and then slipped off, receiving a violent contusion in his fall. Before he could recover his legs he was washed off by the surge, in which he supported himself by swimming till the returning wave dashed him against the back of the cavern. Here he laid hold of a small projection of the rock, but was so benumbed that he was on the point of quitting it, when a seaman, who had already gained a footing, extended his hand and assisted him till he could secure himself on a little shelf of the rock, from which he clambered still higher till he was out of the reach of the surf.

Mr. Rogers, the third mate, remained with the captain and the ladies nearly twenty minutes after Mr. Meriton had left the ship. The latter had not long quitted the roundhouse, before the captain inquired what was become of him, when Mr. Rogers replied, that he had gone upon deck to see what could be done. A heavy sea soon afterwards broke over the ship, upon which the ladies expressed great concern at the apprehension of his loss. Mr. Rogers proposed to go and call him, but this they opposed, fearful lest he might share the same fate.

The sea now broke in at the fore part of the ship, and reached as far as the main mast. Captain Pierce and Mr. Rogers then went together, with a lamp, to the stern gallery, where, after viewing the rocks, the captain asked Mr. Rogers if he thought there was any possibility of saving the girls. He replied, he feared not ; for they could discover nothing but the black surface of the perpendicular rock, and not the cavern which afforded shelter to those who had escaped. They then returned to the round-house, where captain Pierce again seated himself between his two daughters, struggling to suppress the parental tear which then started into his eye.

The sea continuing to break in very fast, Mr. Rogers, Mr. Schutz, and Mr. M'Manus, a midshipman, with a view to attempt their escape, made their way to the poop. They had scarcely reached it, when a heavy sea breaking over the wreck, the round-house gave way, and they heard the ladies shriek at intervals, as if the water had reached them ; the noise of the sea at other times drowning their voices.

Mr. Brimer had followed Mr. Rogers to the poop, where, on the coming of the fatal sea, they jointly seized a hen-coop, and the same wave which whelmed those who remained below in destruction, carried him and his companion to the rock, on which they were dashed with great violence and miserably bruised.

On this rock were twenty- seven men ; but it was low water, and being convinced that, upon the flowing of the tide, they must all be washed off, many endeavored to get to the back or sides of the cavern beyond the reach of the returning sea. Excepting Mr. Rogers and Mr. Brimer, scarcely more than six succeeded in this attempt. Of the remainder, some experienced the fate they sought to avoid, others perished in endeavoring to get into the cavern.

Mr. Rogers and Mr. Brimer, however, having reached the cavern, climbed up the rock, on the narrow shelves of which they fixed themselves. The former got so near to his friend, Mr. Meriton, as to exchange congratulations with him; but between these gentlemen there were about twenty men, none of whom could stir but at the most imminent hazard of his life. When Mr. Rogers reached this station his strength was so nearly exhausted, that had the struggle continued a few mintes longer he must inevitably have perished.

They soon found that though many who had reached the rocks below, had perished in attempting to ascend, yet that a considerable number of the crew, seamen, soldiers, and some of the inferior officers, were in the same situation with themselves. What that situation was they had still to learn. They had escaped immediate death ; but they were yet to encounter a thousand hardships for the precarious chance of escape. Some part of the ship was still discernible, and they cheered themselves, in this dreary situation, with the hope that it would hold together till day-break. Amidst their own misfortunes the sufferings of the females filled their minds with the acutest anguish ; every returning sea increased their apprehensions for the safety of their amiable and helpless companions.

But, alas ! too soon were these apprehensions realized. A few minutes after Mr. Rogers had gained the rock, a general shriek, in which the voice of female distresses was lamentably distinguishable, announced the dreadful catastrophe ! In a few moments all was hushed, excepting the warring winds and the dashing waves. The wreck was whelmed in the bosom of the deep, and not an atom of it was ever discovered. Thus perished the Halsewell— and with her, worth, honor, skill, beauty, and accomplishments !

This stroke was a dreadful aggravation of woe to the trembling and scarcely half-saved wretches, who were clinging about the sides of the horrid cavern. They felt for themselves, but they wept for wives, parents, fathers, brothers, sisters perhaps lovers !— all cut off from their dearest, fondest hopes !

Their feelings were not less agonized by the subsequent events of that ill-fated night. Many who had gained the precarious stations on the rocks, exhausted with fatigue, weakened by bruises, and benumbed with cold, quitted their holds, and falling headlong, either upon the rocks below, or into the surf, perished beneath the feet of their wretched associates, and by their dying groans and loud exclamations, awakened terrific apprehensions of a similar fate in the survivors.

At length, after three hours of the keenest misery, the day broke on them, but, far from bringing with it the expected relief, it served only to discover to them all the horrors of their situation. They were convinced that, had the country been alarmed by the guns of distress, which they continued to fire several hours before the ship struck, but which, from the violence of the storm, were unheard, they could neither be observed by the people above, as they were completely ingulphed in the cavern, and overhung by the cliff; nor was any part of the wreck remaining to indicate their probable place of refuge. Below, no boat could live to search them out, and had it been possible to acquaint those who were willing to assist them with their exact situation, they were at a loss to conceive how any ropes could be conveyed into the cavern to facilitate their escape.

The only method that afforded any prospect of success was to creep along the side to its outer extremity, to turn the corner on a ledge scarcely as broad as a man's hand, and to climb up the almost perpendicular precipices, nearly two hundred feet in height. In this desperate attempt some succeeded, while others, trembling with terror, and exhausted with bodily and mental fatigue, lost their precarious footing and perished.

The first men who gained the summit of the cliff were the cook, and James Thompson, a quarter- master. By their individual exertions they reached the top, and instantly hastened to the nearest house, to make known the situation of their fellow-sufferers. Eastington, the habitation of Mr. Garland, steward, or agent, to the proprietors of the Purbeck quarries, was the house at which they first arrived. That gentleman immediately assembled the workmen under his direction, and with the most zealous humanity exerted every effort for the preservation of the surviving part of the crew of the unfortunate ship.

Mr. Meriton had, by this time, almost reached the edge of the precipice. A soldier, who preceded him, stood upon a small projecting rock, or stone, and upon the same stone Mr. Meriton had fastened his hands to assist his progress. Just at this moment the quarrymen arrived, and seeing a man so nearly within their reach they dropped a rope, of which he immediately laid hold. By a vigorous effort to avail himself of the advantage, he loosened the stone, which giving way, Mr. Meriton must have been precipitated to the bottom, had not a rope been lowered to him at the instant, which he seized, while in the act of falling, and was safely drawn to the summit.

The fate of Mr. Brimer was peculiarly severe. He had been married only nine days before the ship sailed, to the daughter of Captain Norman, of the Royal Navy, came on shore, as it has been observed, with Mr. Rogers, and, like him, got up the side of the cavern.

Here he remained till the morning, when he crawled out; a rope was thrown him, but he was either so benumbed with the cold as to fasten it about him improperly, or so agitated as to neglect to fasten it at all. Whatever was the cause, the effect proved fatal ; at the moment of his supposed preservation he fell from his stand, and was unfortunately dashed to pieces, in sight of those who could only lament the deplorable fate of an amiable man and skilful officer.

The method of affording help was remarkable, and does honor to the humanity and intrepidity of the quarrymen. The distance from the top of the rock to the cavern, over which it projected, was at least one hundred feet : ten of these formed a declivity to the edge, and the remainder was perpendicular. On the very brink of this precipice stood too daring fellows, with a rope tied round them, and fastened above to a strong iron bar fixed into the ground. Behind these, in like manner, stood others, two and two. A strong rope, likewise properly secured, passed between them, by which they might hold, and support themselves from falling. Another rope, with a noose ready fixed, was then let down below the cavern, and the wind blowing hard, it was sometimes forced under the projecting rock, so that the sufferers could reach it without crawling to the edge. Whoever laid hold of it put the nose round his waist, and was drawn up with the utmost care and caution by their intrepid deliverers.

In this attempt, however, many shared the fate of the unfortunate Mr. Brimer. Unable, through cold, perturbation of mind, weakness, or the inconvenience of the stations they occupied, to avail themselves of the succor that was offered them, they were precipitated from the stupendous cliff, and either dashed to pieces on the rocks, or falling into the surge, perished in the waves.

Among these unhappy sufferers the death of a drummer was attended with circumstances of peculiar distress. Being either washed off the rocks by the sea, or falling into the surf, he was carried by the returning waves beyond the breakers. His utmost efforts to regain them were ineffectual, he was drawn farther out to sea, and being a remarkable good swimmer, continued to struggle with the wares, in the view of his commiserating companions, till his strength was exhausted, and he sunk, to rise no more!

It was late in the day when all the survivors were carried to a place of safety, excepting William Trenton, a soldier, who remained on his perilous stand till the morning of Saturday, the 7th, exposed to the united horrors of extreme personal danger, and the most acute disquietude of mind.

The surviving officers, seamen, and soldiers, being assembled at the house of their benevolent deliverer, Mr. Garland, they were mustered, and found to amount to 74, out of rather more than 240, which was nearly the number of the crew, and passengers, when she sailed through the Downs. Of the rest it is supposed that fifty or more sunk with the Captain and the ladies in the round-house, and that upwards of seventy reached the rocks, but were washed off, or perished, in falling from the cliffs. All those who reached the summit survived, excepting two or three, who expired while being drawn up, and a black, who died a few hours after he was brought to the house. Many, however, were so miserably bruised, that their lives were doubtful, and it was a considerable time before they perfectly recovered their strength.

The benevolence and generosity of the master of the Crown Inn, at Blanford, deserves the highest praise. When the distressed seamen arrived at that town he sent for them all to his house, and having given them the refreshment of a comfortable dinner, he presented each man with half crown to help him on his journey.

Andrus and Starr
Remarkable Shipwrecks, or a Collection of Interesting Accounts of Naval Disasters, With Many Particulars of the Extraordinary Adventures and Sufferings of the Crews of Vessels Wrecked at Sea or on Distant Shores. Together with an Account of the Deliverance of Survivors.

At the time of the wreck, it was customary for those on shore to help themselves to anything from a stricken ship. In some places ships were deliberately lured on to rocks so local people could plunder them. The fate of the *Halsewell* is remarkable because the villagers of Worth Matravers helped the sailors, using skills and equipment they had from working in the Purbeck quarries.

SNOWDROPS

"When did you first see snowdrops?"
"The day I was born
With candles by the cradle
  And frost upon the lawn,
Icicles on the laurels
  And nothing yet begun
Except the march of snowdrops
  Behind the winter sun."

Fredegond Shove
Daybreak

THE SNOWDROP

Many, many welcomes,
February fair-maid!
Ever as of old time,
Solitary firstling,
Coming in the cold time,
Prophet of the gay time,
Prophet of the May time,
Prophet of the roses,
Many, many welcomes,
February fair-maid!

Alfred, Lord Tennyson

Alfred, Lord Tennyson (1809–1892) was not at first successful as a poet, but ten years after his first book failed, his second book of poems was acclaimed. He continued to be successful, becoming Poet Laureate in 1850, and created a baron in 1884.

WINTER

There are dreadful mornings in January that chill one's heart. I awoke on this particular day with a vague feeling of anxiety. It had thawed during the night, and when I cast my eyes over the country from the threshold, it looked to me like an immense dirty grey rag, soiled with mud and rent to tatters.

The horizon was shrouded in a curtain of fog, in which the oak-trees along the walk lugubriously extended their dark arms, like a row of spectres guarding the vast mass of vapour spreading out behind them. The fields had sunk, and were covered with great sheets of water, at the edge of which hung the remnants of dirty snow. The loud roar of the Durance was increasing in the distance.

Winter imparts health and strength to one's frame when the sun is clear and the ground dry. The air makes the tips of your ears tingle, you walk merrily along the frozen pathways, which ring with a silvery sound beneath your tread. But I know of nothing more saddening than dull, thawing weather: I hate the damp fogs which weigh one's shoulders down.

I shivered in the presence of that copper-like sky, and hastened to retire indoors, making up my mind that I would not go out into the fields that day. There was plenty of work in and around the farm-buildings.

Jacques had been up a long time. I heard him whistling in a shed, where he was helping some men remove sacks of corn. The boy was already eighteen years old; he was a tall fellow, with strong arms. He had not had an uncle Lazare to spoil him and teach him Latin, and he did not go and dream beneath the willows at the riverside. Jacques had become a real peasant, an untiring worker, who got angry when I touched anything, telling me I was getting old and ought to rest.

And as I was watching him from a distance, a sweet lithe creature, leaping on my shoulders, clapped her little hands to my eyes, inquiring:

"Who is it?"

I laughed and answered:

"It's little Marie, who has just been dressed by her mamma."

The dear little girl was completing her tenth year, and for ten years she had been the delight of the farm. Having come the last, at a time when we could no longer hope to have any more children, she was doubly loved. Her precarious health made her particularly dear to us. She was treated as a young lady; her mother absolutely wanted to make a lady of her, and I had not the heart to oppose her wish, so little Marie was a pet, in lovely silk skirts trimmed with ribbons.

Marie was still seated on my shoulders.

"Mamma, mamma," she cried, "come and look; I'm playing at horses."

Babet, who was entering, smiled. Ah! my poor Babet, how old we were! I remember we were shivering with weariness, on that day, gazing sadly at one another when alone.

Our children brought back our youth.

Lunch was eaten in silence. We had been compelled to light the lamp. The reddish glimmer that hung round the room was sad enough to drive one crazy.

"Bah!" said Jacques, "this tepid rainy weather is better than intense cold that would freeze our vines and olives."

And he tried to joke. But he was as anxious as we were, without knowing why. Babet had had bad dreams. We listened to the account of her nightmare, laughing with our lips but sad at heart.

"This weather quite upsets one," I said to cheer us all up.

"Yes, yes, it's the weather," Jacques hastened to add. "I'll put some vine branches on the fire."

There was a bright flame which cast large sheets of light upon the walls. The branches burnt with a cracking sound, leaving rosy ashes. We had seated ourselves in front of the chimney; the air, outside, was tepid; but great drops of icy cold damp fell from the ceilings inside the farmhouse. Babet had taken little Marie on her knees; she was talking to her in an undertone, amused at her childish chatter.

"Are you coming, father?" Jacques inquired of me. "We are going to look at the cellars and lofts."

I went out with him. The harvests had been getting bad for some years past. We were suffering great losses: our vines and trees were caught by frost, whilst hail had chopped up our wheat and oats. And I sometimes said that I was growing old, and that fortune, who is a woman, does not care for old men. Jacques laughed, answering that he was young, and was going to court fortune.

I had reached the winter, the cold season. I felt distinctly that all was withering around me. At each pleasure that departed, I thought of uncle Lazare, who had died so calmly; and with fond remembrances of him, asked for strength.

Daylight had completely disappeared at three o'clock. We went down into the common room. Babet was sewing in the chimney corner, with her head bent over her work; and little Marie was seated on the ground, in front of the fire, gravely dressing a doll. Jacques and I had placed ourselves at a mahogany writing-table, which had come to us from uncle Lazare, and were engaged in checking our accounts.

The window was as if blocked up; the fog, sticking to the panes of glass, formed a perfect wall of gloom. Behind this wall stretched emptiness, the unknown. A great noise, a loud roar, alone arose in the silence and spread through the obscurity.

We had dismissed the workpeople, keeping only our old woman-servant, Marguerite, with us. When I raised my head and listened, it seemed to me that the farmhouse hung suspended in the middle of a chasm. No human sound came from the outside. I heard naught but the riot of the abyss. Then I gazed at my wife and children, and experienced the cowardice of those old people who feel themselves too weak to protect those surrounding them against unknown peril.

The noise became harsher, and it seemed to us that there was a knocking at the door. At the same instant, the horses in the stable began to neigh furiously, whilst the cattle lowed as if choking. We had all risen, pale with anxiety, Jacques dashed to the door and threw it wide open.

A wave of muddy water burst into the room.

The Durance was overflowing. It was it that had been making the noise, that had been increasing in the distance since morning. The snow melting on the mountains had transformed each hillside into a torrent which had swelled the river. The curtain of fog had hidden from us this sudden rise of water.

It had often advanced thus to the gates of the farm, when the thaw came after severe winters. But the flood had never increased so rapidly. We could see through the open door that the courtyard was transformed into a lake. The water already reached our ankles.

Babet had caught up little Marie, who was crying and clasping her doll to her. Jacques wanted to run and open the doors of the stables and cowhouses; but his mother held him back by his clothes, begging him not to go out. The water continued rising. I pushed Babet towards the staircase.

"Quick, quick, let us go up into the bedrooms," I cried.

And I obliged Jacques to pass before me. I left the ground-floor the last.

Marguerite came down in terror from the loft where she happened to find herself. I made her sit down at the end of the room beside Babet, who remained silent, pale, and with beseeching eyes. We put little Marie into bed; she had insisted on keeping her doll, and went quietly to sleep pressing it in her arms. This child's sleep relieved me; when I turned round and saw Babet, listening to the little girl's regular breathing, I forgot the danger, all I heard was the water beating against the walls.

But Jacques and I could not help looking the peril in the face. Anxiety made us endeavour to discover the progress of the inundation. We had thrown the window wide open, we leant out at the risk of falling, searching into the darkness. The fog, which was thicker, hung above the flood, throwing out fine rain which gave us the shivers. Vague steel-like flashes were all that showed the moving sheet of water, amidst the profound obscurity. Below, it was splashing in the courtyard, rising along the walls in gentle undulations. And we still heard naught but the anger of the Durance, and the affrighted cattle and horses.

The neighing and lowing of these poor beasts pierced me to the heart. Jacques questioned me with his eyes; he would have liked to try and deliver them. Their agonising moans soon became lamentable, and a great cracking sound was heard. The oxen had just broken down the stable doors. We saw them pass before us, borne away by the flood, rolled over and over in the current. And they disappeared amid the roar of the river.

Then I felt choking with anger. I became as one possessed, I shook my fist at the Durance. Erect, facing the window, I insulted it.

"Wicked thing!" I shouted amidst the tumult of the waters, "I loved you fondly, you were my first sweetheart, and now you are plundering me. You come and disturb my farm, and carry off my cattle. Ah! cursed, cursed thing.—Then you gave me Babet, you ran gently at the edge of my meadows. I took you for a good mother. I remembered uncle Lazare felt affection for your limpid stream, and I thought I owed you gratitude. You are a barbarous mother, I only owe you my hatred—"

But the Durance stifled my cries with its thundering voice; and, broad and indifferent, expanded and drove its flood onward with tranquil obstinacy.

I turned back to the room and went and kissed Babet, who was weeping. Little Marie was smiling in her sleep.

"Don't be afraid," I said to my wife. "The water cannot always rise. It will certainly go down. There is no danger."

"No, there is no danger," Jacques repeated feverishly. "The house is solid."

At that moment Marguerite, who had approached the window, tormented by that feeling of curiosity which is the outcome of fear, leant forward like a mad thing and fell, uttering a cry. I threw myself before the window, but could not prevent Jacques plunging into the water. Marguerite had nursed him, and he felt the tenderness of a son for the poor old woman. Babet had risen in terror, with joined hands, at the sound of the two splashes. She remained there, erect, with open mouth and distended eyes, watching the window.

I had seated myself on the wooden handrail, and my ears were ringing with the roar of the flood. I do not know how long it was that Babet and I were in this painful state of stupor, when a voice called to me. It was Jacques who was holding on to the wall beneath the window. I stretched out my hand to him, and he clambered up.

Babet clasped him in her arms. She could sob now; and she relieved herself.

No reference was made to Marguerite. Jacques did not dare say he had been unable to find her, and we did not dare question him anent his search.

He took me apart and brought me back to the window.

"Father," he said to me in an undertone, "there are more than seven feet of water in the courtyard, and the river is still rising. We cannot remain here any longer."

Jacques was right. The house was falling to pieces, the planks of the outbuildings were going away one by one. Then this death of Marguerite weighed upon us. Babet, bewildered, was beseeching us. Marie alone remained peaceful in the big bed? with her doll between her arms, and slumbering with the happy smile of an angel.

The peril increased at every minute. The water was on the point of reaching the handrail of the window and pouring into the room. Any one would have said that it was an engine of war making the farmhouse totter with regular, dull, hard blows. The current must be running right against the facade, and we could not hope for any human assistance.

"Every minute is precious," said Jacques in agony. "We shall be crushed beneath the ruins. Let us look for boards, let us make a raft."

He said that in his excitement. I would naturally have preferred a thousand times to be in the middle of the river, on a few beams lashed together, than beneath the roof of this house which was about to fall in. But where could we lay hands on the beams we required? In a rage I tore the planks from the cupboards, Jacques broke the furniture, we took away the shutters, every piece of wood we could reach. And feeling it was impossible to utilise these fragments, we cast them into the middle of the room in a fury, and continued searching.

Our last hope was departing, we understood our misery and want of power. The water was rising; the harsh voice of the Durance was calling to us in anger. Then, I burst out sobbing, I took Babet in my trembling arms, I begged Jacques to come near us. I wished us all to die in the same embrace.

Jacques had returned to the window. And, suddenly, he exclaimed:

"Father, we are saved!—Come and see."

The sky was clear. The roof of a shed, torn away by the current, had come to a standstill beneath our window. This roof, which was several yards broad, was formed of light beams and thatch; it floated, and would make a capital raft, I joined my hands together and would have worshipped this wood and straw.

Jacques jumped on the roof, after having firmly secured it. He walked on the thatch, making sure it was everywhere strong. The thatch resisted; therefore we could adventure on it without fear.

"Oh! it will carry us all very well," said Jacques joyfully. "See how little it sinks into the water! The difficulty will be to steer it."

He looked around him and seized two poles drifting along in the current, as they passed by.

"Ah! here are oars," he continued. "You will go to the stern, father, and I forward, and we will manoeuvre the raft easily. There are not twelve feet of water. Quick, quick! get on board, we must not lose a minute."

My poor Babet tried to smile. She wrapped little Marie carefully up in her shawl; the child had just woke up, and, quite alarmed, maintained a silence which was broken by deep sobs. I placed a chair before the window and made Babet get on the raft. As I held her in my arms I kissed her with poignant emotion, feeling this kiss was the last.

The water was beginning to pour into the room. Our feet were soaking. I was the last to embark; then I undid the cord. The current hurled us against the wall; it required precautions and many efforts to quit the farmhouse.

The fog had little by little dispersed. It was about midnight when we left. The stars were still buried in mist; the moon which was almost at the edge of the horizon, lit up the night with a sort of wan daylight.

The inundation then appeared to us in all its grandiose horror. The valley had become a river. The Durance, swollen to enormous proportions and washing the two hillsides, passed between dark masses of cultivated land, and was the sole thing displaying life in the inanimate space bounded by the horizon. It thundered with a sovereign voice, maintaining in its anger the majesty of its colossal wave. Clumps of trees emerged in places, staining the sheet of pale water with black streaks. Opposite us I recognised the tops of the oaks along the walk; the current carried us towards these branches, which for us were so many reefs. Around the raft floated various kinds of remains, pieces of wood, empty barrels, bundles of grass; the river was bearing along the ruins it had made in its anger.

To the left we perceived the lights of Dourgues—flashes of lanterns moving about in the darkness. The water could not have risen as high as the village; only the low land had been submerged. No doubt assistance would come. We searched the patches of light hanging over the water; it seemed to us at every instant that we heard the sound of oars.

We had started at random. As soon as the raft was in the middle of the current, lost amidst the whirlpools of the river, anguish of mind overtook us again; we almost regretted having left the farm. I sometimes turned round and gazed at the house, which still remained standing, presenting a grey aspect on the white water. Babet, crouching down in the centre of the raft, in the thatch of the roof, was holding little Marie on her knees, the child's head against her breast, to hide the horror of the river from her. Both were bent double, leaning forward in an embrace, as if reduced in stature by fear. Jacques, standing upright in the front, was leaning on his pole with all his weight; from time to time he cast a rapid glance towards us, and then silently resumed his task. I seconded him as well as I could, but our efforts to reach the bank remained fruitless. Little by little, notwithstanding our poles, which we buried into the mud until we nearly broke them, we drifted into the open; a force that seemed to come from the depths of the water drove us away. The Durance was slowly taking possession of us.

Struggling, bathed in perspiration, we had worked ourselves into a passion; we were fighting with the river as with a living being, seeking to vanquish, wound, kill it. It strained us in its giant-like arms, and our poles in our hands became weapons which we thrust into its breast. It roared, flung its slaver into our faces, wriggled beneath our strokes. We resisted its victory with clenched teeth. We would not be conquered. And we had mad impulses to fell the monster, to calm it with blows from our fists.

We went slowly towards the offing. We were already at the entrance to the oak-tree walk. The dark branches pierced through the water, which they tore with a lamentable sound. Death, perhaps, awaited us there in a collision. I cried out to Jacques to follow the walk by clinging close to the branches. And it was thus that I passed for the last time in the middle of this oak-tree alley, where I had walked in my youth and ripe age. In the terrible darkness, above the howling depth, I thought of uncle Lazare, and saw the happy days of my youth smiling at me sadly.

The Durance triumphed at the end of the alley. Our poles no longer touched the bottom. The water bore us along in its impetuous bound of victory. And now it could do what it pleased with us. We gave ourselves up. We went downstream with frightful rapidity. Great clouds, dirty tattered rags hung about the sky; when the moon was hidden there came lugubrious obscurity. Then we rolled in chaos. Enormous billows as black as ink, resembling the backs of fish, bore us along, spinning us round. I could no longer see either Babet or the children. I already felt myself dying.

I know not how long this last run lasted. The moon was suddenly unveiled, and the horizon became clear. And in that light I perceived an immense black mass in front of us which blocked the way, and towards which we were being carried with all the violence of the current. We were lost, we would be broken there.

Babet had stood upright. She held out little Marie to me:

"Take the child," she exclaimed. "Leave me alone, leave me alone!"

Jacques had already caught Babet in his arms. In a loud voice he said:

"Father, save the little one—I will save mother."

We had come close to the black mass. I thought I recognised a tree. The shock was terrible, and the raft, split in two, scattered its straw and beams in the whirlpool of water.

I fell, clasping little Marie tightly to me. The icy cold water brought back all my courage. On rising to the surface of the river, I supported the child, I half laid her on my neck and began to swim laboriously. If the little creature had not lost consciousness but had struggled, we should both have remained at the bottom of the deep.

And, whilst I swam, I felt choking with anxiety. I called Jacques, I tried to see in the distance; but I heard nothing save the roar of the waters, I saw naught but the pale sheet of the Durance. Jacques and Babet were at the bottom. She must have clung to him, dragged him down in a deadly strain of her arms. What frightful agony! I wanted to die; I sunk slowly, I was going to find them beneath the black water. And as soon as the flood touched little Marie's face, I struggled again with impetuous anguish to get near the waterside.

It was thus that I abandoned Babet and Jacques, in despair at having been unable to die with them, still calling out to them in a husky voice. The river cast me on the stones, like one of those bundles of grass it leaves on its way. When I came to myself again, I took my daughter, who was opening her eyes, in my arms. Day was breaking. My winter night was at an end, that terrible night which had been an accomplice in the murder of my wife and son.

At this moment, after years of regret, one last consolation remains to me. I am the icy winter, but I feel the approaching spring stirring within me. As my uncle Lazare said, we never die. I have had four seasons, and here I am returning to the spring, there is my dear Marie commencing the everlasting joys and sorrows over again.

Emile Zola
Jean Gourdon's Four Days, Part IV

This short story by the French novelist Emile Zola (1840–1902) describes a man's life by looking at it as four different days. Zola, one of France's greatest writers, was sentenced to imprisonment after he wrote an open letter, 'J'accuse', supporting the Jewish army officer Alfred Dreyfus, wrongly accused of treachery. Zola escaped to England; when he returned to France after Dreyfus had been found innocent he was a national hero.

DESTRUCTION OF THE INTERIOR OF YORK MINSTER

On Monday morning last, this magnificent structure was discovered to be on fire. Soon after the alarm was given, the bells of twenty-three churches announced the dismal tidings; but for some time the people looked upon the report as a hoax, and it was not until after the lapse of an hour that the city was fairly roused to a sense of the impending calamity.

On the Sunday evening previous, there was service in the Minster, as usual, and all appeared to be left safe. A light was, however, observed in the building, by a man passing through the Minster-yard, about four o'clock on Monday morning; but he supposed some workmen were employed there, and passed on without inquiry. Between six and seven o'clock, the discovery was made in an extraordinary manner. One of the choristers passing through the Minster-yard, accidentally stepping on a piece of ice, was thrown on his back, in which position he saw a quantity of smoke issuing from the roof.

In a letter dated York, February 2nd, the writer thus hastily describes the extent of the conflagration: The first appearance I observed was the issue of an immense volume of smoke from the junction of the western towers with the nave, a smaller column from the great tower, and a third column from the roof of the choir, thus presenting the appearance of the building being on fire in all parts, whilst a dense smoke filled the interior to such a degree as to preclude the immediate entrance of the firemen. At length, the engines were rolled into the august edifice, when a scene beyond all description presented itself; the interior of the choir enveloped in flames, reflected upon the beautiful stained glass. The flames soon burst through the roof of the choir, and in less than an hour the whole was in a blaze, and the melted lead poured down the spouting. The roof soon fell in, in about five or six dreadful crashes. Every effort was made to prevent the flames spreading to the transept and nave, and I trust with success, for though the engines are now (midnight) still playing, I do not find that there is any other fire than the remains of the roof on the floor of the choir.

The damage may be summed up thus: The roof of the choir quite gone, the wood work on each side consumed, the matchless organ entirely destroyed, many monuments broken, and the communion plate melted. On the other hand, the east window is entire to the surprise of every one, the screen is uninjured, although immediately below the organ, the records in the vestry, the horn of Ulphus,[2] the coronation chair, and the brass eagle are saved, and the wills in the Prerogative office are all safely lodged in Belfrey's Church. For some time the city was in considerable danger; flakes of fire were carried as far as the Lord Mayor's Walk; providentially there was very little wind.

From another account we learn that communication with the roof was not at first apprehended, but the roof of the choir being very dry wood, soon joined in the conflagration. It is impossible to describe the awful picture of the flames rising above this majestic building. The effect produced by the glare of light upon the stained glass of the windows exceeds description. On the falling of the roof, the house of prayer, which but the evening before had resounded with the voices of worshippers, and where all was order and harmony, now resembled a fiery furnace. The pillars, which once served to divide the choir from the two side aisles, now stood alone, the whole being an open space, with the roof burning on the ground, and nothing above but the blue canopy of heaven.

Mr. Britton, in his valuable work on York Cathedral, gives a minute description of that part of the Minster which has been destroyed; from which the following is extracted:-- "After passing through the screen, the visiter is introduced to the choir, which is grand in scale and rich in adornment. On each side is a series of 20 stalls, with 12 at the west end, beneath the organ. These are of oak, and are peculiarly rich in their canopies and carved decorations. Each seat, or stall, has its movable miserecordia, with projecting rests for the elbows, from which rise two detached slender columns, supporting an elaborate canopy. At the eastern end of the choir is the altar-table, raised above the regular floor by a series of 15 steps.

"On the north side of the altar, over the grated window that lights the crypt, is an ancient pew, or gallery, to which there is an ascent by a flight of narrow stairs, of solid blocks of oak. The exterior of this gallery is very neat, and it is certainly older than the Reformation.

"Behind the stalls of the choir are closets, some of which are used as vestries by the singing-men: modern staircases have been constructed, leading to the galleries erected above, and which disfigure the view into the aisles. These closets are fronted, next the aisles, by open screens of oak, some of which are of excellent carving, and more elaborate than others. In the centre of the choir stands a desk for the vicars-choral to chant the litany in; it is enclosed in a pew of carved wood."

The Minster was lighted with gas, to which the conflagration was at first attributed; but the fire appears to have originated in one of the vestries. When we remember the beauty of the carved work which has thus been destroyed, and the elaborate skill which had been bestowed on its execution, our sympathies are deeply awakened for its fate. Indeed, the most listless admirer of art, as well as the antiquarian devotee, has just cause to lament this accident; especially as the taste and labours of our times fall far short of the olden glories of architecture. When we think of the "unsubstantial pageant" of the recent "Festival," and associate its fleeting show with the desert remains of this venerable pile, our feelings deepen into melancholy, and the smoking fragments of art seem to breathe--

> Tell thou the lamentable fall of me,
> And send the hearers weeping to their beds.

The Mirror of Literature, Amusement and Instruction, Vol. 13, No. 355
Feb. 7, 1829

York Minster has suffered several fires. One early fire was in 1137, when the entire Minster was left in ruins. It was not rebuilt until 1171. A fire in the South Transept in 1753 seems to have been started by workmen leaving coal burning. The conflagration described in this account was the work of Jonathan Martin, who deliberately set fire to the choir: he was declared insane. On 20 May 1840 William Groves of Leeds was repairing the clock, and a candle he left burning in the tower resulted in a blaze that destroyed the belfry, nave roof and vault. More recently, lightning struck the roof of the South Transept, causing considerable damage. Below: detail of the suitably terrifying Doomstone in the crypt.

LADY FRANKLIN'S LAMENT

We were homeward bound one night on the deep
Swinging in my hammock I fell asleep
I dreamed a dream and I thought it true
Concerning Franklin and his gallant crew

With a hundred seamen he sailed away
To the frozen ocean in the month of May
To seek a passage around the pole
Where we poor sailors do sometimes go

Through cruel hardships they vainly strove
Their ships on mountains of ice were drove
Only the Eskimo with his skin canoe
Was the only one that ever came through

In Baffin's Bay where the whale fish blow
The fate of Franklin no man may know
The fate of Franklin no tongue can tell
Lord Franklin alone with his sailors do dwell

And now my burden it gives me pain
For my long-lost Franklin I would cross the main
Ten thousand pounds I would freely give
To know on earth, that my Franklin do live.

Anon.

Sir John Franklin (1786–1847) had a distinguished career in the navy. He was given the command of an expedition to find the North-west Passage in 1845: two ships, the *Erebus* and *Terror*, set sale for Arctic Canada on 24 May, with 110 men and 24 officers. A whaler, the *Prince of Wales*, saw the two ships in Lancaster Sound, but after that there was no news. After two years, Lady Franklin asked the Admiralty to search, but it took another year before any attempt was made to find Franklin and the two ships. Some forty expeditions, official and unofficial, were launched, but it was not until 1859 that Inuit hunters revealed that the two ships had become ice-bound and the men had tried to walk to safety. It was many years before the complete truth was known: Franklin had died in 1847, and the rest of the crew had succumbed at various points to starvation, hypothermia, tuberculosis, lead poisoning and scurvy. Jane Franklin's increasingly desperate efforts to find out what had happened to her husband inspired a number of popular songs.

TWO LETTERS

Since the weather of a district is undoubtedly part of its natural history, I shall make no further apology for the four following letters, which will contain many particulars concerning some of the great frosts and a few respecting some very hot summers, that have distinguished themselves from the rest during the course of my observations.

As the frost in January 1768 was, for the small it lasted, the most severe that we had then known for many years, and was remarkably injurious to evergreens, some account of its rigour, and reason of its ravages, may be useful, and not unacceptable to persons that delight in planting and ornamenting; and may particularly become a work that professes never to lose sight of utility.

For the last two or three days of the former year there were considerable falls of snow, which lay deep and uniform on the ground without any drifting, wrapping up the more humble vegetation in perfect security. From the first day to the fifth of the new year more snow succeeded; but from that day the air became entirely clear; and the heat of the sun about noon had a considerable influence in sheltered situations.

It was in such an aspect that the snow on the author's evergreens was melted every day, and frozen intensely every night; so that the laurustines, bays, laurels, and arbutuses looked, in three or four days, as if they had been burnt in the fire; while a neighbour's plantation of the same kind, in a high cold situation, where the snow was never melted at all, remained uninjured.

From hence I would infer that it is the repeated melting and freezing of the snow that is so fatal to vegetation, rather than the severity of the cold. Therefore it highly behaves every planter, who wishes to escape the cruel mortification of losing in a few days the labour and hopes of years, to bestir himself on such emergencies; and, if his plantations are small, to avail himself of mats, cloths, pease-haum, straw, reeds, or any such covering, for a short time; or, if his shrubberies are extensive, to see that his people go about with prongs and forks, and carefully dislodge the snow from the boughs, since the naked foliage will shift much better for itself, than where the snow is partly melted and frozen again.

It may perhaps appear at first like a paradox; but doubtless the more tender trees and shrubs should never be planted in hot aspects; not only for the reason assigned above, but also because, thus circumstanced, they are disposed to shoot earlier in the spring, and grow on later in the autumn than they would otherwise do, and so are sufferers by lagging or early frosts. For this reason also plants from Siberia will hardly endure our climate: because, on the very first advances of spring, they shoot away, and so are cut off by the severe nights of March or April.

Dr. Fothergill and others have experienced the same inconvenience with respect to the more tender shrubs from North America; which they therefore plant under north walls. There should also perhaps be a wall to the east to defend them from the piercing blasts from that quarter.

This observation might without any impropriety be carried into animal life; for discerning bee-masters now find that their hives should not in the winter be exposed to the hot sun, because such unseasonable warmth awakens the inhabitants too early from their slumbers; and, by putting their juices into motion too soon, subjects them afterwards to inconveniences when rigorous weather returns.

The coincidents attending this short but intense frost were, that the horses fell sick with an epidemic distemper, which injured the winds of many, and killed some; that colds and coughs were general among the human species; that it froze under people's beds for several nights; that meat was so hard frozen that it could not be spitted, and could not be secured but in cellars; that several redwings and thrushes were killed by the frost; and that the large titmouse continued to pull straw lengthwise from the eaves of thatched houses and barns in a most adroit manner, for a purpose that has been explained already.* (* See Letter XLI to Mr. Pennant.)

On the 3d of January, Benjamin Martin's thermometer within doors, in a close parlour where there was no fire, fell in the night to 20, and on the 4th to 18, and the 7th to 17.5, a degree of cold which the owner never since saw in the same situation; and he regrets much that he was not able at that juncture to attend his instrument abroad. All this time the wind continued north and north-east; and yet on the eighth roost-cocks, which had been silent, began to sound their clarions, and crows to clamour, as prognostic of milder weather; and, moreover, moles began to heave and work, and a manifest thaw took place. From the latter circumstance we may conclude that thaws often originate under ground from warm vapours which arise; else how should subterraneous animals receive such early intimations of their approach? Moreover, we have often observed that cold seems to descend from above; for, when a thermometer hangs abroad in a frosty night, the intervention of a cloud shall immediately raise the mercury ten degrees; and a clear sky shall again compel it to descend to its former gauge.

And here it may be proper to observe, on what has been said above, that though frosts advance to their utmost severity by somewhat of a regular gradation, yet thaws do not usually come on by as regular a declension of cold; but often take place immediately from intense freezing; as men in sickness often mend at once from a paroxysm.

To the great credit of Portugal laurels and American junipers, be it remembered that they remained untouched amidst the general havoc: hence men should learn to ornament chiefly with such trees as are able to withstand accidental severities, and not subject themselves to the vexation of a loss which may befall them once perhaps in ten years, yet may hardly be recovered through the whole course of their lives.

As it appeared afterwards the ilexes were much injured, the cypresses were half destroyed, the arbutuses lingered on, but never recovered; and the bays, laurustines, and laurels, were killed to the ground; and the very wild hollies, in hot aspects, were so much affected that they cast all their leaves.

By the 14th of January the snow was entirely gone; the turnips emerged not damaged at all, save in sunny places; the wheat looked delicately, and the garden plants were well preserved; for snow is the most kindly mantle that infant vegetation can be wrapped in; were it not for that friendly meteor no vegetable life could exist at all in northerly regions. Yet in Sweden the earth in April is not divested of snow for more than a fortnight before the face of the country is covered with flowers.

* * *

There were some circumstances attending the remarkable frost in January 1776 so singular and striking, that a short detail of them may not be unacceptable.

The most certain way to be exact will be to copy the passages from my journal, which were taken from time to time as things occurred. But it may be proper previously to remark that the first week in January was uncommonly wet, and drowned with vast rains from every quarter: from whence may be inferred, as there is great reason to believe is the case, that intense frosts seldom take place till the earth is perfectly glutted and chilled with water;* and hence dry autumns are seldom followed by rigorous winters. (* The autumn preceding January 1768 was very wet, and particularly the month of September, during which there fell at Lyndon, in the county of Rutland, six inches and an half of rain. And the terrible long frost of 1739-40 set in after a rainy season, and when the springs were very high.)

January 7th. — Snow driving all the day, which was followed by frost, sleet, and some snow, till the 12th, when a prodigious mass overwhelmed all the works of men, drifting over the tops of the gates and filling the hollow lanes.

On the 14th the writer was obliged to be much abroad; and thinks he never before or since has encountered such rugged Siberian weather. Many of the narrow roads were now filled above the tops of the hedges; through which the snow was driven into most romantic and grotesque shapes, so striking to the imagination as not to be seen without wonder and pleasure. The poultry dared not to stir out of their roosting-places; for cocks and hens are so dazzled and confounded by the glare of snow that they would soon perish without assistance. The hares also lay sullenly in their seats, and would not move until compelled by hunger; being conscious, poor animals, that the drifts and heaps treacherously betray their footsteps, and prove fatal to numbers of them.

From the 14th the snow continued to increase, and began to stop the road waggons and coaches, which could no longer keep on their regular stages; and especially on the western roads, where the fall appears to have been deeper than in the south. The company at Bath, that wanted to attend the Queen's birth-day, were strangely incommoded: many carriages of persons, who got, in their way to town from Bath, as far as Marlborough, after strange embarrassments, here met with a ne plus ultra. The ladies fretted, and offered large rewards to labourers, if they would shovel them a track to London; but the relentless heaps of snow were too bulky to be removed; and so the 18th passed over, leaving the company in very uncomfortable circumstances at the Castle and other inns.

On the 20th the sun shone out for the first time since the frost began; a circumstance that has been remarked before much in favour of vegetation. All this time the cold was not very intense, for the thermometer stood at 29, 28, 25, and thereabout; but on the 21st it descended to 20. The birds now began to be in a very pitiable and starving condition. Tamed by the season, skylarks settled in the streets of towns, because they saw the ground was bare; rooks frequented dunghills close to houses; and crows watched horses as they passed, and greedily devoured what dropped from them; hares now came into men's gardens, and, scraping away the snow, devoured such plants as they could find.

On the 22nd the author had occasion to go to London through a sort of Laplandian-scene, very wild and grotesque indeed. But the metropolis itself exhibited a still more singular appearance than the country; for, being bedded deep in snow, the pavement of the streets could not be touched by the wheels or the horses' feet, so that the carriages ran about without the least noise. Such an exception from din and clatter was strange, but not pleasant; it seemed to convey an uncomfortable idea of desolation:

... ipsa silentia terrent.

On the 27th much snow fell all day, and in the evening the frost became very intense. At South Lambeth, for the four following nights, the thermometer fell to 11, 7, 6, 6; and at Selborne to 7, 6, 10; and on the 31st January, just before sunrise, with rime on the trees and on the tube of the glass, the quicksilver sunk exactly to zero, being 32 degrees below the freezing point; but by eleven in the morning, though in the shade, it sprung up to 16.5 * — a most unusual degree of cold this for the south of England! During these four nights the cold was so penetrating that it occasioned ice in warm chambers and under beds; and in the day the wind was so keen that persons of robust constitutions could scarcely endure to face it. The Thames was at once so frozen over both above and below bridge that crowds ran about on the ice. The streets were now strangely incumbered with snow, which crumbled and trod dusty; and, turning grey, resembled bay-salt; what had fallen on the roofs was so perfectly dry that, from first to last, it lay twenty-six days on the houses in the city; a longer time than had been remembered by the oldest housekeepers living. According to all appearances we might now have expected the continuance of this rigorous weather for weeks to come, since every night increased in severity; but behold, without any apparent cause, on the 1st of February a thaw took place, and some rain followed before night; making good the observation above, that frosts often go off as it were at once, without any gradual declension of cold. On the second of February the thaw persisted; and on the 3d swarms of little insects were frisking and sporting in a court-yard at South Lambeth, as if they had felt no frost. Why the juices in the small bodies and smaller limbs of such minute beings are not frozen is a matter of curious inquiry. (* At Selborne the cold was greater than at any other place that the author could hear of with certainty: though some reported at the time that at a village in Kent, the thermometer fell two degrees below zero, viz., 34 degrees below the freezing point. The thermometer used at Selborne was graduated by Benjamin Martin.)

Severe frosts seem to be partial, or to run in currents; for, at the same juncture, as the author was informed by accurate correspondents, at Lyndon in the county of Rutland, the thermometer stood at 19: at Blackburn, in Lancashire, at 19: and at Manchester at 21, 20, and 18. Thus does some unknown circumstance strangely overbalance latitude, and render the cold sometimes much greater in the southern than in the northern parts of this kingdom.

The consequences of this severity were, that in Hampshire, at the melting of the snow, the wheat looked well, and the turnips came forth little injured. The laurels and laurustines were somewhat damaged, but only in hot aspects. No evergreens were quite destroyed; and not half the damage sustained that befell in January, 1768. Those laurels that were a little scorched on the south-sides were perfectly untouched on their north-sides. The care taken to shake the snow day by day from the branches seemed greatly to avail the author's evergreens. A neighbour's laurel-hedge, in a high situation, and facing to the north, was perfectly green and vigorous; and the Portugal laurels remained unhurt.

As to the birds, the thrushes and blackbirds were mostly destroyed; and the partridges, by the weather and poachers, were so thinned that few remained to breed the following year.

Gilbert White
A Natural History of Selborne, Letter LXI and Letter LXII to the
Honourable Daines Barrington

BARON MUNCHAUSEN TRAVELS IN WINTER

I set off from Rome on a journey to Russia, in the midst of winter, from a just notion that frost and snow must of course mend the roads, which every traveller had described as uncommonly bad through the northern parts of Germany, Poland, Courland, and Livonia. I went on horseback, as the most convenient manner of travelling; I was but lightly clothed, and of this I felt the inconvenience the more I advanced north-east. What must not a poor old man have suffered in that severe weather and climate, whom I saw on a bleak common in Poland, lying on the road, helpless, shivering, and hardly having wherewithal to cover his nakedness? I pitied the poor soul: though I felt the severity of the air myself, I threw my mantle over him, and immediately I heard a voice from the heavens, blessing me for that piece of charity, saying—

"You will be rewarded, my son, for this in time."

I went on: night and darkness overtook me. No village was to be seen. The country was covered with snow, and I was unacquainted with the road.

Tired, I alighted, and fastened my horse to something like a pointed stump of a tree, which appeared above the snow; for the sake of safety I placed my pistols under my arm, and laid down on the snow, where I slept so soundly that I did not open my eyes till full daylight. It is not

easy to conceive my astonishment to find myself in the midst of a village, lying in a churchyard; nor was my horse to be seen, but I heard him soon after neigh somewhere above me. On looking upwards I beheld him hanging by his bridle to the weather-cock of the steeple. Matters were now very plain to me: the village had been covered with snow overnight; a sudden change of weather had taken place; I had sunk down to the churchyard whilst asleep, gently, and in the same proportion as the snow had melted away; and what in the dark I had taken to be a stump of a little tree appearing above the snow, to which I had tied my horse, proved to have been the cross or weather-cock of the steeple!

Without long consideration I took one of my pistols, shot the bridle in two, brought the horse, and proceeded on my journey.

He carried me well—advancing into the interior parts of Russia. I found travelling on horseback rather unfashionable in winter, therefore I submitted, as I always do, to the custom of the country, took a single horse sledge, and drove briskly towards St. Petersburg. I do not exactly recollect whether it was in Eastland or Jugemanland, but I remember that in the midst of a dreary forest I spied a terrible wolf making after me, with all the speed of ravenous winter hunger. He soon overtook me. There was no possibility of escape. Mechanically I laid myself down flat in the sledge, and let my horse run for our safety. What I wished, but hardly hoped or expected, happened immediately after. The wolf did not mind me in the least, but took a leap over me, and falling furiously on the horse, began instantly to tear and devour the hind-part of the poor animal, which ran the faster for his pain and terror. Thus unnoticed and safe myself, I lifted my head slyly up, and with horror I beheld that the wolf had ate his way into the horse's body; it was not long before he had fairly forced himself into it, when I took my advantage, and fell upon him with the butt-end of my whip. This unexpected attack in his rear frightened him so much, that he leaped forward with all his might: the horse's carcase dropped on the ground, but in his place the wolf was in the harness, and I on my part whipping him continually: we both arrived in full career safe at St. Petersburg, contrary to our respective expectations, and very much to the astonishment of the spectators.

Rudolph Erich Raspe
The Surprising Adventures of Baron Munchausen

Rudolphe Raspe (1736–1794) was a clever man – a librarian, writer and scientist – with a criminal streak. Born in Hanover, he had to fly to England in 1775 when he was found to have sold valuables belonging to the Landgrave of Hesse-Cassel and kept the money: he was meant to have used it to buy curios in Italy. This was by no means his only dishonest activity, though he worked perfectly legitimately writing books on artistic and scientific subjects and in the mining industry. His stories about Baron Münchausen – a real traveller and soldier, given to boasting about his exploits – were intended as satire, and as some could also be called libellous, were published anonymously. It was not until 1824 that Raspe was generally recognised as the author of the stories.

EPITHALAMION VPON FREDERICK COUNT PALATINE AND THE LADY ELIZABETH MARRYED ON ST. VALENTINES DAY

Haile Bishop Valentine, whose day this is,
All the Aire is thy Diocis,
And all the chirping Choristers
And other birds are thy Parishioners,
Thou marryest every yeare
The Lirique Larke, and the grave whispering Dove,
The Sparrow that neglects his life for love,
The household Bird, with the red stomacher,
Thou mak'st the black bird speed as soone,
As doth the Goldfinch, or the Halcyon;
The husband cocke lookes out, and straight is sped,
And meets his wife, which brings her feather-bed.
This day more cheerfully then ever shine.
This day, which might enflame thy self, Old Valentine.

Till now, Thou warmd'st with multiplying loves
Two larkes, two sparrowes, or two Doves,
All that is nothing unto this,
For thou this day couplest two Phoenixes,
Thou mak'st a Taper see
What the sunne never saw, and what the Arke
(Which was of foules, and beasts, the cage, and park,)
 Did not containe, one bed containes, through Thee,
Two Phoenixes, whose joyned breasts
Are unto one another mutuall nests,
Where motion kindles such fires, as shall give
Yong Phoenixes, and yet the old shall live.
Whose love and courage never shall decline,
But make the whole year through, thy day, O Valentine.

Up then faire Phoenix Bride, frustrate the Sunne,
Thy selfe from thine affection
Takest warmth enough, and from thine eye
All lesser birds will take their Jollitie.
Up, up, faire Bride, and call,
Thy starres, from out their severall boxes, take
Thy Rubies, Pearles, and Diamonds forth, and make
Thy selfe a constellation, of them All,
And by their blazing, signifie,
That a Great Princess falls, but doth nor die;
Bee thou a new starre, that to us portends
Ends of much wonder; And be Thou those ends,
Since thou dost this day in new glory shine,
May all men date Records, from this thy Valentine.

Come forth, come forth, and as one glorious flame
Meeting Another, growes the same,
So meet thy Fredericke, and so
To an unseparable union goe,
Since separation Falls not on such things as are infinite,
Nor things which are but one, can disunite.
You'are twice inseparable, great, and one;
Goe then to where the Bishop staies,
To make you one, his way, which divers waies
Must be effected; and when all is past,
And that you'are one, by hearts and hands made fast,
You two have one way left, your selves to'entwine,
Besides this Bishops knot, O Bishop Valentine.

But oh, what ailes the Sunne, that here he staies,
Longer to day, then other daies?
Staies he new light from these to get?
And finding here such store, is loth to set?
And why doe you two walke,
So slowly pac'd in this procession?
Is all your care but to be look'd upon,
And be to others spectacle, and talke?
The feast, with gluttonous delaies,

Is eaten, and too long their meat they praise,
The masquers come too late, and'I thinke, will stay,
Like Fairies, till the Cock crow them away.
Alas, did not Antiquity assigne
A night, as well as day, to thee, O Valentine?

They did, and night is come; and yet wee see
Formalities retarding thee.
What meane these Ladies, which (as though
They were to take a clock in peeces,) goe
So nicely about the Bride;
A Bride, before a good night could be said,
Should vanish from her cloathes, into her bed,
As Soules from bodies steale, and are not spy'd.
But now she is laid; What though shee bee?
Yet there are more delayes, For, where is he?
He comes, and passes through Spheare after Spheare.
First her sheetes, then her Armes, then any where,
Let not this day, then, but this night be thine,
Thy day was but the eve to this, O Valentine.

Here lyes a shee Sunne, and a hee Moone here,
She gives the best light to his Spheare,
Or each is both, and all, and so
They unto one another nothing owe,
And yet they doe, but are
So just and rich in that coyne which they pay,
That neither would, nor needs forbeare nor stay,
Neither desires to be spar'd, nor to spare,
They quickly pay their debt, and then
Take no acquittance, but pay again;
They pay, they give, they lend, and so let fall,
No such occasion to be liberall.
More truth, more courage in these two do shine,
Then all thy turtles have, and sparrows, Valentine.

And by this act of these two Phenixes
Nature againe restored is,
For since these two are two no more,
Ther's but one Phenix still, as was before.
Rest now at last, and wee
As Satyres watch the Sunnes uprise, will stay
Waiting, when your eyes opened, let out day.
Onely desir'd, because your face wee see;
Others neare you shall whispering speake,
And wagers lay, at which side day will breake,
And win by'observing, then, whose hand it is
That opens first a curtaine, hers or his;
This will be tryed to morrow after nine,
Till which houre, wee thy day enlarge, O Valentine.

John Donne

Before he took orders in 1615, the poet John Donne (1572–1631) wrote an epithalamium, or wedding song, to celebrate the marriage of James I's daughter Elizabeth to Frederick the Elector Palatine. The ceremony was held on 14 February, St Valentine's Day, and Donne uses the traditional belief that this was the day that birds got married in his poem. The Princess Elizabeth, subject of this poem, is Elizabeth of Bohemia, mentioned in John Evelyn's Diary entry below.

STORM DAMAGE

17th February, 1662. I went with my Lord of Bristol to see his house at Wimbledon, newly bought of the Queen-Mother, to help contrive the garden after the modern. It is a delicious place for prospect and the thickets, but the soil cold and weeping clay. Returned that evening with Sir Henry Bennett.

This night was buried in Westminster Abbey the Queen of Bohemia, after all her sorrows and afflictions being come to die in the arms of her nephew, the King; also this night and the next day fell such a storm of hail, thunder, and lightning, as never was seen the like in any man's memory, especially the tempest of wind, being southwest, which subverted, besides huge trees, many houses, innumerable chimneys (among others that of my parlor at Sayes Court), and made such havoc at land and sea, that several perished on both. Divers lamentable fires were also kindled at this time; so exceedingly was God's hand against this ungrateful and vicious nation and Court.

John Evelyn
Diary

ELEPHANT ISLAND

The twenty-two men who had been left behind on Elephant Island were under the command of Wild, in whom I had absolute confidence, and the account of their experiences during the long four and a half months' wait while I was trying to get help to them, I have secured from their various diaries, supplemented by details which I obtained in conversation on the voyage back to civilization.

The first consideration, which was even more important than that of food, was to provide shelter. The semi-starvation during the drift on the ice-floe, added to the exposure in the boats, and the inclemencies of the weather encountered after our landing on Elephant Island, had left its mark on a good many of them. Rickenson, who bore up gamely to the last, collapsed from heart-failure. Blackborrow and Hudson could not move. All were frost-bitten in varying degrees and their clothes, which had been worn continuously for six months, were much the worse for wear. The blizzard which sprang up the day that we landed at Cape Wild lasted for a fortnight, often blowing at the rate of seventy to ninety miles an hour, and occasionally reaching even higher figures. The tents which had lasted so well and endured so much were torn to ribbons, with the exception of the square tent occupied by Hurley, James, and Hudson. Sleeping-bags and clothes were wringing wet, and the physical discomforts were tending to produce acute mental depression. The two remaining boats had been turned upside down with one gunwale resting on the snow, and the other raised about two feet on rocks and cases, and under these the sailors and some of the scientists, with the two invalids, Rickenson and Blackborrow, found head-cover at least. Shelter from the weather and warmth to dry their clothes was imperative, so Wild hastened the excavation of the ice-cave in the slope which had been started before I left.

The high temperature, however, caused a continuous stream of water to drip from the roof and sides of the ice-cave, and as with twenty-two men living in it the temperature would be practically always above freezing, there would have been no hope of dry quarters for them there. Under the direction of Wild they, therefore, collected some big flat stones, having in many cases to dig down under the snow which was covering the beach, and with these they erected two substantial walls four feet high and nineteen feet apart.

"We are all ridiculously weak, and this part of the work was exceedingly laborious and took us more than twice as long as it would have done had we been in normal health. Stones that we could easily have lifted at other times we found quite beyond our capacity, and it needed two or three of us to carry some that would otherwise have been one man's load. Our difficulties were added to by the fact that most of the more suitable stones lay at the farther end of the spit, some one hundred and fifty yards away. Our weakness is best compared with that which one experiences on getting up from a long illness; one 'feels' well, but physically enervated.

"The site chosen for the hut was the spot where the stove had been originally erected on the night of our arrival. It lay between two large boulders, which, if they would not actually form the walls of the hut, would at least provide a valuable protection from the wind. Further protection was provided to the north by a hill called Penguin Hill at the end of the spit. As soon as the walls were completed and squared off, the two boats were laid upside down on them side by side. The exact adjustment of the boats took some time, but was of paramount importance if our structure was to be the permanent affair that we hoped it would be. Once in place they were securely chocked up and lashed down to the rocks. The few pieces of wood that we had were laid across from keel to keel, and over this the material of one of the torn tents was spread and secured with guys to the rocks. The walls were ingeniously contrived and fixed up by Marston. First he cut the now useless tents into suitable lengths; then he cut the legs of a pair of seaboots into narrow strips, and using these in much the same way that the leather binding is put round the edge of upholstered chairs, he nailed the tent-cloth all round the insides of the outer gunwales of the two boats in such a way that it hung down like a valance to the ground, where it was secured with spars and oars. A couple of overlapping blankets made the door, superseded later by a sack-mouth door cut from one of the tents. This consisted of a sort of tube of canvas sewn on to the tent-cloth, through which the men crawled in or out, tying it up as one would the mouth of a sack as soon as the man had passed through. It is certainly the most convenient and efficient door for these conditions that has ever been invented.

"Whilst the side walls of the hut were being fixed, others proceeded to fill the interstices between the stones of the end walls with snow. As this was very powdery and would not bind well, we eventually had to supplement it with the only spare blanket and an overcoat. All this work was very hard on our frost-bitten fingers, and materials were very limited.

"At last all was completed and we were invited to bring in our sodden bags, which had been lying out in the drizzling rain for several hours; for the tents and boats that had previously sheltered them had all been requisitioned to form our new residence.

"We took our places under Wild's direction. There was no squabbling for best places, but it was noticeable that there was something in the nature of a rush for the billets up on the thwarts of the boats.

"Rickenson, who was still very weak and ill, but very cheery, obtained a place in the boat directly above the stove, and the sailors having lived under the Stancomb Wills for a few days while she was upside down on the beach, tacitly claimed it as their own, and flocked up on to its thwarts as one man. There was one 'upstair' billet left in this boat, which Wild offered to Hussey and Lees simultaneously, saying that the first man that got his bag up could have the billet. Whilst Lees was calculating the pros and cons Hussey got his bag, and had it up just as Lees had determined that the pros had it. There were now four men up on the thwarts of the Dudley Docker, and the five sailors and Hussey on those of the Stancomb Wills, the remainder disposing themselves on the floor."

The floor was at first covered with snow and ice, frozen in amongst the pebbles. This was cleared out, and the remainder of the tents spread out over the stones. Within the shelter of these cramped but comparatively palatial quarters cheerfulness once more reigned amongst the party. The blizzard, however, soon discovered the flaws in the architecture of their hut, and the fine drift-snow forced its way through the crevices between the stones forming the end walls. Jaeger sleeping-bags and coats were spread over the outside of these walls, packed over with snow and securely frozen up, effectively keeping out this drift.

At first all the cooking was done outside under the lee of some rocks, further protection being provided by a wall of provision-cases. There were two blubber-stoves made from old oil-drums, and one day, when the blizzard was unusually severe, an attempt was made to cook the meals inside the hut. There being no means of escape for the pungent blubber-smoke, the inmates had rather a bad time, some being affected with a form of smoke-blindness similar to snow-blindness, very painful and requiring medical attention.

A chimney was soon fitted, made by Kerr out of the tin lining of one of the biscuit-cases, and passed through a close-fitting tin grummet sewn into the canvas of the roof just between the keels of the two boats, and the smoke nuisance was soon a thing of the past. Later on, another old oil-drum was made to surround this chimney, so that two pots could be cooked at once on the one stove. Those whose billets were near the stove suffered from the effects of the local thaw caused by its heat, but they were repaid by being able to warm up portions of steak and hooshes left over from previous meals, and even to warm up those of the less fortunate ones, for a consideration. This consisted generally of part of the hoosh or one or two pieces of sugar.

The cook and his assistant, which latter job was taken by each man in turn, were called about 7 a.m., and breakfast was generally ready by about 10 a.m.

Provision-cases were then arranged in a wide circle round the stove, and those who were fortunate enough to be next to it could dry their gear. So that all should benefit equally by this, a sort of "General Post" was carried out, each man occupying his place at meal-times for one day only, moving up one the succeeding day. In this way eventually every man managed to dry his clothes, and life began to assume a much brighter aspect.

The great trouble in the hut was the absence of light. The canvas walls were covered with blubber-soot, and with the snowdrifts accumulating round the hut its inhabitants were living in a state of perpetual night. Lamps were fashioned out of sardine-tins, with bits of surgical bandage for wicks; but as the oil consisted of seal-oil rendered down from the blubber, the remaining fibrous tissue being issued very sparingly at lunch, by the by, and being considered a great delicacy, they were more a means of conserving the scanty store of matches than of serving as illuminants.

Wild was the first to overcome this difficulty by sewing into the canvas wall the glass lid of a chronometer box. Later on three other windows were added, the material in this case being some celluloid panels from a photograph case of mine which I had left behind in a bag. This enabled the occupants of the floor billets who were near enough to read and sew, which relieved the monotony of the situation considerably.

"Our reading material consisted at this time of two books of poetry, one book of 'Nordenskjold's Expedition,' one or two torn volumes of the 'Encyclopaedia Britannica,' and a penny cookery book, owned by Marston. Our clothes, though never presentable, as they bore the scars of nearly ten months of rough usage, had to be continually patched to keep them together at all."

As the floor of the hut had been raised by the addition of loads of clean pebbles, from which most of the snow had been removed, during the cold weather it was kept comparatively dry. When, however, the temperature rose to just above freezing-point, as occasionally happened, the hut became the drainage-pool of all the surrounding hills. Wild was the first to notice it by remarking one morning that his sleeping-bag was practically afloat. Other men examined theirs with a like result, so baling operations commenced forthwith. Stones were removed from the floor and a large hole dug, and in its gloomy depths the water could be seen rapidly rising. Using a saucepan for a baler, they baled out over 100 gallons of dirty water. The next day 150 gallons were removed, the men taking it in turns to bale at intervals during the night; 160 more gallons were baled out during the next twenty-four hours, till one man rather pathetically remarked in his diary, "This is what nice, mild, high temperatures mean to us: no wonder we prefer the cold." Eventually, by removing a portion of one wall a long channel was dug nearly down to the sea, completely solving the problem. Additional precautions were taken by digging away the snow which surrounded the hut after each blizzard, sometimes entirely obscuring it.

A huge glacier across the bay behind the hut nearly put an end to the party. Enormous blocks of ice weighing many tons would break off and fall into the sea, the disturbance thus caused giving rise to great waves. One day Marston was outside the hut digging up the frozen seal for lunch with a pick, when a noise "like an artillery barrage" startled him. Looking up he saw that one of these tremendous waves, over thirty feet high, was advancing rapidly across the bay, threatening to sweep hut and inhabitants into the sea. A hastily shouted warning brought the men tumbling out, but fortunately the loose ice which filled the bay damped the wave down so much that, though it flowed right under the hut, nothing was carried away. It was a narrow escape, though, as had they been washed into the sea nothing could have saved them.

Although they themselves gradually became accustomed to the darkness and the dirt, some entries in their diaries show that occasionally they could realize the conditions under which they were living.

"The hut grows more grimy every day. Everything is a sooty black. We have arrived at the limit where further increments from the smoking stove, blubber-lamps, and cooking-gear are unnoticed. It is at least comforting to feel that we can become no filthier. Our shingle floor will scarcely bear examination by strong light without causing even us to shudder and express our disapprobation at its state. Oil mixed with reindeer hair, bits of meat, sennegrass, and penguin feathers form a conglomeration which cements the stones together. From time to time we have a spring cleaning, but a fresh supply of flooring material is not always available, as all the shingle is frozen up and buried by deep rifts. Such is our Home Sweet Home."

"All joints are aching through being compelled to lie on the hard, rubbly floor which forms our bedsteads."

Again, later on, one writes: "Now that Wild's window allows a shaft of light to enter our hut, one can begin to 'see' things inside. Previously one relied upon one's sense of touch, assisted by the remarks from those whose faces were inadvertently trodden on, to guide one to the door. Looking down in the semi-darkness to the far end, one observes two very small smoky flares that dimly illuminate a row of five, endeavouring to make time pass by reading or argument. These are Macklin, Kerr, Wordie, Hudson, and Blackborrow—the last two being invalids.

"The centre of the hut is filled with the cases which do duty for the cook's bed, the meat and blubber boxes, and a mummified-looking object, which is Lees in his sleeping-bag. The near end of the floor space is taken up with the stove, with Wild and McIlroy on one side, and Hurley and James on the other. Marston occupies a hammock most of the night—and day—which is slung across the entrance. As he is large and the entrance very small, he invariably gets bumped by those passing in and out. His vocabulary at such times is interesting.

"In the attic, formed by the two upturned boats, live ten unkempt and careless lodgers, who drop boots, mitts, and other articles of apparel on to the men below. Reindeer hairs rain down incessantly day and night, with every movement that they make in their moulting bags. These, with penguin feathers and a little grit from the floor, occasionally savour the hooshes. Thank heaven man is an adaptable brute! If we dwell sufficiently long in this hut, we are likely to alter our method of walking, for our ceiling, which is but four feet six inches high at its highest part, compels us to walk bent double or on all fours.

"Our doorway—Cheetham is just crawling in now, bringing a shower of snow with him—was originally a tent entrance. When one wishes to go out, one unties the cord securing the door, and crawls or wriggles out, at the same time exclaiming 'Thank goodness I'm in the open air!' This should suffice to describe the atmosphere inside the hut, only pleasant when charged with the overpowering yet appetizing smell of burning penguin steaks.

"From all parts there dangles an odd collection of blubbery garments, hung up to dry, through which one crawls, much as a chicken in an incubator. Our walls of tent-canvas admit as much light as might be expected from a closed Venetian blind. It is astonishing how we have grown accustomed to inconveniences, and tolerate, at least, habits which a little time back were regarded with repugnance. We have no forks, but each man has a sheath-knife and a spoon, the latter in many cases having been fashioned from a piece of box lid. The knife serves many purposes. With it we kill, skin, and cut up seals and penguins, cut blubber into strips for the fire, very carefully scrape the snow off our hut walls, and then after a perfunctory rub with an oily penguin-skin, use it at meals. We are as regardless of our grime and dirt as is the Esquimaux. We have been unable to wash since we left the ship, nearly ten months ago. For one thing we have no soap or towels, only bare necessities being brought with us; and, again, had we possessed these articles, our supply of fuel would only permit us to melt enough ice for drinking purposes. Had one man washed, half a dozen others would have had to go without a drink all day. One cannot suck ice to relieve the thirst, as at these low temperatures it cracks the lips and blisters the tongue. Still, we are all very cheerful."

During the whole of their stay on Elephant Island the weather was described by Wild as "simply appalling." Stranded as they were on a narrow, sandy beach surrounded by high mountains, they saw little of the scanty sunshine during the brief intervals of clear sky. On most days the air was full of snowdrift blown from the adjacent heights. Elephant Island being practically on the outside edge of the pack, the winds which passed over the relatively warm ocean before reaching it clothed it in a "constant pall of fog and snow."

On April 25, the day after I left for South Georgia, the island was beset by heavy pack-ice, with snow and a wet mist. Next day was calmer, but on the 27th, to quote one of the diaries, they experienced "the most wretched weather conceivable. Raining all night and day, and blowing hard. Wet to the skin." The following day brought heavy fog and sleet, and a continuance of the blizzard. April ended with a terrific windstorm which nearly destroyed the hut. The one remaining tent had to be dismantled, the pole taken down, and the inhabitants had to lie flat all night under the icy canvas. This lasted well into May, and a typical May day is described as follows: "A day of terrific winds, threatening to dislodge our shelter. The wind is a succession of hurricane gusts that sweep down the glacier immediately south-south-west of us. Each gust heralds its approach by a low rumbling which increases to a thunderous roar. Snow, stones, and gravel are flying about, and any gear left unweighted by very heavy stones is carried away to sea."

Heavy bales of sennegrass, and boxes of cooking-gear, were lifted bodily in the air and carried away out of sight. Once the wind carried off the floor-cloth of a tent which six men were holding on to and shaking the snow off. These gusts often came with alarming suddenness; and without any warning. Hussey was outside in the blizzard digging up the day's meat, which had frozen to the ground, when a gust caught him and drove him down the spit towards the sea. Fortunately, when he reached the softer sand and shingle below high-water mark, he managed to stick his pick into the ground and hold on with both hands till the squall had passed.

On one or two rare occasions they had fine, calm, clear days. The glow of the dying sun on the mountains and glaciers filled even the most materialistic of them with wonder and admiration. These days were sometimes succeeded by calm, clear nights, when, but for the cold, they would have stayed out on the sandy beach all night.

About the middle of May a terrific blizzard sprang up, blowing from sixty to ninety miles an hour, and Wild entertained grave fears for their hut. One curious feature noted in this blizzard was the fact that huge ice-sheets as big as window-panes, and about a quarter of an inch thick, were being hurled about by the wind, making it as dangerous to walk about outside as if one were in an avalanche of splintered glass. Still, these winds from the south and south-west, though invariably accompanied by snow and low temperatures, were welcome in that they drove the pack-ice away from the immediate vicinity of the island, and so gave rise on each occasion to hopes of relief. North-east winds, on the other hand, by filling the bays with ice and bringing thick misty weather, made it impossible to hope for any ship to approach them.

Towards the end of May a period of dead calm set in, with ice closely packed all round the island. This gave place to north-east winds and mist, and at the beginning of June came another south-west blizzard, with cold driving snow. "The blizzard increased to terrific gusts during the night, causing us much anxiety for the safety of our hut. There was little sleep, all being apprehensive of the canvas roof ripping off, and the boats being blown out to sea."

Thus it continued, alternating between south-west blizzards, when they were all confined to the hut, and north-east winds bringing cold, damp, misty weather.

On June 25 a severe storm from north-west was recorded, accompanied by strong winds and heavy seas, which encroached upon their little sandy beach up to within four yards of their hut.

Towards the end of July and the beginning of August they had a few fine, calm, clear days. Occasional glimpses of the sun, with high temperatures, were experienced, after south-west winds had blown all the ice away, and the party, their spirits cheered by Wild's unfailing optimism, again began to look eagerly for the rescue ship.

The first three attempts at their rescue unfortunately coincided with the times when the island was beset with ice, and though on the second occasion we approached close enough to fire a gun, in the hope that they would hear the sound and know that we were safe and well, yet so accustomed were they to the noise made by the calving of the adjacent glacier that either they did not hear or the sound passed unnoticed. On August 16 pack was observed on the horizon, and next day the bay was filled with loose ice, which soon consolidated. Soon afterwards huge old floes and many bergs drifted in. "The pack appears as dense as we have ever seen it. No open water is visible, and 'ice-blink' girdles the horizon. The weather is wretched—a stagnant calm of air and ocean alike, the latter obscured by dense pack through which no swell can penetrate, and a wet mist hangs like a pall over land and sea. The silence is oppressive. There is nothing to do but to stay in one's sleeping-bag, or else wander in the soft snow and become thoroughly wet." Fifteen inches of snow fell in the next twenty-four hours, making over two feet between August 18 and 21. A slight swell next day from the north-east ground up the pack-ice, but this soon subsided, and the pack became consolidated once more. On August 27 a strong west-south-west wind sprang up and drove all this ice out of the bay, and except for some stranded bergs left a clear ice-free sea through which we finally made our way from Punta Arenas to Elephant Island.

As soon as I had left the island to get help for the rest of the Expedition, Wild set all hands to collect as many seals and penguins as possible, in case their stay was longer than was at first anticipated. A sudden rise in temperature caused a whole lot to go bad and become unfit for food, so while a fair reserve was kept in hand too much was not accumulated.

At first the meals, consisting mostly of seal meat with one hot drink per day, were cooked on a stove in the open. The snow and wind, besides making it very unpleasant for the cook, filled all the cooking-pots with sand and grit, so during the winter the cooking was done inside the hut.

A little Cerebos salt had been saved, and this was issued out at the rate of three-quarters of an ounce per man per week. Some of the packets containing the salt had broken, so that all did not get the full ration. On the other hand, one man dropped his week's ration on the floor of the hut, amongst the stones and dirt. It was quickly collected, and he found to his delight that he had enough now to last him for three weeks. Of course it was not ALL salt. The hot drink consisted at first of milk made from milk-powder up to about one-quarter of its proper strength.

This was later on diluted still more, and sometimes replaced by a drink made from a pea-soup-like packing from the Bovril sledging rations. For midwinter's day celebrations, a mixture of one teaspoonful of methylated spirit in a pint of hot water, flavoured with a little ginger and sugar, served to remind some of cock-tails and Veuve Cliquot.

At breakfast each had a piece of seal or half a penguin breast. Luncheon consisted of one biscuit on three days a week, nut-food on Thursdays, bits of blubber, from which most of the oil had been extracted for the lamps, on two days a week, and nothing on the remaining day. On this day breakfast consisted of a half-strength sledging ration. Supper was almost invariably seal and penguin, cut up very finely and fried with a little seal blubber.

There were occasionally very welcome variations from this menu. Some paddies—a little white bird not unlike a pigeon—were snared with a loop of string, and fried, with one water-sodden biscuit, for lunch. Enough barley and peas for one meal all round of each had been saved, and when this was issued it was a day of great celebration. Sometimes, by general consent, the luncheon biscuit would be saved, and, with the next serving of biscuit, was crushed in a canvas bag into a powder and boiled, with a little sugar, making a very satisfying pudding. When blubber was fairly plentiful there was always a saucepan of cold water, made from melting down the pieces of ice which had broken off from the glacier, fallen into the sea, and been washed ashore, for them to quench their thirst in. As the experience of Arctic explorers tended to show that sea-water produced a form of dysentery, Wild was rather diffident about using it. Penguin carcasses boiled in one part of sea-water to four of fresh were a great success, though, and no ill-effects were felt by anybody.

The ringed penguins migrated north the day after we landed at Cape Wild, and though every effort was made to secure as large a stock of meat and blubber as possible, by the end of the month the supply was so low that only one hot meal a day could be served. Twice the usual number of penguin steaks were cooked at breakfast, and the ones intended for supper were kept hot in the pots by wrapping up in coats, etc. "Clark put our saucepanful in his sleeping-bag to-day to keep it hot, and it really was a great success in spite of the extra helping of reindeer hairs that it contained. In this way we can make ten penguin skins do for one day."

Some who were fortunate enough to catch penguins with fairly large undigested fish in their gullets used to warm these up in tins hung on bits of wire round the stove.

"All the meat intended for hooshes is cut up inside the hut, as it is too cold outside. As the boards which we use for the purpose are also used for cutting up tobacco, when we still have it, a definite flavour is sometimes imparted to the hoosh, which, if anything, improves it."

Their diet was now practically all meat, and not too much of that, and all the diaries bear witness to their craving for carbohydrates, such as flour, oatmeal, etc. One man longingly speaks of the cabbages which grow on Kerguelen Island. By June 18 there were only nine hundred lumps of sugar left, i.e., just over forty pieces each. Even my readers know what shortage of sugar means at this very date, but from a different cause. Under these circumstances it is not surprising that all their thoughts and conversation should turn to food, past and future banquets, and second helpings that had been once refused.

A census was taken, each man being asked to state just what he would like to eat at that moment if he were allowed to have anything that he wanted. All, with but one exception, desired a suet pudding of some sort—the "duff" beloved of sailors. Macklin asked for many returns of scrambled eggs on hot buttered toast. Several voted for "a prodigious Devonshire dumpling," while Wild wished for "any old dumpling so long as it was a large one." The craving for carbohydrates, such as flour and sugar, and for fats was very real. Marston had with him a small penny cookery book. From this he would read out one recipe each night, so as to make them last. This would be discussed very seriously, and alterations and improvements suggested, and then they would turn into their bags to dream of wonderful meals that they could never reach. The following conversation was recorded in one diary:

"WILD: 'Do you like doughnuts?'

"McILROY: 'Rather!'

"WILD: 'Very easily made, too. I like them cold with a little jam.'

"McILROY: 'Not bad; but how about a huge omelette?'

"WILD: 'Fine!' (with a deep sigh).

"Overhead, two of the sailors are discussing, some extraordinary mixture of hash, apple-sauce, beer, and cheese. Marston is in his hammock reading from his penny cookery book. Farther down, some one eulogizes Scotch shortbread. Several of the sailors are talking of spotted dog, sea-pie, and Lockhart's with great feeling. Some one mentions nut-food, whereat the conversation becomes general, and we all decide to buy one pound's worth of it as soon as we get to civilization, and retire to a country house to eat it undisturbed. At present we really mean it, too!"

Midwinter's day, the great Polar festival, was duly observed. A "magnificent breakfast" of sledging ration hoosh, full strength and well boiled to thicken it, with hot milk was served. Luncheon consisted of a wonderful pudding, invented by Wild, made of powdered biscuit boiled with twelve pieces of mouldy nut-food. Supper was a very finely cut seal hoosh flavoured with sugar.

After supper they had a concert, accompanied by Hussey on his "indispensable banjo." This banjo was the last thing to be saved off the ship before she sank, and I took it with us as a mental tonic. It was carried all the way through with us, and landed on Elephant Island practically unharmed, and did much to keep the men cheerful. Nearly every Saturday night such a concert was held, when each one sang a song about some other member of the party. If that other one objected to some of the remarks, a worse one was written for the next week.

The cook, who had carried on so well and for so long, was given a rest on August 9, and each man took it in turns to be cook for one week. As the cook and his "mate" had the privilege of scraping out the saucepans, there was some anxiety to secure the job, especially amongst those with the larger appetites. "The last of the methylated spirit was drunk on August 12, and from then onwards the King's health, 'sweethearts and wives,' and 'the Boss and crew of the Caird,' were drunk in hot water and ginger every Saturday night."

The penguins and seals which had migrated north at the beginning of winter had not yet returned, or else the ice-foot, which surrounded the spit to a thickness of six feet, prevented them from coming ashore, so that food was getting short. Old seal-bones, that had been used once for a meal and then thrown away, were dug up and stewed down with sea-water. Penguin carcasses were treated likewise. Limpets were gathered from the pools disclosed between the rocks below high tide, after the pack-ice had been driven away. It was a cold job gathering these little shell-fish, as for each one the whole hand and arm had to be plunged into the icy water, and many score of these small creatures had to be collected to make anything of a meal. Seaweed boiled in sea-water was used to eke out the rapidly diminishing stock of seal and penguin meat. This did not agree with some of the party. Though it was acknowledged to be very tasty it only served to increase their appetite—a serious thing when there was nothing to satisfy it with! One man remarked in his diary: "We had a sumptuous meal to-day—nearly five ounces of solid food each."

It is largely due to Wild, and to his energy, initiative, and resource, that the whole party kept cheerful all along, and, indeed, came out alive and so well. Assisted by the two surgeons, Drs. McIlroy and Macklin, he had ever a watchful eye for the health of each one. His cheery optimism never failed, even when food was very short and the prospect of relief seemed remote. Each one in his diary speaks with admiration of him. I think without doubt that all the party who were stranded on Elephant Island owe their lives to him. The demons of depression could find no foothold when he was around; and, not content with merely "telling," he was "doing" as much as, and very often more than, the rest. He showed wonderful capabilities of leadership and more than justified the absolute confidence that I placed in him. Hussey, with his cheeriness and his banjo, was another vital factor in chasing away any tendency to downheartedness.

Once they were settled in their hut, the health of the party was quite good. Of course, they were all a bit weak, some were light-headed, all were frost-bitten, and others, later, had attacks of heart failure. Blackborrow, whose toes were so badly frost-bitten in the boats, had to have all five amputated while on the island. With insufficient instruments and no proper means of sterilizing them, the operation, carried out as it was in a dark, grimy hut, with only a blubber-stove to keep up the temperature and with an outside temperature well below freezing, speaks volumes for the skill and initiative of the surgeons. I am glad to be able to say that the operation was very successful, and after a little treatment ashore, very kindly given by the Chilian doctors at Punta Arenas, he has now completely recovered and walks with only a slight limp. Hudson, who developed bronchitis and hip disease, was practically well again when the party was rescued. All trace of the severe frost-bites suffered in the boat journey had disappeared, though traces of recent superficial ones remained on some. All were naturally weak when rescued, owing to having been on such scanty rations for so long, but all were alive and very cheerful, thanks to Frank Wild.

August 30, 1916, is described in their diaries as a "day of wonders." Food was very short, only two days' seal and penguin meat being left, and no prospect of any more arriving. The whole party had been collecting limpets and seaweed to eat with the stewed seal bones. Lunch was being served by Wild, Hurley and Marston waiting outside to take a last long look at the direction from which they expected the ship to arrive. From a fortnight after I had left, Wild would roll up his sleeping-bag each day with the remark, "Get your things ready, boys, the Boss may come to-day." And sure enough, one day the mist opened and revealed the ship for which they had been waiting and longing and hoping for over four months. "Marston was the first to notice it, and immediately yelled out 'Ship O!' The inmates of the hut mistook it for a call of 'Lunch O!' so took no notice at first. Soon, however, we heard him pattering along the snow as fast as he could run, and in a gasping, anxious voice, hoarse with excitement, he shouted, 'Wild, there's a ship! Hadn't we better light a flare?' We all made one dive for our narrow door. Those who could not get through tore down the canvas walls in their hurry and excitement. The hoosh-pot with our precious limpets and seaweed was kicked over in the rush. There, just rounding the island which had previously hidden her from our sight, we saw a little ship flying the Chilian flag.

"We tried to cheer, but excitement had gripped our vocal chords. Macklin had made a rush for the flagstaff, previously placed in the most conspicuous position on the ice-slope. The running-gear would not work, and the flag was frozen into a solid, compact mass so he tied his jersey to the top of the pole for a signal.

"Wild put a pick through our last remaining tin of petrol, and soaking coats, mitts, and socks with it, carried them to the top of Penguin Hill at the end of our spit, and soon, they were ablaze.

"Meanwhile most of us had gathered on the foreshore watching with anxious eyes for any signs that the ship had seen us, or for any answering signals. As we stood and gazed she seemed to turn away as if she had not seen us. Again and again we cheered, though our feeble cries could certainly not have carried so far. Suddenly she stopped, a boat was lowered, and we could recognize Sir Ernest's figure as he climbed down the ladder. Simultaneously we burst into a cheer, and then one said to the other, 'Thank God, the Boss is safe.' For I think that his safety was of more concern to us than was our own.

"Soon the boat approached near enough for the Boss, who was standing up in the bows, to shout to Wild, 'Are you all well?' To which he replied, 'All safe, all well,' and we could see a smile light up the Boss's face as he said, 'Thank God!'

"Before he could land he threw ashore handsful of cigarettes and tobacco; and these the smokers, who for two months had been trying to find solace in such substitutes as seaweed, finely chopped pipe-bowls, seal meat, and sennegrass, grasped greedily.

"Blackborrow, who could not walk, had been carried to a high rock and propped up in his sleeping-bag, so that he could view the wonderful scene.

"Soon we were tumbling into the boat, and the Chilian sailors, laughing up at us, seemed as pleased at our rescue as we were. Twice more the boat returned, and within an hour of our first having sighted the boat we were heading northwards to the outer world from which we had had no news since October 1914, over twenty-two months before. We are like men awakened from a long sleep. We are trying to acquire suddenly the perspective which the rest of the world has acquired gradually through two years of war. There are many events which have happened of which we shall never know.

"Our first meal, owing to our weakness and the atrophied state of our stomachs, proved disastrous to a good many. They soon recovered though. Our beds were just shake-downs on cushions and settees, though the officer on watch very generously gave up his bunk to two of us. I think we got very little sleep that night. It was just heavenly to lie and listen to the throb of the engines, instead of to the crack of the breaking floe, the beat of the surf on the ice-strewn shore, or the howling of the blizzard.

"We intend to keep August 30 as a festival for the rest of our lives."

You readers can imagine my feelings as I stood in the little cabin watching my rescued comrades feeding.

Ernest Shackleton
South!

FEBRUARY

When my mum first came to England from Jamaica she embarked on an evening class. She can't recall what the class was about but she can remember the essay she was asked to produce so her writing ability could be assessed.

'Describe winter in your own words', was the task my mum was set.

Now, not being very long in England, my mum was not that familiar with British winters. So she described the winters in Jamaica – her childhood Februaries. And there the 'Christmas breeze' blew its cooling air on her skin. Succulent avocado pears and soft ripe mangoes were at last upon the dining table. The ortaniques, stolen from the tree, squelched their sweet and sticky juice on to her fingers. In the garden the gentle early evening rains scattered droplets, bright as diamonds, on to the flaming red poinsettias. And the fragrant white euphorbia bloomed …

When my mum got this essay back from being marked she'd only got a C minus for all her effort. She was a little surprised. But then she read the reason written large in green ink.

'But this,' the teacher wrote, 'is not what February is like at all!'

Andrea Levy
Six Stories & an Essay

Andrea Levy (1956–) is a British writer whose parents came from Jamaica to London in 1948, on the *Empire Windrush*. A keen reader, she found plenty of books by black Americans but very few by black British writers. Her first novel, *Every Light in the House Burnin'*, published in 1994, was well reviewed, but she struggled to find publishers for subsequent work. However, *Small Island*, which came out in 2004, won several major prizes, and established her as a serious and important author.

an archygram

the wood louse sits on a splinter
and sings to the rising sap
aint it awful how winter
lingers in springtimes lap

Don Marquis
archy's life of mehitabel

WINTER'S END

Rise up, my love, my fair one, and come away.
For, lo, the winter is past,
The rain is over and gone;
The flowers appear on the earth;
The time of the singing of birds is come,
And the voice of the turtle is heard in our land.

Song of Solomon, 2, vv. 10–12

ACKNOWLEDGEMENTS

The editor and publishers gratefully acknowledge permission to reprint copyright material in this book as follows:

U. A. Fanthorpe: 'West Bay In Winter' from *Queueing for the Sun* (Peterloo Poets, 2003). Reprinted by permission of Dr R V Bailey.

Carolyn King: 'First Snow'. Reprinted by permission of the author.

Andrea Levy: 'Friday', from *Six Stories & an Essay* (The Tinder Press, 2014). Reprinted by permission of Headline Publishing Group.

Peter Levi: 'In Midwinter a Wood Was' from *The Gravel Ponds* (André Deutsch, 1960). Reprinted by permission of Carlton Publishing Group.

Fredegond Shove: 'Winter' and 'Snowdrops' from *Daybreak* (The Hogarth Press, 1918). Reprinted by permission of Madame Sophie Ilbert Decaudaveine.

Every effort has been made to trace copyright holders, but if any omissions have been made, please let us know and acknowledgements will be made in the next edition.

Illustrations courtesy of the Library of Congress except: pages 2, 33, 63, 81, 87, 96, 103, 108, 137, 186, 233, 237, 246, 261, 286, 332 courtesy of the British Library; page 209 Russian icon of the late 15th century, p225 Adoration of the Magi by Albrecht Dürer, p266 wolf statue, p302 detail of the Doomstone in the crypt of York Minster, all Creative Commons licensed.